Intersections

Gender, Culture, and Politics in the Middle East

Leila Ahmed, miriam cooke, Simona Sharoni, *and* Suad Joseph, *Series Editors*

Other titles in Gender, Culture, and Politics in the Middle East

Intersections
Gender, Nation, and Community
in Arab Women's Novels

* * *

Edited by Lisa Suhair Majaj,
Paula W. Sunderman, *and* Therese Saliba

SYRACUSE UNIVERSITY PRESS

Copyright © 2002 by Syracuse University Press
Syracuse, New York 13244-5160

All Rights Reserved

First Edition 2002
02 03 04 05 06 07   6 5 4 3 2 1

The paper used in this publication meets the minimum requirements of
American National Standard for Information Sciences—Permanence
of Paper for Printed Library Materials, ANSI Z39.48–1984.∞™

Library of Congress Cataloging-in-Publication Data

Intersections : gender, nation, and community in Arab women's
novels / edited by Lisa Suhair Majaj, Paula W. Sunderman,
and Therese Saliba. — 1st ed.
p. cm.—(Gender, culture, and politics in the Middle East)
Includes bibliographical references and index.
ISBN 0-8156-2951-6 — ISBN 0-8156-2976-1 (pbk.)
1. Arabic fiction—Women authors—History and criticism.
2. Arabic fiction—20th century—History and criticism. 3. Feminism
and literature—Arab countries. 4. Gender identity in literature.
5. Sex role in literature. 6. Politics in literature. 7. Women—
Social conditions—Arab countries. I. Majaj, Lisa Suhair.
II. Sunderman, Paula W. III. Saliba, Therese. IV. Series.
PJ7525.2.I55 2002
892.7'3099287'0904—dc21
2002011956

Manufactured in the United States of America

For Andreas, Nadia, and Nicolas
and in memory of Isa J. and Jean C. Majaj

For Frank E. Cotton, Jr. and in memory of Evelyn Sunderman

For Helen and Ron Saliba and in memory of Victoria Saliba

Contents

Illustrations

Acknowledgments

O ur thanks, first of all, to our contributors, whose essays made this book possible, and to the Arab women authors whose works continue to inspire us.

We are grateful to the Women's Studies Internet list that provided the forum in which Paula Sunderman and Lisa Suhair Majaj first met, leading to the conception of this book. Special thanks to Souad Dajani for generously reading and commenting on an earlier version of the manuscript. We are grateful to Tayne Hodges Leonard for formatting and printing the first version of our manuscript, and to Gene E. Boggess for his help with converting different word processing programs used by contributors to a uniform standard. We also wish to thank Kana Shephard and Abigail Fowler for their technical and research support in the final manuscript preparation. Great thanks to Simona Sharoni and Mary Selden Evans for their editorial enthusiasm for this project.

Therese Saliba would like to thank her family for their encouragement and support throughout the years. Thanks also to her friends and colleagues, especially Carolyn Allen, Lisa Suhair Majaj, and Alice Nelson, who have offered inspiration and insights along the way. Special thanks to Tom Wright for his attentive editing and his humor, patience, and commitment to the struggle, and to Samia for brightening the days.

Paula W. Sunderman is grateful to the friends and family members whose support over the years helped make this book possible. And special thanks to her husband, Frank E. Cotton, Jr., for his love, understanding, and encouragement.

Lisa Suhair Majaj is deeply grateful to friends and family members for their encouragement and support over the years; it has made all the difference. Particular thanks to Pauline Kaldas and Laura Porter, who saw me through this project from inception to conclusion. Most of all, thanks to Andreas N. Alexandrou for his ongoing faith and love, and to Nadia and Nicolas for bringing joy.

The editors gratefully acknowledge permission to reprint the following:

"Framing Nawal El Saadawi: Arab Feminism in a Transnational World," by Amal Amireh. Originally published in *Signs: Journal of Women in Culture and Society* 26, no. 1 (autumn 2000): 215–49. Copyright 2000 by The University of Chicago. All rights reserved. Reprinted by permission.

"Reenvisioning National Community in Salwa Bakr's *The Golden Chariot*," by Magda M. Al-Nowaihi. Originally published in *Arab Studies Journal* 7, no. 2/8, no. 1 (fall 1999/spring 2000): 8–24. Reprinted by permission.

"The Fourth Language: Subaltern Expression in Djebar's *Fantasia*," by Nada Elia. A version of this essay was originally published in her book *Trances, Dances, and Vociferations: Agency and Resistance in Africana Women's Narratives*, pages 11–34 (Garland, 2001). Reprinted by permission of Routledge, Inc.

Contributors

Amal Amireh is assistant professor of world literature and postcolonial theory at George Mason University. She is author of *The Factory Girl and the Seamstress: Imagining Gender and Class in Nineteenth-Century American Fiction* (2000), and is coeditor (with Lisa Suhair Majaj) of *Going Global: The Transnational Reception of Third World Women* (2000) and *Etel Adnan: Critical Reflections* (2001). Her essays and reviews on Arab women and Arabic literature have appeared in *Signs: Journal of Women in Culture and Society, Against the Current, The Women's Review of Books, World Literature Today,* and *Edebiyat: The Journal of Middle Eastern Literatures.* Her current work focuses on gender and nationalism in the Palestinian context.

Nada Elia is visiting associate professor in the Department of Africana Studies at Brown University. She is the author of *Trances, Dances, and Vociferations: Agency and Resistance in Africana Women's Narratives* (2001), and is currently at work on a second manuscript, "Spell-Bound, Un-Bound: Conjuring as the Practice of Freedom," an examination of spiritual and psychological empowerment through survivals of African religions in the diaspora. She has published numerous articles on postcolonial and Africana feminist resistance in such journals as *World Literature Today, Research in African Literatures,* and *Callaloo.*

Mona Fayad is assistant professor of English literature at Salem State College in Massachusetts. She has published many essays on Arab and European women writers, and is a contributor to *Al-Jadid.* She has completed a book about Arab women writers and the question of identity, "Identifying Arab Women," and has written a novel, *Chameleon Tracks,* about the Arab-American immigrant experience.

Sabah Ghandour teaches comparative literature at the University of Balamand, Lebanon, where she is chair of the Department of Languages and Literature. She has published several articles on contemporary Lebanese literature, as well as translations of poems and short stories, and is the author of forewords for Elias Khoury's translated novels *Gates of the City* and *The Journey of Little Gandhi.* She is currently working on a manuscript about discourse in the Lebanese novel.

Barbara Harlow is professor of English and teaches English and comparative literature at the University of Texas at Austin. She also has taught in Egypt, Ireland, and South Africa and has traveled in the Middle East, Central America, and Europe. She is the author of *Resistance Literature* (1987), *Barred: Women, Writing, and Political Detention* (1992), and *After Lives: Legacies of Revolutionary Writing* (1996), and is coeditor, with Mia Carter, of *Imperialism and Orientalism: A Documentary Sourcebook* (1999).

Salma Khadra Jayyusi is the author of the two-volume critical history *Trends and Movements in Modern Arabic Poetry* (1977) and editor of *Modern Arabic Poetry: An Anthology* (1987), *Literature of Modern Arabia* (1988), *Anthology of Modern Palestinian Literature* (1992), *The Legacy of Muslim Spain* (1992), *Modern Arabic Drama: An Anthology* (1995), *Modern Arabic Fiction* (forthcoming), and *Human Rights in Arabic Texts* (in Arabic and in English translation, forthcoming). She is also the editor of some twenty-seven single-author works (novels, poetry collections, short story collections, and books of social and intellectual critique). She taught at several Arab and American universities before leaving to direct *PROTA* (Project of Translation from Arabic), which she founded in 1980. In 1992 she also founded *East-West Nexus* for the dissemination of Arabic thought and culture.

Mary N. Layoun is professor of comparative literature and faculty director of Chadbourne Residential College at the University of Wisconsin at

Madison, where she teaches and writes about comparative modern literatures and cultures (Arabic, Greek, Japanese, and Anglophone and Francophone African), nationalism and gender, politics and culture, disciplinary histories, institutional politics, and pedagogy. Her books include *Travels of a Genre: Ideology and the Modern Novel* (1990, and *Choice* Outstanding Academic Book Award for 1991), and *Wedded to the Land?: Gender, Boundaries, and Nationalism in Crisis* (2001).

Lisa Suhair Majaj writes and teaches on postcolonial, Arab, and ethnic American literature. She is coeditor, with Amal Amireh, of *Going Global: The Transnational Reception of Third World Women Writers* (2000) and of *Etel Adnan: Critical Reflections* (2001). Her articles and essays have appeared in various journals and collections, including *Arabs in America: Building a New Future* (1999) and *Postcolonial Theory and the United States* (2000). She also publishes poetry and creative essays. In 1997 she was a U.S. Information Services writer and lecturer in Jerusalem, the West Bank, and Jordan.

Magda M. Al-Nowaihi has taught at Harvard and Princeton universities, and is currently assistant professor of Arabic literature at Columbia University. She is the author of *The Poetry of Ibn Khafajah: A Literary Analysis* (1993) and of a number of articles and book chapters on modern Arabic narratives.

Therese Saliba is faculty of Third World feminist studies at Evergreen State College, Washington. She is editor, with Carolyn Allen and Judith A. Howard, of *Gender, Politics, and Islam* (2002). Her essays on postcolonial literature, media representations, and feminist issues have appeared in various journals and collections, including *Signs* (2000), *Arabs in America: Building a New Future* (1999), and *Going Global* (2000). From 1995 to 1996 she was Senior Fulbright Scholar at Bethlehem University, West Bank.

Paula W. Sunderman is associate professor emerita of English and applied linguistics at Mississippi State University. Her articles, essays, and interviews on feminist studies, applied linguistics, speech act theory, and stylistics have appeared in various journals and collections, including *Language and Style, Phoebe, Michigan Quarterly Review, The Literary Review, Meisei Review* (Japan), and *The Indian Journal of Linguistics*. She is also the author of *Connections: Writing Across Disciplines* (1985). In 1996–97, she was a visiting professor of English at Meisei University, Tokyo.

Introduction

A proliferation of Arab women's texts in the last century has changed the face of Arabic literature. Arab women writers have emerged as important players in the modern and postmodern literary renaissance of the Arab world, their rich diversity of style and subject matter opening critical avenues of discussion in social, political, and cultural arenas. While little of this writing was previously available outside of the Arab world, in recent years Arab women's literature has become much more readily available in English translation, and it is often published by mainstream as well as alternative presses. As a result, Arab women's texts are used in literature and women's studies courses with growing frequency, and Arab women writers have gained increasing recognition in English-speaking literary contexts.

This expanded interest in Arab women's literature has led to a corresponding growth in scholarship on Arab women's writing.[1] However, the volume of secondary sources on Arab women's literature does not fully reflect either the availability of this literature or its significance. As teachers, readers, and scholars of Arab women's literature, we have felt the need for critical work on Arab women's writing that would help to situate these texts for English-speaking students and readers and that would delineate major themes in this literature as well as focus closely on individual texts. To this end, this collection brings together original essays on contemporary Arab women writers from Algeria, Egypt, Lebanon, and Palestine, ex-

---

1. For some book-length critical studies of Arab women's literature and of the representation of women in Arab literature, see Accad 1978 and 1990; Al-Ali 1994; Arebi 1994; Cooke 1988 and 1997; Malti-Douglas 1991 and 1995a; Mikhail 1988; and Zeidan 1995.

ploring the engagement of novels by these authors with contemporary phenomena of nationalism, postcolonialism, war, transnationalism, and societal change. While each essay focuses on a single author, the juxtaposition of essays, and their shared attention to the political, historical, social, and discursive contexts situating texts, suggests points of intersection among Arab women's texts as they challenge and rewrite traditional boundaries of gender, nation, and community.

Western interest in Arab women has been growing in recent decades, as evidenced not only by the increasing availability of Arab women's texts in translation, but also by anthropological and sociological studies of Arab women's lives. But this attention is double-edged. As Amal Amireh observes, "Historically, the West's interest in Arab women is part of its interest in and hostility to Islam" (1996b, 10). This interest, Amireh points out, is furthermore grounded in "the colonialist project, which casts women as victims to be rescued from Muslim male violence" (10), and is more recently linked to the rise in anti-Islamic discourse following the 1979 Iranian revolution against the pro-U.S. Shah. (Although Iran is not an Arab country, the perceived threat of the revolution's success spreading throughout the predominately Muslim Arab world has contributed both to anti-Islamic media images in the West and to U.S. and European foreign policies in the region.) Western discussions of Arab women have typically situated feminism in implicit or explicit opposition to Arab or Islamic culture, suggesting that Arab women are in need of being "saved" from their own cultures.

However, since the publication of Margot Badran and miriam cooke's groundbreaking anthology *Opening the Gates: A Century of Arab Feminist Writing* (1990), the common perception of "Arab feminism" as either an oxymoron or a Western import has been far less easy to sustain. This growing awareness of the complexities of Arab women's experiences is similarly reflected in the increasing inclusion of and attention to Arab women writers in books and essay collections on postcolonialism, transnationalism, global feminism, and political resistance.[2] By situating discus-

---

2. For instance, Barbara Harlow (1987 and 1992) includes discussion of several Arab women writers in her book-length studies, as does Nada Elia (2001). For a collection of es-

sions about Arab women within the complexities of postcolonial experience, such texts have helped to dispel the persistent Orientalist fascination with Arab women that reduces their lives to gender and sexual oppression under the purportedly unchanging, backward traditions of Arab-Islamic society. This increasing attentiveness to the location of Arab women within the larger "imagined community" of Third World women and transnational feminist writers makes it possible to explore with greater precision the impact of political, economic, and military forces on Arab women's lives.

However, it is also true that Orientalist fascination remains a significant factor in discussions of Arab women, and that transnational contexts of global feminism implicitly construct what Chandra Talpade Mohanty has called " 'the third world woman' as a singular monolithic subject" (1991, 51). In this collection we seek to challenge simplistic readings of Arab women's lives that would privilege gender above all other categories of analysis, and to underscore instead the complexities of the postcolonial contradictions experienced and voiced by Arab women writers. The novelists discussed here write within the turbulent postcolonial context of the post-1960s, a period marked in the Arab world by the rise of national liberation movements, the defeat of Arab nationalism, the fragmentation of Arab identity, and the increasing militarism of the Israeli state. They contend with the intersecting hierarchies of gender, religion, class, and ethnicity within their societies, as well as with the patriarchal, colonialist, Zionist, and militarized violence linked to these hierarchies. Situating gender issues within these historical moments of flux and change, these authors seek to recast national narratives and to redefine boundaries of identity and community. Their texts, shaped by what Lebanese novelist Etel Adnan calls intersecting "circles of oppression" and "circles of repression" (1982, 104), explore the possibilities of representation as a site of re-

---

says on the Lebanese/Arab-American writer and artist Etel Adnan, see Majaj and Amireh, forthcoming. A number of collections on postcolonialism and feminism include essays on Arab women writers. See, for instance, Amireh and Majaj 2000; Ghosh and Bose 1996; Green et al. 1996; Grewal and Kaplan 1994; Mohanty, Russo, and Torres 1991; and Parker et al. 1992.

sistance even as they appeal to human rights and communal compassion to right societal and political injustice.

We have chosen to limit the geographical scope of this collection to Egypt, Lebanon, Palestine, and Algeria for several reasons. On a practical level, the greater availability in English translation of literature from Egypt, Lebanon, Palestine, and Algeria makes the project of situating and discussing these texts within English-speaking contexts of particular importance. On a historical level, these countries have played a central role in the development of feminism and the rise of postcolonialism in the Arab world. The feminist consciousness that had begun to find expression among Arab women by the 1870s was largely centered in Egypt; indeed, the first public identification of Arab women as feminists coincided with the founding of the Egyptian Feminist Union in 1923. Egyptian feminism was also embedded within the context of the nationalist movement against British occupation, and women struggled "concurrently as feminists and nationalists" (Badran 1988, 16). This theme of "dual liberation" similarly informs women's struggles for political and social transformation in Lebanon, Palestine, and Algeria. Although the meanings and implications of the terms *feminism* and *nationalism* vary from author to author, an emphasis on critiquing both social and political structures plays a significant role in women's writings from these countries.

The authors included here all write within a postcolonial context—or, in the case of Palestinians, the context of a continuing struggle against Israeli annexation of their homeland—and their texts are informed by this context. While colonialist policies and atrocities have contributed to present conflicts in the region, fueling sectarian and class divisions as well as nationalist resistance movements, the colonial legacy has also complicated women's struggles for gender equality within their own societies. For instance, although the Algerian struggle for independence from French settler colonialism (1954–62) proved to be a beacon for Third World anticolonialist struggles, it also served as a critical warning for many Arab and Third World women of the conflicts women face between their allegiances to nationalist interests and to their liberation as women. The Algerian experience of decolonization is thus particularly pertinent to the struggles of women in Lebanon and Palestine who confront the intersecting forces of colonialist legacies, patriarchy, and militarized violence.

This collection includes both Arabic and Francophone writers, whose literary languages reflect the various forms that colonialism took in the countries under discussion. While both Egypt and Palestine experienced a history of British occupation and mandate (in the case of Egypt, 1882–1952; in the case of Palestine, 1917–48), the predominantly military and economic nature of these occupations for the most part allowed Egyptians and Palestinians to maintain their native Arabic language and educational systems. This is evident in the fact that most of the Egyptian and both of the Palestinian writers included in the collection wrote their novels in their native Arabic. In contrast, Algeria was subjected to an intensive form of French settler colonialism (1830–1962) that carried out its "civilizing mission" through the French school system and through education in the French language. When Britain and France divided up the remains of the defeated Ottoman Empire in the post–World War I era, France also gained control of Syria-Lebanon, establishing a French mandate for Greater Lebanon (1918–42) that institutionalized confessionalism and the Maronite Christian hegemony. As in Algeria, the establishment of French schools and institutions in Lebanon created an educational system that privileged the French language among an earlier generation of writers. As a result of these colonial histories, several writers in the collection, including Algerian Assia Djebar, Lebanese Etel Adnan, and Egyptian-born, Paris-based Andrée Chedid, write originally in French (and, in the case of Adnan, in English). In the postcolonial era, however, this linguistic overdetermination is beginning to be challenged. Thus, for instance, a younger generation of Lebanese writers, including Hoda Barakat and Hanan al-Shaykh, write in Arabic. Such linguistic negotiations are emblematic of the hybrid, transnational, and transcultural experiences of many Arab women writers. Indeed, of the writers discussed in this collection, several have lived in or taken up residence in Europe or the United States, although they continue to locate their work predominately in the Arab world.

In situating Arab women's texts for English-speaking readers, we do not wish to suggest that the relationship between Arab texts and non-Arab readers is unidirectional, with Arab women's texts simply providing the raw material for Western critical discussions. Nor do we wish to imply that these critical discussions occur in isolation from the debates and contexts reflected in the texts themselves. As Arab women's texts are put into global circulation through processes of translation, publication, and marketing, the critical discussions about these texts also circulate transnationally.[3] The critics whose essays appear in this collection write from a variety of critical, geographical, and cultural locations. Their discussions situate them within the ongoing debates about feminism, nationalism, postcolonialism, sexuality, and identity taking place across national and transnational lines.

⚜

Intersections begins with a historical overview by Salma Khadra Jayyusi of the Arab women writers who appeared on the cultural scene from the turn of the twentieth century to the mid-1950s. Discussing the general tenor of feminist thought in the Arab world during this period, and focusing on the feminist writers Mai Ziyada, Nazira Zeineddin, Durriyya Shafik, and Nazik al-Mala'ika, Jayyusi charts the background from which contemporary Arab women novelists have emerged. Although the work of these early writers lay in the realm of ideas rather than fiction, it is the efforts of these feminists, Jayyusi argues, that provided the foundation for the achievements of contemporary Arab women novelists. Women such as Ziyada, Zeineddin, Shafik, and al-Mala'ika were pioneers in both the feminist struggle and the realm of Arab women's letters. Their writings, whether poetry, criticism, or fiction, were informed by a feminist consciousness that made possible the post-1960s generation of writers discussed in this book. It is this consciousness, Jayyusi argues, that underlies the energy and independence of female novelists in the contemporary Arab world.

Following this introduction to the Arab feminist context from which

---

3. On the impact of transnational circulation on Third World women writers, including Arab women, see Amireh and Majaj 2000.

contemporary writers have emerged, the collection is organized into three parts: 1, "Gender and Community"; 2, "Narrating the Nation"; and 3, "Embodied Voices and Histories." In order to dismantle the monolithic view of "the Arab woman" and to introduce readers to a variety of contemporary Arab women novelists, many of whom are little known in the West, each essay focuses on the work or works of a particular author, delineating the geographic, historical, or social context from which these writings emerge.

Part 1, "Gender and Community," situates Arab women's writing at the intersection of local and transnational communities, examining the reception of their texts within a global marketplace of unequal exchange and exploring authors' attempts to redefine concepts of identity and community. At the local level, Arab women writers address issues specific to their own locations, critiquing and reinventing their communities both within and beyond the frameworks of gender and nationalism.

However, the reception of their work within an international context means that their texts are often constructed or reconstructed to fit First World expectations of Arab women. The tensions between local definitions of women's struggles and the reinterpretation of these struggles through the processes of globalization are of increasing significance to feminists as they seek to establish transnational solidarity among women without thereby obscuring the specificity of women's experiences.

Amal Amireh's essay focuses on the problem of interpretations of Arab women's writing that ignore the political, discursive, and material structures governing the circulation and reception of non-Western texts in Western contexts. Taking as her example the fiction and nonfiction of Nawal El Saadawi, Amireh argues that this author's emergence into visibility in the West is a function of the circumstances in which she is read, "circumstances determined by the political economy of First World-Third World relations of production and consumption." Her essay examines the ways in which Western discourse constructs El Saadawi to fit First World expectations, as well as the extent to which El Saadawi herself both contests and participates in this construction. The visibility that El Saadawi has gained in the West accentuates the need to analyze the context of reception that situates Arab women writers in general. In opening the collection with this essay, we seek not only to bring to the foreground the problematics of marketing and reception faced by all the Arab women writers discussed in this collection, but also to emphasize the complex role occupied by Third World women within the context of a transnational feminist community.

Magda Al-Nowaihi's essay on Egyptian author Salwa Bakr shifts attention to local definitions and negotiations of community. In contrast to what Al-Nowaihi terms El Saadawi's "bleak novelistic universe of tragic essentialism," Bakr's working-class novel *The Golden Chariot* lays bare Egyptian social norms and beliefs through the use of humor, parody, and a "poetics of disorientation." In her discussion of this novel, Al-Nowaihi examines Bakr's juxtaposition of stylistic and thematic spaces, a juxtaposition that works to disorient readers and to challenge much that has become normative in contemporary Egyptian society. By setting her narrative within a women's prison, a space that functions "both as a microcosm of and an oppositional space to the nation," Bakr redefines traditional norms of community. Throughout the story, female voices from various classes and affiliations intersect and diverge in a communal performance that sharply criticizes contemporary Egyptian society and that transforms marginal spaces into new communities based on negotiation and compassion. Bakr's strategy of forcing readers to disengage tangled layers of meaning to find points of connection makes the act of reading itself "a 'strategy of affiliation' and an invitation to rebuild at least the desire for community." As a result, Al-Nowaihi suggests, Bakr's novel not only makes clear the need to rewrite social norms, but also posits narrative and the accompanying act of reading as ways of recreating modes of community.

In an essay on Egyptian-born Andrée Chedid's novels *The Sixth Day* and *The Return to Beirut,* Mary Layoun similarly focuses on concepts of community, this time within a more broadly defined context of illness, death, and war. Chedid's novels—set respectively within an Egyptian village plagued by cholera and a Lebanon devastated by war—stand as interlocutors to each other, their contexts of shared misfortune providing the occasion for an exploration of what Layoun terms "the potential of im/possible community in recognizing, sharing, and allotting the 'misfortune' of human mortality and death." Implicitly redefining the conventional understanding of community as grounded primarily in group identity, Layoun suggests that community has to do not with the accident of linguistic commonality or geographical proximity, but rather with choice and commitment. This sense of commitment finds expression through the act of witnessing and testifying to misfortune, for it is in such acts that commonalities are made clear. Readers participate in this establishment of community through their positioning as witnesses; indeed, the possibility of community rests upon their recognition of the commonality of misfortune. As Al-Nowaihi does in her discussion of Bakr's novel, Layoun points toward the role of readers in recreating a community based on compassion, suggesting that Chedid's texts function not simply as literary artifacts but as tools of social transformation.

Part 2, "Narrating the Nation," focuses more specifically on the tensions that arise when women, and sometimes men, attempt to negotiate between nationalist and gendered imperatives in the context of political struggle. Nationalist causes often situate women between two extremes, viewing them either as emblems of cultural authenticity locked within traditional roles or as participants in masculinist political struggles—struggles that typically impel women to lay aside female roles in response to nationalist exigencies, most often for temporary gains. Men also may struggle with constructions of the masculinized fighter that define both their sexuality and their duties to family and nation. These issues are of particular significance to Palestinian and Lebanese women, whose experiences of war and nationalism play significant roles in their attempts to negotiate gender issues. The essays in this section address the ways in which Palestinian and Lebanese women have rewritten nationalist narratives in an attempt to make space both for themselves and for alternative sexualities that defy the gendered constructions of war and nationalism.

Situating her discussion within the concrete historical events of Palestine, Barbara Harlow, in an essay on Sahar Khalifeh, examines the "sexualized and gendered tension between a nation's honor and its people's dishonor." Harlow argues that Khalifeh's mapping of gendered arenas of struggle—within a political economy dependent on Israel, a developmentalism that has destroyed agrarian life, a nationalism conducted by leaders in exile, and a traditionalism that confines women to the symbolic thresholds of society—challenges the hierarchies created by military occupation and exacerbated by class, religious, and ethnic divisions among Palestinians. In depicting the intersection of feminist and nationalist projects, Harlow asserts, Khalifeh collapses the distinction between public and private, "at once internaliz[ing] the public and political debate, and externaliz[ing] the otherwise privatized issues of women's lives in a compelling argument for the reciprocities of the conversations that build communities and the diplomacies that establish states." This growing emphasis in Khalifeh's later fiction on the place of women's voices and women's spaces in the Palestinian national agenda of state-building accentuates the crucial need to recognize women's rights as human rights within the context of the nationalist struggle.

Turning to the Palestinian diaspora experience, Therese Saliba traces the meanings of Palestinian exile in the narratives of Liana Badr, emphasizing the contradictions and inadequacies of nationalist constructions of identity articulated without a land base. Chronicling a series of exiles in Jordan and Lebanon as well as shifting representations of gender and nationalism over twenty years of struggle, Badr's novels demonstrate the necessity of addressing Palestinian women's concerns within the context of nationalism. However, Saliba argues, Badr subverts masculine narratives of nationalism by placing women at the center and by rewriting gendered metaphors of the nation, reconfiguring Palestinian nationalism as a transnational struggle based on human rights. While Badr's narratives make clear the centrality of nationalism to Palestinian women's struggles, they also make clear that this nationalism is situated within the context of "the search for individual and collective humanity." Like Harlow, Saliba emphasizes the intersection between women's rights and human rights, insisting that Palestinian women's gender struggles cannot be understood in separation from their political struggles for justice, human rights, and a homeland.

Mona Fayad's essay on Hoda Barakat's novel *The Stone of Laughter* explores the possibility of rescripting gender and nationalism within the Lebanese war context. In this novel, Fayad argues, Barakat draws on the concept of androgyny to critique not just male/female binarisms but also the dependence of notions of communal and national identity on such binarisms. Through its portrayal of the overdetermination of gendered and communal identity in wartime contexts, Barakat's novel "reveals the mechanisms through which collectivity is established, and the ways in which identity itself becomes nothing more than a construct that serves the interest of various systems of control." Barakat's depiction of a character that has not yet accepted the mark of gender makes possible an investigation into the processes by which masculinity and femininity are defined, as well as into the status of representation itself. Indeed, argues Fayad, through the process of representation Barakat is able to create an alternative, resistant, androgynous space that challenges that of the masculine national subject. To this end, the novel locates resistance not in the main character, who eventually trades his conflicted gay male identity for that of the masculinized fighter, but in the narrator, who continues to occupy a place outside the normative boundaries of community. Through her analysis of Barakat's novel, Fayad demonstrates how the rewriting of gender roles necessarily intersects with the rewriting of national and communal identities.

Part 3, "Embodied Voices and Histories," includes essays on Arab women writers who further critique the rigid gender divisions upon which hierarchies of power, violence, and the violation of women's bodies are predicated. Writing out of contexts of war and death, particularly the Algerian war of independence and the Lebanese war, these authors consciously problematize both the use of the oppressor's language and their own tools of representation. Their attempts at subversion and reinvention enable them to create resistant narrative voices and strategies. In their texts, these authors both express and repair the schism between body and voice that results from the colonial, patriarchal, and militarized discourses silencing women.

Nada Elia's essay on Algerian author and filmmaker Assia Djebar explores the ways in which subaltern women's bodies become sites of feminine alterity and a medium for preverbal, physical expression. This bodily expression makes possible a "fourth language" that captures the primal resistant scream of the Algerian struggle for independence. Critiquing French feminism's concept of *écriture féminine* and its failure to address non-Western experience, Elia shows that Djebar, as a bilingual, bicultural author, writes through the colonized female body and through the bodies of illiterate Algerian women fighters. While Djebar is acutely conscious of her own problematic relationship to the oppressor's language in which she writes, she is nonetheless able to subvert the colonial language to her own purposes, recovering both women's voices and their embodied realities. In her work the act of subaltern expression stands as a site of resistance to both physical and representational aspects of the colonial legacy, translating into the "wild collective voice" (Djebar 1993, 56) of Algerian resistance.

In an essay on Etel Adnan's novel *Sitt Marie Rose,* Lisa Suhair Majaj similarly explores processes of representation and narration as sites of resistance, situating Adnan's critique of gendered and political binarisms within an investigation of the effectiveness and limitations of artistic representation in bearing witness to situations of injustice and violence. As Adnan's novel makes clear, acts of representation carried out within overdetermined contexts of political power and violence are fraught with anxiety and complexity, often becoming complicit with structures of oppressive power. Examining the mediating role of the artist/intellectual, the tension between individual agency and structural overdetermination, and the ways in which violent power creates a schism between body and voice, Majaj traces Adnan's negotiations of these representational tensions through the novel's narrative form as well as through its thematic focus on the silenced subalterns of Lebanon. Grounded in the complicated relationship between what Barbara Harlow calls "writing human rights and righting political wrongs" (1992, 256), *Sitt Marie Rose* makes clear the difficulties confronting resistance literature. Yet the novel nonetheless affirms the possibility of speaking out against, and beyond, the silencing power of violence and oppression.

In her essay on Hanan al-Shaykh's novel *The Story of Zahra,* Sabah Ghandour charts al-Shaykh's narrative challenge to the patriarchal history of the Lebanese state. Zahra's story, Ghandour points out, is not just the story of an individual woman. Rather, the novel traces the violations of a speechless Lebanon fragmented by war onto the body of Zahra, whose own embodied history disrupts the official state narrative. As Ghandour demonstrates, the novel's gendered counter-narrative is conveyed through the tension between the voices of Zahra the narrator and Zahra the character. On the level of discourse, the temporary merging of the voices of the narrator and character heals the schism between Zahra's body and voice. On the level of narrative, Zahra's ambivalent, yet transformative, healing is portrayed through her escape from a patriarchal marriage in Africa and her return to Lebanon, where she experiences her suppressed sexuality and bodily memories in the arms of a Lebanese sniper. Although Zahra dies in the end, Ghandour argues, the narrative voice representing both the consciousness of Zahra and the voice of Lebanon cannot be silenced, but stands as a challenge to the official history of Lebanon and its social formation.

ಲ೦ಠ

During the years since the inception of this collection, the Middle East has continued to be transformed by the processes of globalization, "normalization," and various peace efforts. In the past ten years, the Lebanese war has ended; Israel has withdrawn its troops from South Lebanon; Algeria has endured a brutal civil war; and Israeli and Palestinian leaders have negotiated over numerous peace proposals that, as of this writing, have led no closer to resolving the fundamental issues underlying the Israeli-Palestinian conflict. Reading Arab women's literature within the context of these ongoing changes brings to the foreground the necessary "worldliness," to use Edward Said's phrase (1983, 4), of Arab women's texts as well as of critical discussions of these texts. As Said notes, "The realities of power and authority—as well as the resistances offered by men, women, and social movements to institutions, authorities, and orthodoxies—are the realities that make texts possible, that deliver them to their readers, that solicit the attention of critics" (5).

It is these realities of power and of resistance that inform the essays in this book. The critics included here, like the authors they analyze, are concerned with political as well as social transformations of the region. Their essays situate literary analysis within the historical and political events that shape Arab women's lives, even as they implicitly and explicitly critique the masculinist narratives that justify violence and exclude women's voices. As critical analysis and cultural resistance, *Intersections* seeks to interrogate and critique ahistorical and overdetermined assumptions about Arab women, gender oppression, and the possibilities of resistance. At the same time, it seeks to establish new points of intersection within transnational spaces—between Arab women from different countries, between Arab women and Arab men, between Arab writers and English-speaking readers, between writers and critics, and among literary and historical and political contexts. It is in this spirit of transnational interchange that we encourage readers to negotiate these intersecting interpretations for themselves, and to transgress the boundaries of this collection's categories in their reading of Arab women's literature and lives.

Intersections

1 Modernist Arab Women Writers
A Historical Overview

SALMA KHADRA JAYYUSI _____

When I feel a sense of exhilaration at the contemporary profusion of Arab women authors, both scholars and creative writers, I wonder whether this kind of wonderment will ever be the privilege of a woman scholar living in the year 2050, allowing for the two generations that will separate us. I feel she will perhaps have transcended the age when this kind of joyful amazement could fill her heart at the creative and intellectual skills shown by women, at their audacity and courage, at the brisk overflow of their talent and creativity, at their determined entry into an arena reserved, for too many centuries, for the male gender.[1] By the year 2050 the appearance of an important woman writer will, I imagine, have become a natural expectation, not an explosive event. And without being a commonplace happening (the appearance of a good writer is never a commonplace incident) it will have assumed the normalcy that befits it. Indeed, in the light of what the future can be expected to bring—women writing, creating, and radically changing the Arab cultural scene—an elated reaction like the one we now experience at the contemporary surge of women into the world of letters may well create feelings of discomfort

---

1. I was invited to open the First Book Fair of Arab Women in Cairo on November 16, 1995, and was pleasantly surprised to see the great number of books, on a wide variety of subjects and disciplines, already published by Arab women from all over the Arab world, including the Gulf area.

1

in the coming generation. For the moment, however, one can only feel boundless joy.

The fact that women have, throughout the history of world literature, lagged behind men must be put down in part to problems of direction, preparation, expectation, and the little leisure allowed to women by virtue of the traditional roles imposed on them as mothers, wives, and guardians of the family hearth. Virginia Woolf's *A Room of One's Own* (1929) is a modern complaint about this state of affairs, imposed on women by the fact of their gender. Perhaps more important, though, is the fact that often little or no attention has been paid to women's output in a male-dominated world, and that much of this output has been suppressed. The case of classical Arabic literature is a good example. There seems to have been a good repertoire of Arab women's poetry in classical times that has not, however, been fully preserved. We read in books of literary history how poets and professional transmitters of poetry (*ruwat*), such as the famous Hammad al-Rawiya, memorized, quite apart from men's poetry, thousands of verses of women's poetry. The paucity of Arab women's poetry preserved for us over the centuries must, therefore, spring from extraneous factors. Women's verse seems to have held little attraction for the famous anthologists of Arabic poetry in classical times. Abu Tammam (804–45) and al-Buhturi (822–98), two of the most important poets of the Arab/Islamic Empire at its peak in the Abbasid period, each assembled an anthology of poetry, calling their collections, in each case, *Diwan al-Hamasa* (The diwan of chivalry).[2] This choice of title points to their major interest in the theme of *hamasa*—of poetry speaking, in a heroic tone, of courage in war and of the chivalry, virility, and manly qualities considered necessary to ward off raids and protect the honor and integrity of the tribe. Women's poetry was, I suspect, neglected because women did not much concern themselves with this *hamasa* theme. The only woman's verse transmitted to us as a full body of poetry is that of al-Khansa', most probably because she wrote in the same vein as her male colleagues: her elegies on her slain brother Sakhr are full of motifs of chivalry and man-

---

2. *Diwan* refers to a collection of poems on various subjects, while *Diwan al-Hamasa* refers to a collection dealing with various subjects, but particularly with poems of chivalry.

hood attributed to a valiant brother, rendered in the elevated tone that has remained an outstanding feature of the poetry of male Arab poets right up to present time. The preferences of Arabic culture were not, it seems, attuned to a quality of poetry mirroring women's experiences and moods in those times, and great quantities of women's verse must have been dropped in the process.[3] This is a pertinent example of what has happened to women's creativity through the ages.

Up to the middle of the twentieth century, Arab women, therefore, had no established female poetic traditions to draw upon. With the enlightenment and the availability of education to some women since the end of the nineteenth century, however, women had begun to contribute to the cultural and literary currents of their times. Although their efforts were mainly in the realm of ideas written in prose, poetry remained a quest of aspiring women. Thus, we find that some of the women who became famous for their ideas on woman's rights and status in society, such as Mai Ziyada (1886–1941) and Malak Hafni Nasif (1886–1918), also tried their hands at poetry. However, women poets before the mid-twentieth century did not leave a strong creative legacy behind them, and the importance to posterity of their contribution lies rather in their ideas and nonfictional prose output. It was only in the 1950s that a real foundation for a feminine tradition in Arabic poetry was established with the rise of Nazik al-Mala'ika (b. 1923), Fadwa Tuqan (b. 1917), and one or two others.

In the realm of prose, Arabic fiction, in the first few decades of the

3. It is essential to establish here that poetry, being the most "private" literary art, was the major means of literary expression afforded to women in those remote days. All other genres, which were oral at the time, demanded a social and public framework not usually open to women. In contrast to what is generally believed, there was no paucity of oral fictional tales even in pre-Islamic times, that is, before the seventh century A.D. However, these were created, like the poetry of chivalry, mainly in the "heroic" mode, centering on heroic action and exploits in war, with varied fantastic and metaphysical inclusions. Moreover, these were mainly propagated by men: anthologists, reciters, and entertainers. There must have been many women who told stories to their children and to each other, but these stories are not known to have been recorded, perhaps because they did not make heroic action their mainspring, or address a general audience outside the women's immediate circle of family and neighbors.

twentieth century, was highly experimental and unsure of itself. It was at
the mid-century that the novel's inception into Arabic as a serious major
genre was established, due to the work of a few experimentalists, mainly
from Egypt, and to the genius of Naguib Mahfouz, who was the novel's
prime exponent. By 1951, Mahfouz had already published eight novels,
gradually establishing the form in Arabic. However, it was the publication
in 1956–57 of his famous *Trilogy*—*Bayna al-qasrayn* (*Palace Walk*), *Qasr
al-shawq* (*Palace of Desire*), and *al-Sukkariyah* (*Sugar Street*)—a family
saga in three volumes, that was the turning point in contemporary Arabic
fiction. Mahfouz's work was a firm bridge over which the Arab novelist
crossed to new horizons of modernity and fictional dexterity. By the time
that young Arab women, from all parts of the Arab world, had become
ready to envisage genuine literary careers for themselves, the art of fiction
had become entrenched as a major literary genre in Arabic, attracting,
around the 1970s and 1980s, a multitude of female talents.[4] These modern fiction writers are not only indebted to the rise of the novel at the
hands of male authors, however, but are also indebted to the courage and
modernist outlook of a woman writer: the Lebanese Layla Baalbakki,
whose revolutionary fiction—her 1958 novel *Ana ahya* (I live) and her
1962 short story collection *Safinat hanan ila l-qamar* (Spaceship of tenderness to the moon)—assailed the sensibility of Arab readers, ushering in
a fresh approach to feminist problems and laying bare the major hin-
drances to women's freedom and dignity in Arabic culture.

◑◉◐

This collection of critical essays focuses on women writers of fiction: of
novels and short stories. These women had to fight a silent but determined battle on many fronts; and since nothing is nurtured without labor,
they took time out (which many of them did not really have) to practice
their craft, building on a still unsure foundation, trying to forge a tradition
of feminine and often feminist literature independent of men. Far from re-

---

4. See my introduction to my *Anthology of Modern Arabic Fiction*, forthcoming from
Columbia Univ. Press.

sorting to a romantic, sentimental fiction of love and emotional escape, they moved straight to problematic issues, probing the questions most pertinent to their society and abstaining, spontaneously I think, from writing for the sake of amusement or diversion, or to give momentary solace to the repressed sexual desires of their audience. (We do not have a female Yusuf Siba'i or Ihsan Abdul Quddus, the two Egyptian novelists famous for this genre of sentimental fiction.) Rather, they addressed, with candor, alacrity, and sometimes great audacity, the serious, perturbing, and vital problems that afflicted their gender and their lives.

The women writers who form the background to this generation of new authors were mostly writers of discourse. I shall therefore focus here on women writing in the realm of ideas, whose works form the bastion of the present-day audacity and independence seen in the new women writers of fiction in the Arab world. In order to reveal a connecting thread throughout the twentieth century, I shall briefly discuss Mai Ziyada, an important feminist active during the earlier part of the twentieth century. After demonstrating the flow of feminist ideas in the Arab world as of the end of the nineteenth century, I will then concentrate on three major feminists: the Lebanese Nazira Zeineddin (1908–1976), the Egyptian Durriyya Shafik (1907–1975), and the Iraqi Nazik al-Mala'ika (b. 1923), writers whose work, for all its particular distinction, originality, timeliness, and brilliant argument, was, for one reason or another, suppressed or at least forgotten soon after the mid-twentieth century had passed. The fate of these writers is similar to that of the creative woman's situation in classical times, for in the twentieth century, as in earlier periods, women's literary and intellectual endeavors had been overlooked, often dismissed, and sometimes committed to oblivion.

◊◊◊

My own small generation of women writers grew up with the name of Mai Ziyada (1886–1941) echoing all around us with a glorious resonance. Mai, with her many accomplishments, her elegant literary salon, and her circle of personages from among the choicest of Egypt's literati, was indeed a unique individual, one who would have been every bit as distinguished now, in this generation of so many distinguished women authors.[5] She reminded one of the times of the early Muslims, when, in the first century of Islam (seventh to eighth century A.D.), the beautiful and cultivated Sukaina bint al-Husain, great granddaughter of the Prophet, had her own famous literary salon open to poets and other men of letters in the very neighborhood of the holy shrines.[6] The dazzling image of Mai ("the form of heavenly spirits . . . the figure of light," as the Egyptian poet Ismail Sabri, a faithful frequenter of her Tuesday literary salon, is believed to have called her in one of his finest poems [see Sabri 1938, 107–9]), was probably the most vivid reminder to us, growing up as we did in an atmosphere still charged with her personal achievement, of the capacity of women to overcome their social inheritance and assert their own talents and personhood. Yet the story of her tragic end, as victim to a male assault on her integrity, is also a reminder of the difficulties women constantly faced (and still face) in a male-dominated world.[7]

For all her courage and self-confidence, Mai was circumspect in her assessment of women's situation in the Arab world. Her writings were marked by a careful handling of ideas, by tact, and by a respect for those traditions she felt to be deep-seated in Arab culture. Nor was there any posturing in this, for all she said and wrote was undoubtedly governed by an inner, instinctive decorum. "I read sometimes," she wrote in one of her many epigrams, "what makes me wonder whether this is the candor of an audacious writer or of an uncultivated one" (Ziyada 1975, 14). Mai's kind of morality was part and parcel of the idealistic moral enlightenment illus-

5. Like everyone else, I grew up thinking of Mai Ziyada as "Mai" and will so call her in this essay, refraining from the formal "Ziyada." I shall also often call the other women writers by their first names, as they are usually called in Arabic.

6. Many in the contemporary battle for Muslim women's freedom and rights have tried to find fault with Islam itself, but Sukaina's precedence tells us more of Islam and its regard for and faith in women and their personhood than all the zealous third-century jurists, who laid down many of the "religious" laws that suppressed women's freedom, could ever attempt to tell.

7. To get hold of her inheritance, her cousin accused her of madness and, despite the attempts of many people to free her from his grip, committed her to a mental institution where she died.

trated by a number of avant-garde writers of her generation, such as Khalil Gibran (1883–1931) and Amin al-Rihani (1876–1940), writers who blended the best of their inherited values with values adopted from their contact with Western culture. The sexual revolution and the preoccupation with problems of the female body that were later to absorb a number of feminist writers such as Nawal El Saadawi still lay in the future.

In a 1914 lecture titled "Woman and civilization," Mai asserted that the continued misery of humanity, for all the advance in civilization, lies in "the backward status of women, who represent half of humanity" (Ziyada 1982, 29).[8] It is interesting to see her describe, in the same lecture, the roles that contemporary feminist critics the world over note as being assigned to women throughout history: servant, doll, mannequin. Woman, she says, began as a humiliated slave, then developed into a brainless child, then into a toy with which the masters played at their leisure, then into a statue bedecked with silken robes and precious jewels. In sum, Mai states, woman's history is one of long and painful martyrdom (33). After an attack on the Greek philosophers, especially Plato, for their contempt toward women, she speaks of Christ and Muhammad, who were the first to elevate women and give them their rights (30–31). Now, however, she argues, civilization is flourishing, and the twentieth century would be, as Victor Hugo had predicted, the century of woman, for women were now opening their eyes to the light in all parts of the world (36).

There were several other women in the Arab world at this time who wrote on women, edited journals on women's issues, and voiced a truly feminist consciousness. However, this nascent feminist literature formed only a very small portion of the general literary corpus, still written mostly by men, the greatest number of whom were either oblivious to the possibilities of women or simply had no faith in their potential. Even in their present writings on modernity one finds very little about the feminist question and its intricate implications for all other avenues of life. It seems, sometimes, that philosophy and the whole realm of ideas, economic and

---

8. The lecture "Al-Mar'a wa al-tamaddun" (Women and civilization) was delivered on April 23, 1914, at the Oriental Club in Cairo to a large audience of the club's members, who were accompanied by their wives and daughters.

political life, the struggle against colonialism, the whole edifice of living and planning can go on robustly without the question of feminine co-sharing and responsibility being seriously addressed.

A number of men, however, also took part in the battle for women's liberation—as early, indeed, as the end of the nineteenth century. The writer who springs to mind is, of course, Qasim Amin, who was the first man to address the issue at length. It comes as a great surprise, therefore, to find that his earliest writings were directed against the liberation of women. At the end of the nineteenth century, on his return from France, he wrote several articles attacking the Egyptian woman and demanding that she stay at home and confine herself to domestic duties. But it was a woman who set him right. Princess Nazli Fadil, daughter of Mustafa Fadil (who owned the largest library of his time, which subsequently became the Dar al-Kutub), had a salon in her house where she received such elite Cairene figures as Sa'd Zaghlol, Ibrahim al-Muwailhi, Shaikh Mohammad Abdo, and the Syrian Adib Ishaq. Taking offense at Qasim Amin, she asked Shaikh Mohammad Abdo to persuade him to refrain from such attacks because Egyptian women were not as backward as he described them. Abdo invited Qasim Amin to visit Nazli in his company, and it was this, it is said, that changed Amin. He began, subsequently, to call for the emancipation of women, publishing, in 1899, a series of articles in the paper *Al-Mu'ayyad,* which he collected in the same year in his famous book *Tahrir al-mar'a* (The liberation of women) (Khalifa 1973, 27–28).[9] But the work of Qasim Amin, like other champions of the feminine issue, both male and female, reflects a hesitant attitude toward women's liberation, at least at the outset of his career: a general lack of direction, a tendency to flirt with stale traditions, and an apologetic tone designed to assuage the conservatives.

Women in Egypt began demanding the vote as early as 1920, the first being Munira Thabit, who, between 1920 and 1923, wrote several articles on the subject in the newspapers *Al-Sufur* and *Al-Ahram,* and who then, in 1925, founded her review *Al-Amal,* in which she demanded women's right to vote and to become members of Parliament. There are interesting

---

9. See also Amin's book *Al-Mar'a al-jadida* (The new woman, 1900).

cultural parallels here, as it was only in 1919 that Lady Astor was elected and took her seat as the first British woman member of Parliament; and it was in 1920, too, that the Nineteenth Amendment gave women the vote in the United States. It is therefore with a pleasant surprise that one reads that the General Syrian Congress convening in Damascus at the end of March 1920 to establish the charter of the constitution for the new post–World War I Arab government in Damascus, formed under Prince Faisal ibn al-Husain (later King Faisal I of Iraq), included, in the various articles discussed, one designed to give women the vote and the right to be elected as members of Parliament. Unfortunately the congress, which discussed the articles one by one, was prevented from establishing the whole body of the charter by the French invasion, and a most commendable effort at liberalization was sadly forestalled. As for the actual article dealing with the rights of women, it was decided after heated controversy, and in order to avert a rift with the reactionaries, to set down that "all Syrians may vote and be members of parliament." The Palestinian historian Muhammad 'Izzat Darwaza (then regarded, like all Palestinians, as a citizen of greater Syria) maintains that the article was coined in this way so as to include women too (1993, 460–62).

As this example shows, there was, from the beginning of the enlightenment, a liberal atmosphere in certain Arab quarters that, without the intervention of colonialism, might have seen an earlier liberation for women in Greater Syria and consequently in other parts of the Arab world as well. Later a more resolute conservatism, beginning in the 1930s and growing stronger with the years, was nurtured by two strong forces: the hegemony of colonialism, which produced an adverse reaction among the Arabs against Western liberalism and the social freedom it embraced, and the various religious-bound movements in the Arab world, whose rise was also largely dictated by colonialism. Following Saudi Arabia's hegemony from the early 1980s on, this spirit of conservatism came to be ever more strongly felt over much of the Arab world.

Until the mid-1950s the Egyptian woman was still unable to vote, a situation endorsed by such scholars and writers as 'Aisha 'Abd al-Rahman. Women, she asserted, were born to work productively as capable mothers, this being a sensitive and distinctive role fulfilling a major need in

Egyptian society. It is astonishing to see how even a woman with a distinguished career ahead of her, one proving the full capacity of women to excel in fields of learning reserved in the past for men alone, could degrade her gender, excluding women from a more diversified role in society according to their particular aptitudes and endowments. But Dr. ʿAbd al-Rahman was a conservative at heart, never reconciled to the modernist notion of a woman living freely at large in society (Khalifa 1973, 173).[10] However, such conservative attitudes were eloquently challenged by the rise of some magnificent speakers for women's rights and freedom. Among these were the feminists mentioned above, Nazira Zeineddin, Durriyya Shafik, and Nazik al-Malaʾika, whose work I will now discuss in more detail.

Nazira Zeineddin

Nazira Zeineddin (1908–1976) suddenly rose to fame in Lebanon with the appearance of her book *al-Sufur wa al-hijab* (Lifting the veil; wearing the veil) in 1928, when she was only twenty years old. She has proved to be the major woman feminist to date in Lebanon and adjacent countries east of the Mediterranean. The book, a long argument against the veil, the rigorous segregation of Muslim women, and the suppression of their volition and rights, was written as a discussion depending not only on pure secular argument, but also relying strongly on the Quran and the traditions of the Prophet, which must have been a considerable feat at the time.

It seems that, initially, Nazira had not intended to write a whole book but rather a short lecture. She says in her preface: "As soon as I began to understand the meaning of rights [and] freedom. . . . I began studying . . . the situation of women in [the Orient] . . . the events of last summer

10. Speaking on women in modern Arabic literature at the Conference on Modern Arabic Literature (Rome, October 1961), ʿAbd al-Rahman made Layla Baalbakki's revolutionary drive in fiction for the liberation of women the butt of her attack, receiving loud rebuttals from such attendant conferees as the famous Algerian playwright Katib Yasin. See her lecture in *Al-Adab al-ʿArabi al-muʿasir* (Contemporary Arabic literature), ed. Tawfiq Sayigh (1962).

in Damascus, when a great repression was imposed on Muslim women and they were not allowed to unveil . . . prompted me to take up my pen . . . to express . . . the pain I felt" (Zeineddin 1928, n.p.). Throughout the book Zeineddin quotes ideas opposing the liberation of women and offers reasoned rebuttals. As noted above, she emphasizes her dependence both on the words of the Quran and the Prophet's traditions and on logic and the judgment of the intellect. The two were implicitly enmeshed, she argued, for religion and intellect support each other and cannot be separated (55).

Bent as she was on arguing the validity of lifting the veil, and armed with solid proofs from the sacred sources, Nazira elicited a major reaction in the form of letters to her and articles in the newspapers in Lebanon and in other parts of the Arab world. The appearance of her book also produced a reaction among the Arab community in the Americas. Particularly interesting were the many favorable reactions she received from prominent Arab writers and intellectuals. However, she received, at the same time, many hostile ripostes. She was severely chastised from the pulpits of mosques and accused of apostasy and falsehood, and several attempts were made on her life. The noise lasted a whole year, after which Nazira collected the most solid of these responses, both the positive and the negative, and, preceding these with a long discussion further expostulating her ideas, published them in 1929 in a new book titled *al-Fatat wa al-shuyukh* (The young woman and the savants).

In a letter she wrote to the French High Commissioner (April 3, 1928) on the appearance of her first book, Nazira said:

> I am a Muslim Lebanese Oriental young woman. My father gave me the chance to study and to exercise my freedom of thought. I studied with an open mind . . . the civilization of the Orient and its social conditions, just as I studied Western civilization and its social phenomena. I also studied in depth the principles of our religion and all that pertains to the two civilizations and their social standards, particularly those relating to the rights of woman, her freedom and equality [with men]. I was deeply grieved to see that our civilization and the principles of our society were

built on customs, traditions and ancient heresies that contradicted the spirit of our Book and the traditions of our Prophet, just as they contradict logic and rationality. (Zeineddin 1929, 102–3)

She speaks then of the rigidity of mind of the Muslim savants and their resistance to development. This rigidity is upheld, she says, by two factors: first, the belief of the world powers that ignorance and submission to traditions on the part of the majority will support their hegemony, and second, the leveling of accusations of apostasy and heresy against all those who attempt change (103). Asserting that she had enough strength of spirit to allow her, through proof and argument, to reveal the truth and to lift the screen from the eyes of those who are blindfolded and cannot see it, she explains: "I have deep belief in God's book [the Quran] and His Prophet, and my pen is led by my mind, free and unshackled . . . lighting the lamps of knowledge from those [Divine] lights. So I wrote a series of lectures . . . treating our social ills" (104).

Nazira's most important points—proved, she says, through logical testimony and by drawing on verses from God's Holy Book and the Prophet's traditions—include these arguments:

1. The veiling of women in Islam is a mere pernicious custom inherited from idol worshippers and has no proof whatsoever in the principles of the (Islamic) religion.

2. Women's freedom and their sitting with men are allowed in the *shari'a* (Islamic law).

3. Men are not more perfect than women in intellect or worship; nor do men deserve freedom more.

4. Men and women must share the same kind of education at the same level.

5. In God's law, a woman is a complete person, not a deficient slave.

6. Rule in the Islamic religion is democratic, and men and women must share it, especially in the right to vote.

11. God and His Prophet are the champions of woman, while some religious savants are her enemies.

13. The Quran is the lamp of enlightenment . . . but the interpreters

did not understand its essence, and made errors in thinking, constricting us [the women] to a narrow and difficult corner.

16. The Muslim is instructed to take wisdom wherever he finds it. He should take all he can from the wisdom of the West. (Zeineddin 1929, 104–6)

Nazira's arguments are cogent and convincing. It is of great interest to see her, in defending her admiration for Western civilization, reveal her belief that the world will embrace a "harmonious unified civilization" (Zeineddin 1929, 53)—a view that is apt for our days of globalization. She envisages a world in which a global unity would be achieved and the human family would be strong and bonded.

The major figure among her attackers was Shaikh Mustafa al-Ghalayini, a famous Muslim savant who, relying on the fact that she had studied in missionary schools where grasp of the Arabic language and knowledge of Islam would often be curtailed, claimed she was not the actual author of the book. However, in her second book, she argued with him point for point. "Can you deny that the Muslims took some of their religion from a woman?" she asked, reminding him that collectors relied, in the early days of Islam, on what a woman had memorized, and that they had copied the Holy Quran from the sheets of the Quran kept in the custody of another woman (Zeineddin 1929, 10).[11]

These arguments received a great many favorable responses from a number of Arab writers in the Arab world and in the Americas, including the famous Amin al-Rihani. This reaction illustrates the liberal currents blowing over the Arab world at the end of the 1920s, reveals a readiness in

---

11. Reference here is to Aisha, wife of the Prophet. One of his traditions says, "Take your religion from this red-head." See also Zeineddin 1928, 63. It is also known that the Prophet's wife Hafsa, daughter of the second Orthodox Caliph Omar, was entrusted by her father with the first sheets of the Quran, later collected by the third Orthodox Caliph, 'Uthman. The Prophet's wives were certainly a major source of his sayings and traditions, and the Muslims took many of these from their mouths. For a single reference, see Rida 1932. See page 53 for Aisha's erudition and knowledge of these traditions; page 62 for Um Salama's and Juwairiyya's; and page 64 for Um Habiba's and Maimuna's.

Arab society to adopt new ideas about women and their status in society, and proves the capacity of Arabic culture at the time to embrace a liberal social address.

It is tragic that these arguments of the 1920s are still relevant today, and are not simply part of a foregone era. It is as if, in many quarters throughout the Arab world, all these intervening years between Nazira's times and ours, and the actual emergence, in many spheres, of the Arab woman from her traditional enclosure, had simply not happened. Modern Arabs might have expected to see this argument conclusively resolved long since, particularly as the Arab world passed through a much more liberal period during the 1940s, 1950s, and 1960s. However, since the mid-1970s, the argument has been resumed and threatens to undo the progress achieved by so many women and men in modern times.

Nazira seems to have led a more or less quiet life when, eventually, the noise calmed down. She got married in 1938 and had three children. Happily for her, she did not receive the unseemly male retaliation that other feminists did. It was her books that suffered neglect—a phenomenon that would repeat itself with other feminists. However, it is necessary now to bring these and similar feminist books and writings out from the shadows to which they have been committed. A silent rejection has afflicted many women writers in the cause of women's liberation. Bringing to light these writings is of particular significance now, as women face present-day attempts to reshape the Arab world according to reactionary concepts that would rob them both of the rights they have already achieved and of their legitimate longing for full liberation.[12]

---

12. I have benefited from two extra references: the first, a short published biography of Nazira Zeineddin by Nadia Nuweihed, "Nazira Zeineddin, the Woman More Mysterious," published in Beirut in the *Al-Duha Review* (May 1998), kindly sent to me by the author; and the second, an unpublished assessment by Nouri Jarrah, a feminist journalist and editor of the avant-garde review *Al-Katiba* (London), devoted to women's issues. I thank both authors very much.

Durriyya Shafik

One of the mid-twentieth century's most interesting feminists was Durriyya Shafik (1907–1975), a poet, essayist, and human rights activist. Her story is a heart-wrenching tale of courage and despair, of resounding manifestation and enforced silence, of noble endeavor and tragic defeat. Moreover, her story is the story of the Middle East following World War II, when a vibrant consciousness of freedom and progress, which had grown steadily over the decades since the enlightenment, encountered a tragically renewed reversal: the replacement of direct, iniquitous colonialism, indifferent at heart to the achievement of genuine progress by the Arabs, by a national independence that, from the late 1940s on, permitted the rise of an equally iniquitous Arab autocracy, strangulating and often brutal in the extreme.

Durriyya Shafik began her feminist struggle in Egypt in the 1940s, after receiving her doctorate (*licence d'état*) with distinction from the Sorbonne in 1940. A few years after Egypt's 1952 revolution, however, she found herself catapulted into a world of organized chaos she never understood; and she paid for her optimism, and her faith in the possibility of equity and justice in this kind of world, with everything she had. Her life and tragic death are a haunting example of the courageous struggle that ends in oblivion, a resonant reminder of the Arab world's short memory for those who, having proved their altruism, lose their power and are committed to loneliness and silence.

The well-known journalist Mustapha Amin paid eloquent tribute to Durriyya Shafik after her suicide:

This woman, who filled the world with noise and declarations, this woman, upon whom the world's lights were directed wherever she went, this woman who was the star of Egyptian, Arab, European and American society. People forgot her charge into parliament, demanding the right to vote; they forgot her hunger strike in 1954 for the rights of women and they forgot that she lost her freedom and her magazines, her money and her husband because she demanded human rights for the Egyptian people. She paid a horrible price for her resistance when other people gave up. (Quoted in Nelson 1996, 274)[13]

Though Amin extolled Durriyya's forgotten accomplishments upon her death, it took an outsider to rediscover her many-faceted personality in a recent biography.[14] Egypt and the Arab world had forgotten her.

There is no space here to speak at adequate length of Durriyya Shafik's work as a prominent feminist; as a determined activist for human rights and democracy; as an international figure spanning two worlds and several cultures with alacrity and grace; as a nationalist proud of her Egyptian, Arab, and Islamic heritage; as founder of several social and political associations intended to enlighten women and to activate them toward liberation of themselves and their country; and as the efficient editor of two journals, *La Femme Nouvelle* and *Bint al-Nil* (the first, in French, inherited from the Femme Nouvelle association, the second in Arabic and her very own creation). It was in the pages of these two journals—both of which centered upon the construction of identity, whether cultural or gender-based—that she articulated her ideas on liberty, women's rights, and the artistic and literary heritage of Egypt (Nelson 1996, 135). *La Femme Nouvelle* addressed cultural issues and was directed both to a highly educated and Westernized Egyptian elite and to a Western public. As such, the review was intended to be a "mirror of present progress [in Egypt]" as well as "the echo of a very old civilization which is being reborn" (quoted in Nelson 1996, 134).[15] *Bint al-Nil,* on the other hand, aimed to "awaken Egyptian and Arab middle-class women to their basic rights and responsibilities" (quoted in Nelson 1996, 135). The two magazines reveal, her biographer says, "how the esthetic and the activist, those

13. Amin's tribute appears in his Arabic account of Shafik, "The Beautiful Leader," in *Masa'il shakhsiyya* (Personal matters) (Cairo 1984), 68.

14. Cynthia Nelson, a professor of anthropology at the American University of Cairo, a lover of poetry and a scholar of sensitivity and insight, devoted years of work to researching and writing Durriyya Shafik's biography.

15. This quote is from the foreword to *La Femme Nouvelle* (December 1947). Subsequent quotes from Nelson are from this foreword.

dual and competing strands in her life, are woven . . . intimately and profoundly into her experience" (135).

Durriyya Shafik's cultural ties with the West were strong. Yet she
proudly kept her Islamic/Egyptian and Arab identity. Her attacks were directed against the establishment, against the entrenched chauvinism of
men, against the inherited disrespect for women's rights and freedom; but,
unlike other activists for women's or human rights, she never attacked
Arab/Islamic civilization, the Islamic religion, or the Arab heritage, as did
so many "modern" intellectuals before and after her. She saw these, on the
contrary, as great monuments of human endeavor and creativity, which
should be brought once more to the attention of the world. Her outlook on
civilizations anticipated the present openness to a world globalization,
which acknowledges the creativity of all peoples and races and the benefit to
be derived from the heritage of all the world. The new woman, Durriyya declared, was a messenger between East and West, bent on making the West
hear her voice, for she will "throw a magnificent bridge between the East
and the West" (quoted in Nelson 1996, 135). As her biographer noted,
Durriya argued that "East and West are not hermetically sealed entities but,
on the contrary, act to complete one another" (Nelson 1996, 136).[16] As
Durriya put it, "There was a time when East and West were two inscrutable
worlds . . . evolving along . . . parallel roads and never meeting. Through
space and time, various civilizations . . . understand one another, unite and
complete one another. This edition [*La Femme Nouvelle*] essentially bears
witness to this reconciliation" (quoted in Nelson 1996, 136).

At the end of 1947 the death of Huda Shaarawi, Egypt's foremost
feminist and head of the Egyptian Feminist Union, gave Durriyya Shafik
new scope, allowing her to fill the gap of feminist leader, spurring her to
"assume the mantle of leadership in the Egyptian woman's struggle to ob-
tain full political rights" (Nelson 1996, 140). The situation in Palestine,
following the UN resolution to partition the country and the struggle that
ensued, convinced Durriyya Shafik that the weakness in the front presented by Arabs to the world was: "The Woman! A nation cannot be liber-

16. All subsequent quotes from Nelson are from "A Bond Between Civilizations" in
La Femme Novelle (December 1949).

ated whether internally or externally while its women are enchained" (quoted in Nelson 1996, 142). It was then, she asserts, that her feminist movement was truly born.

It was early in 1948 that she founded the new movement for the total liberation of the Egyptian woman, which she called the "Bint al-Nil Union." She called two press conferences, one in French and the other in Arabic, to announce the formation of the union. Opening the French press conference with the following bold statement, "The *sine qua non* of Egypt's liberation is woman's liberation" (quoted in Nelson 1996, 147), she explained that this meant delivering women from servitude to men. Asked which form of servitude she meant, she answered: "The worst! That which considers women as inferior beings" (quoted in Nelson 1996, 148). She insisted that men did not care about women's rights, and that women must enter Parliament and take part in the framing of the laws. Asked if she thought Islam was against political rights for women, she firmly answered: "Islam is innocent of such allegations. . . . On the contrary, the true essence of Islam is equality between men and women" (quoted in Nelson 1996, 148).[17]

In the 1951 December issue Durriyya poignantly wrote: "Parliament opened its new session a few days ago. The speaker ignored the political rights of women assuming that we, the women, are mentally retarded and unfit to take part in public life. This implies that ten million Egyptians (half of the population) do not deserve to participate in civic life. Wretched are the men of Egypt who live in houses run by women with no brains!" (quoted in Nelson 1996, 153). She determined to take action by storming the Parliament. She had her direct circle of revolutionary women swear on the Quran (the most binding oath in Islam) to keep this a secret until the planned day. At that time, joined by over a thousand women, they overran Parliament, demanding a promise to give women their rights. Failing to get any such promise from the president of the Chamber, who refused to see them, she contacted Zaki Urabi Pasha, the president of the Senate, who vowed to take up the issue personally. Nothing, though,

17. See also Nelson 1996, 153, for further ideas on Islam and women.

came of this landmark event—except, of course, for an enhanced feminine consciousness.

Durriyya Shafik was to make of the struggle for women's rights and, later on, for general human rights and democracy, a *cause célèbre* all over the world. She carried out the struggle with gusto and a flamboyant demonstration of will. But if the storming of the Egyptian Parliament was a major event in the history of women's struggle for equality, another, even more dramatic, event was to take place in 1954.

Two weeks after General Muhammad Naguib's 1954 coup ousting King Faruq I and declaring a republic, Durriyya Shafik obtained an audience with Naguib, telling him he had accomplished only half a revolution since the liberation of women was still to be achieved. Naguib was hesitant. It was, he explained, too early in the new era to attempt something that might turn a great number of people away from the revolution. Durriyya acquiesced, and, while awaiting future change, backed the revolution in her journals. "Egypt," she wrote, "has turned one of the most beautiful pages of its history" (quoted in Nelson 1996, 187).[18] In the meantime she visited Britain, continuing her connections with Western women's associations.

The announcement, in March 1954, of a projected constitutional committee from which women would be excluded drove Durriyya Shafik to rebellion. She flew into action, sending telegrams to all members of the assembly, to important officials in the military government, to the rector of Al-Azhar, and to members of the press, and then made her way to the Press Syndicate where she announced a hunger strike "unto death" (quoted in Nelson 1996, 197). She was joined by a handful of women in Cairo, while a similar strike was staged by a number of women in Alexandria. The hunger strike lasted ten days, and was called off when a delegate from Naguib agreed to give Durriyya Shafik a written pledge that the new constitution would guarantee women's rights.

By now Durriyya had become a world figure and had gained enormous publicity. After this momentous event, she went on a world tour to raise the reputation of Egypt and its women. Her world tour—to France

18. This is from a special issue of *La Femme Nouvelle* that was published under the title "Egypt's Renaissance."

and Britain, to the United States, to Japan, Pakistan, and India (where she sat with Nehru for two hours)—was highly successful and was deemed to give a fine impression of the modern Egyptian and Arab woman.

During her tour Naguib was placed under house arrest and Nasser assumed full power. The Arab world was inspired by his vision of a united, Pan-Arab world under his leadership, and an impassioned ideology filled the air. Nationalism and anticolonialism were the creeds of the day, and the patriotic waves they raised overflowed the banks of the Nile to engage the whole of the Arab world. Nasser, by far the most charismatic Arab leader of modern times, adored by millions, was bolstering his rule at home with an iron fist.

And Durriyya Shafik took on Nasser! In her single-minded, impassioned pursuit of a great goal, she had reached a point of no return, one only the dedicated can recognize. Yet she was unable, it seems to me, to sense the real changes taking place around her: the developing xenophobia toward the colonial West, the fanatic adherence to a new ideology, and the nascent vision of a possible glorious triumph to vindicate past defeat and humiliation. The Egyptians, and the whole Arab people with them, wanted to wash away the humiliating defeat by Zionism, the memory of an aborted war. Liberation from this burden seemed the most desirable goal at that particular juncture in history, and Nasser, looming large and vigorous on the horizon, speaking in a language the millions understood and adored, seemed the only man capable of bringing about the desired miracle. Durriyya Shafik never saw this reality. Nor did she realize how human nature worked, especially in a traditionally suppressed society that had known little freedom for at least four centuries, and that had long learned to summon caution and circumspection in the face of political menace. None of this found any resonance in her. She behaved as if intoxicated with an ideal, one she believed she, with her courage and determination, and with her liberal humanist philosophy, could achieve single-handedly.

Her last public act was a further hunger strike in 1957, staged at the Indian Embassy. This ended with Nasser's placing her under house arrest, her Egyptian friends and associates abandoning her, her magazines being suppressed and her income curtailed, and, finally, in her husband abandoning her to her fate. Her own writings of poetry and memoirs, along with her two daughters, kept her alive until 1975. Then depression took the upper hand, and she threw herself from her apartment, to death and profound oblivion.

Egypt and the Arab world had not just forgotten her positive struggle toward the liberation of women and the attainment of human rights. This world had become oblivious, too, to her artistic achievement as a poet in French. In my long search for Arab poetic talent in the twentieth century, I have never come across her name as a modern Arab poet. It has, quite simply, not been put down for posterity. Yet reading her poetry now, one is captivated by the delicate imagery and the transparent, benevolent spirit that shines through. The well-known French resistance publisher Pierre Seghers, who published, among others, such great luminaries as Louis Aragon, Paul Eluard, Pierre Reverdy, Pablo Neruda, and Federico García Lorca, and who was her friend and one-time publisher, loved her work.[19] He praised Durriyya's poetry, especially in its later phase (meaning, according to her biographer, her two volumes *Avec Dante aux Enfers* and *Larmes d'Isis* [see Shafik 1979a; 1979b]), for its vigor and strength and considered her a major poet of Egypt who counted "among the best" (quoted in Nelson 1996, 160).[20] Why was Durriyya Shafik committed to obscurity even as a poet? Was it because she combined the intellectual with the aesthetic, the reflective with the practical, national status with international fame, and the outward thrust of leadership and public struggle with luxuriant beauty and elegance? Was it this that provoked the hostility both of male chauvinists and of insecure women? And could it be, too, that the merciless fist of authority made tongues mute, silencing any acknowledgment of her life and work?

19. Pierre Seghers was a highly respected figure in France. On his death in 1987, it was glowingly said of him: "Poetry has lost its most fervent lover, its most active defender" (quoted in Nelson 1996, 159).

20. See also Nelson 1996, 159–61. In fact, it was Cynthia Nelson's discovery of Shafik's poetry in 1983 that prompted the writing of this sensitive biography. See also Nelson's preface, xiii.

Nazik al-Mala'ika

At the beginning of the 1950s, when she was only twenty-nine, Nazik al-Mala'ika, Iraq's foremost woman poet, critic, and erudite writer, already bore the mantle of respect and authority. However, in addition to her literary status and her artistic achievement, Nazik also provided a penetrating analysis of the situation of the Arab woman at the mid-twentieth century, much of which, indeed, still applies, despite the major progress achieved since then.

Al-Mala'ika's contribution to feminist studies began in the early fifties when she had attained full stature in her other fields of expertise. Within just a few years of the establishment of the avant-garde literary review *Al-Adab,* in Beirut in 1953, Nazik had become, through its pages, the uncrowned queen of poetry and poetic criticism, her name a legend, her poetry a constantly amazing source of innovative technique and aesthetic refinement. In the late 1940s she, together with Badr Shakir al-Sayyab, had had the audacity to start a movement that changed the course of Arabic poetry forever, and their pioneering work became the immediate foundation for all later developments. With a daring that could succeed only if matched by genius like theirs, they liberated the Arabic poem from its centuries-old mold of the monorhyme and the two-hemistich form. A number of gifted poets joined the movement, and it was the inspired boldness and confidence of this generation, now termed "the pioneer generation," their untiring search and experimental spirit, and their defiance of false sanctimoniousness, that engendered such dramatic changes in the Arabic poem.

It was Nazik, more than al-Sayyab, who was attacked by hundreds of poetry lovers in Iraq, first perhaps because it was she who described and publicized the experiment with such confidence and youthful verve, but second because she was a woman, daring to approach the holy edifice of Arabic poetry that had for so long been largely the prerogative of men, and to introduce into it what was then seen as dangerous disorder.

Nazik later described to me the very disturbing early months following the appearance, in 1949, of her collection *Shazaya wa ramad* (Ashes and shrapnel) in which she had published eleven poems out of thirty-two in experimental free verse, along with a preface in which she propounded the technique of free verse, proclaiming what she then believed to be its artistic and liberating qualities. She spoke of the telephone that never stopped ringing, the abuse, the raw language. It is testimony to her courage and endurance that she went on with her experimental verse and critical elucidations, writing long articles about poetry that demonstrated her brilliance and erudition.

There had been women poets and writers before her, but none had ever reached her status, to which her endeavor to change the poetic art of the Arabs was an added dimension. Fadwa Tuqan (b. 1917) was then writing her songs of love and spleen, mostly in a style very much in line with what was expected of a woman poet at the time and therefore acceptable to men. Fadwa's genuine achievement (which, to my knowledge, no critic ever noted) lay in the palpable change she introduced in the tone of the Arabic poem and the intimate, completely feminine voice with which she addressed her personal world,[21] in the complete emotional veracity she was able to introduce to poetry, and in the fresh and skillful pliability with which she was quietly forging a new tradition of woman's verse. These qualities crossed the threshold to a new kind of feminine poetic address, facilitating a change of gear from a male-dominated tone and outlook. This was certainly an achievement beyond the power of earlier modern women poets, such as 'Aisha al-Taimuriyya (1840–1902), who wrote a rhetorical poetry more in the inherited tradition.

The names of al-Mala'ika and Tuqan began to circulate together in the mid-fifties, but there were in truth no affinities between them. Nazik al-Mala'ika's complex poetry with its great thematic originality and its feminine but totally robust tone, her erudition, her critical insight, her cogent argument, and her highly courageous stance, in the early 1950s, on

---

21. This tone stood in contrast to that of Arabic poetry written by men, which, as explained above, assumed, through its involvement with chivalry and acts of war, a virile and sonorous tone that has continued up to the present times. This is particularly true of political poetry, which constitutes a considerable part of the contemporary poetic output. This tone has been enhanced by the involvement of poets in the regular poetic festivals in the Arab world, where poets write for large audiences.

behalf of women's rights and integrity were totally different from Tuqan's passive isolation at that time, from her rather sentimental, introspective preoccupations and far simpler verse, before she began to write her more effective poetry of resistance. Nazik's daring leadership in the field of poetic technique, her seriousness and genuine self-confidence, made her quite different from other women writers who felt dependent on men's opinion. Her rise to a focal point of leadership in poetry and poetic criticism during the 1950s was totally unexpected and totally unmatched at the time. She was a puzzle to the men poets and critics, who were simply unable to understand this sudden rise of feminine brilliance to a point never before attained by women in Arab literary history.

Even so, no one anticipated the storm that broke when her book of criticism, *Qadaya al-shi'r al-mu'asir* (Issues in contemporary poetry), appeared in 1962. Her careful reconsideration here of the free verse movement, involving some controversial opinions, gave certain male critics the opportunity for a concentrated attack.[22] She had observed the numerous failed experiments in free verse and the way the venture was flying out of control. With a genuine desire to check what seemed to her a chaotic license, she laid down stringent rules on the free verse that had been the initial focus of a quest for artistic freedom. But as a superior technician herself, she should have realized that in art only the artistically viable could prevail, and that all these failed examples would soon be consigned to oblivion.

Al-Mala'ika, to my knowledge, never joined any movement for feminine liberation. However, her address on women's status in society was probably the most eloquent statement of women's rights so far, her argument set out with lucidity, courage, and incontestable reasoning. Not one of those who easily espouse fashionable causes, Nazik took this stance long before it became popular, exploring the issue in two major lectures in 1953 and 1954.

The first lecture, given at the Women's Union in Baghdad in 1953, was entitled "The [Arab] woman between passivity and strength of character." In this lecture Nazik notes that the history of women has been one

---

22. See Jayyusi 1977, 607 and footnote 5 on 804.

of the "darkest chapter[s]" in "the history of slavery" because women have faced a "complete deprivation of every right in life," gradually losing all they possessed, even their "human value" (Al-Mala'ika 1974, 33). This is seen, she explains, in various things we take as natural, such as the difference in value between maternal and paternal relatives. Society tends to regard the paternal uncle as more important than the maternal, clearly implying that the father is more important than the mother. Another aspect is the fact that the married woman is more elevated than the spinster, enjoying many more privileges, including people's respect. As a result, woman's value in society is not seen to lie in her "personality, culture and behavior" but rather as "a gift from her husband" (33). Consequently, women seek marriage as their major objective in life.

Woman, Nazik maintained, has not helped herself. For example, she has developed the capacity for psychological cover-up—as when she tries to convince herself that what she does at the behest of her father or brother, such as wearing the veil, is really what she wants herself. At the same time, the contemporary man has, in her opinion, a conspiratorial attitude toward woman's freedom. The impediments he puts in her way stem from his feeling that her freedom robs him of his own—and when he does not oppose her liberation, he often takes a passive stance. This attitude results in two different meanings of freedom, one for men and another for women. Pointing out that the subjugation of women results in an equal subjugation of men, she objects to the belief that men and women can live together "and one of them have complete freedom while the other suggests complete subjugation." She objects to the belief that subjugating women must result in an "equal subjugation of men," for it is not logical that both can live together, one in freedom and the other in subjugation (Al-Mala'ika 1974, 32–33).

Nazik raises a very interesting point when she says that women have been burdened with moral commitments not applied to men. This means, in practice, that there are two orders of morality, one feminine and the other masculine. Generosity is a moral quality that can have a double standard because it "ennobles a man and elevates him, but becomes blameworthy in women" (Al-Mala'ika 1974, 36). In Arab culture, it is commendable for the woman to be parsimonious, because men regard money as their own possession, which a woman has no right to give away. Another ambiguous moral area is mourning. Women are supposed to stay at home and wear black for a long time, never seeking any amusement, while men can go out soon after the event and seek a change of scene (37–38).

However, the greatest deprivation woman has faced, Nazik maintains, is that of volition. She offers a brilliant argument here:

> The moral law as applied to women loses the basic condition of every moral law, of what makes us judge a person to be good or bad . . . for there is no meaning to any moral law which does not offer the individual full freedom to break it. This is because every law gains its strength from the supposition that people have the freedom to follow or shun it. It is from this freedom alone that character stems, and it is this which makes us regard character as worthy of commendation or of condemnation. (Al-Mala'ika 1974, 40)

She goes on to point out that compulsory morality is not a virtue. Women are judged in isolation from the constraints that restrict them, yet how can there be character unless there is complete freedom of behavior? To Nazik, freedom produces character, which, in turn, produces personality. And it is personality that gives the "power to think" (Al-Mala'ika 1974, 40).

In her second lecture, entitled "Fragmentation in Arab society," Nazik discusses the ills of contemporary Arab society in general, then moves on to speak about the situation of women in a society divided into two categories: men and women (Al-Mala'ika 1974, 11–30). To her, fragmentation in Arab society is the basic ill that triggers many other negative phenomena. She rightly detests the habit of talking about "women" as an issue among various other political, social, and literary issues, as if all issues belonged to men alone. She also observes that periodicals and radio stations have special women's slots, usually banal and limited in scope, involving only subjects like fashion, hospitality, domestic issues, and other superfluous things (23).

This fragmentation, Nazik continues, leads to a division of work between man and woman based on gender and not on a person's natural affinities and skills. So long as woman is woman, she is supposed to limit her activity to housework, no matter what her talents and inclinations are. Such division of labor has led to deep emotional and social problems reflected in the character and behavior of women. Housework, she asserts, does not use more than a fraction of women's natural mental and psychological capacity. This is not only straightforward waste, unwarranted and unjustifiable, but is also dangerous to woman's general makeup because of the discrepancy imposed on her functional abilities (Al-Mala'ika 1974, 26).

A number of consequences have sprung from this division, Nazik argues. The first is that women's mental powers have become stagnant. This mental stagnation precludes a healthy development of woman's emotional strength, for "emotion cannot be isolated from mental energy, because the mind directs it as it directs the whole body." Thus, a woman without a "developing mind" is not just intellectually, but also emotionally "bankrupt." Since a woman's life is limited to the "experience of raw emotion" by the circumstances imposed upon her, even her "motherhood becomes restricted," for her emotions become "a hindrance to her children, obstructing their emotional independence . . . rather than her love being a source of tender direction and creative guidance" (Al-Mala'ika 1974, 24–25). This deficiency in women's psychological upbringing can be felt in moral characteristics thought by some to be native to women, but which are the result of an arrested psychological development. Examples of these are envy, conceit, obstinacy, hesitation, fear, and suspicion, which Nazik believes characterize women in the Arab world (25).

Another consequence of the division of labor between the two sexes is that woman has "lost confidence in her intellectual power as a result of working continually with her hands" (Al-Mala'ika 1974, 26). This work is restrictive to a woman, Nazik argues, and has gradually resulted in the lowering of her value in the eyes of men. Indeed, the "present division of labor," she notes, "gives rise to a permanent social crisis" (27).

In a third lecture, "Social flaws in the life of the Arab woman," Nazik continued her criticism of the Arab woman's attitude to herself and to life:

> The female characters in the Arabian Nights have left a bad model for the
> Arab woman, the model of the slave girl who . . . lives by her instincts,

and feels she must be beautiful and should offer the man a transient, superficial amusement. This is the model that still haunts [her] life . . . and has not been changed in the least by the fact that she now goes out into public life. All that has changed is her words. We hear her speak of the major social role she will play, of her entering various fields of work, and of her liberation from the slavery of the dark ages. However, the real depth of her life belies this and cancels its effect. . . . She lives like a doll, her highest ideal being an exaggerated elegance. (Al-Mala'ika 1974, 48)

We must remember now, when the feminist movement has engulfed the world, including the Arab world, and has filled the universe with argument and challenge, that Nazik was speaking in the early 1950s. No one in the Arab world had ever argued the issue with greater brilliance. However, in the early 1960s, male critics who found they differed from her regarding ideas on poetry attacked a new book of her criticism as they would never have attacked a fellow man, particularly one with such a history of successful and pioneering leadership. They turned on her, forgetting the unprecedented role she had played and the originality, sensitivity, and brilliance of most of her criticism, and forgetting too one great and abiding quality in her work, which will always bear witness to her intellectual integrity: that she was the coiner of her own ideas, partly perhaps the result of her vast readings in both Arabic and English cultures, but finally her very own, the outcome of her own creativity and brilliance.

Nazik's status was adversely affected after this attack, particularly as she grew increasingly conservative. She herself told me in the 1980s, when I saw her on my visits to Kuwait, that she was a nonbeliever at the beginning of her career but later saw the light. (It was in the late 1960s that a new piety began to surface, first in her poetry, then in her dress.) It is appalling to see how the avant-garde world, in which, less than a decade earlier, she had been a leader and guide, has since been ready to overlook her work—appalling to see how shortsighted and limited contemporary Arabic criticism is. It is unbelievable, for example, that those poems she used to publish consecutively in *Al-Adab*, poems whose appearance always brought wonder and joyful amazement, creating high aesthetic pleasure and real poetic rapture in her contemporaries (myself among them), have now been overlooked, because they happen not to be in the style that has now taken hold of poetry in the Arab world, for better or worse. How can genuine art ever lose its value? How can an artistic creation recede and lose its place, thereby erasing the history or precedent of existing works? And how can a self-respecting critic overlook a once superior poetic experiment because new experiments have taken place? Our age has seen many inferior poets hailed as great simply because they dabbled in political poetry and uttered collective proclamations. And in this age of feminism, when both men and women have entered the feminist battle, some because it is lucrative to espouse fashionable causes, how can her writings, in the early 1950s, in defense of woman's integral rights and independence, be forgotten, when they should be given to every student in the Arab world to study and internalize?

This is not to say that she was forgotten, for quite a few books have been written on her and her life. However, her actual creative output has not been analyzed in all its artistic integrity, and the same applies to the decisive role she played in the history of Arabic poetry, a poetry so entrenched that any radical attempt to turn its course was automatically regarded as a colossal infringement on an almost sacred edifice. In contrast, constant honor and homage are given to poets and critics who are no match for her either in the creative field or in the realm of ideas. For reasons that usually lie outside the realm of art or erudition—politics, friendship, ideology, sectarianism, regionalism, or personal interest—their work is discussed on poetry panels at conferences in the Arab world and abroad, and in books and reviews, and many of them are given prizes and awards, while none of this has been accorded the woman who, with the pride and intelligence of her full personhood, laid a foundation of independence and integrity for other Arab women to follow; who, with unprecedented courage and unrivaled vision, engineered a poetic revolution that changed Arabic poetry for her time and for all future times.

❦

In the above discussion, I have attempted to examine the formative background to the present generation of Arab women writers of fiction. Although they are not the heirs to an established tradition of women's fiction, this generation is not rootless, nor do these writers lack a strong feminist background of writings in modern times to pave the way to a new consciousness of their possibilities and strength. The early twentieth century abounds in women writers whose work established a strong foundation for the self-contained, self-confident attitude that has governed the output of the new generation of fiction writers. The audacity and self-assertive confidence of these precursors have helped the present generation to transcend, probably unconsciously, the many hurdles that confront women rising, suddenly, from their traditional enclosures to enter an open field of creative struggle where competition, male chauvinism, and an inherited lack of esteem for women's output dominate. The new writers have also liberated themselves from the old need of women authors in traditional societies to rely on the opinion and acceptance of men. They constitute an independent, unconstrained new generation of authors, for whom the earlier women writers courageously prepared the way.

Women's voices have echoed untiringly throughout the twentieth century, expostulating women's inherent needs for freedom and equality, arguing, disputing, challenging, defying, raising questions, demanding answers, asserting women's personhood and dignity, and exposing the age-old global strategies limiting their freedom and rights. Without these proud, confident, and highly intelligent feminists, this new generation of women writers would have had a very different experience, and Arab women's literary history would have taken, I believe, quite a different course.

Part One

Gender and Community

2 Framing Nawal El Saadawi
Arab Feminism in a Transnational World

AMAL AMIREH

Nawal El Saadawi. *Courtesy of Nawal El Saadawi*

Nawal El Saadawi is an Egyptian feminist and writer. Born in a small Egyptian village in 1931 to a middle-class family, she was trained as a medical doctor. She became well known in the 1970s for her polemical books exposing the sexual, psychological, and cultural oppression of Arab women. She is a prolific writer of short stories, novels, travel narratives, and autobiography, and her books have been translated into many languages. Among her works translated into English are The Hidden Face of Eve *(1982; Arabic edition 1977),* Woman at Point Zero *(1983; Arabic edition 1979),* God Dies by the Nile *(1985; Arabic edition 1974),* Memoirs from the Women's Prison *(1986; Arabic edition 1983),* The Fall of the Imam *(1988; Arabic edition 1987), and* Memoirs of a Woman Doctor *(1988; Arabic edition 1958). Along with other Egyptian intellectuals, El Saadawi was imprisoned by Sadat in 1981 for her opposition to his policies, and was threatened in the 1990s by Muslim fundamentalist groups, prompting her to leave Egypt for the United Sates. She has taught at the University of Washington, Duke University, and Florida State Univer-*

This chapter was originally published in *Signs: Journal of Women in Culture and Society* 26, no. 1 (autumn 2000): 215–49. Copyright 2000 by The University of Chicago. All rights reserved. Reprinted by permission.

33

sity. El Saadawi resides in Egypt with her husband, Dr. Sherif Hetata, translator of her works into English, and has two children, Mona El Saadawi, a writer, and Atif Hetata, a film director.

The reception of a writer's work, as Nawal El Saadawi recognizes, is neither neutral nor arbitrary: "It's not," she says, "a matter of who's good, who's bad. It's a matter of who has the power—who has the power and writes books" (quoted in el-Faizy 1994). This is particularly true of El Saadawi herself, whose reputation as an Egyptian feminist activist and novelist, I argue, has always been an overtly political matter, especially in the West, where her emergence into visibility has been overdetermined by the political-economic circumstances of First World-Third World relations of production and consumption.[1] In this case study of El Saadawi's reception, I examine both academic and nonacademic writing by and about her, foregrounding the strategies by which the First World reads and understands Arab women's texts and drawing out their implications for issues of cross-cultural inquiry and feminist solidarity. I show that as an Arab feminist, El Saadawi and her work are consumed by a Western audience in a context saturated by stereotypes of Arab culture and that this context of reception, to a large extent, ends up rewriting both the writer and her texts according to scripted First World narratives about Arab women's oppression. To avoid the pitfalls of such reductionist readings of texts and authors, I argue that it is necessary always to historicize and contexualize El Saadawi's work, something I attempt to do in the following pages. Although this chapter is a somewhat narrowly focused case study, it also raises more general ques-

1. I choose to use "First World/Third World" throughout this article although I am well aware of the limitations of such terminology in light of the political-economic changes that make the three worlds theory problematic. But while this terminology is imperfect, it is still useful in highlighting the asymmetry of power between, in this case, Western and Arab intellectuals and in evoking "structural commonalities of struggles" (Shohat 1992, 111) of diverse people. This asymmetry of power is obscured by terms such as "north/south" and "postcolonial." For a critique of the latter term and an argument for retaining Third World terminology, see Shohat 1992.

tions about the difficult and often ambivalent role of Third World feminists and Arab dissident intellectuals in a transnational age.

As a reception study, this chapter emphasizes the politics of location. Reception theory takes meaning to be not an attribute immanent in texts, but rather a product of the larger discursive contexts in which they are read. It considers texts within the circumstances of their production and consumption, that is, within the historical contingencies that make them available for certain readers. From this perspective, what El Saadawi says or writes is less important than the places from which she speaks and writes, the contexts in which her words are received, the audiences who hear and read her, and the uses to which her words are put. This approach recognizes the multiplicity of meanings that a text can have in different contexts. As Linda Alcoff argues, "Not only what is emphasized, noticed, and how it is understood will be affected by the location of both speaker and hearer, but the truth-value or epistemic status will also be affected" (1994, 291). In El Saadawi's case, the relationship between text and context is particularly interesting because El Saadawi does not occupy one fixed location. An Egyptian writer who writes in Arabic for an Arab audience, she is also a "traveling" Third World intellectual who addresses an English-speaking audience through translations of her works and through her lectures and interviews abroad.

The interest in El Saadawi predates the recent attention to Arabic literature generated by Naguib Mahfouz's receipt of the Nobel Prize in 1988. The first of her books to be translated was the nonfictional *al-Wajh al-'ari lil-mar'a al—'arabiyyah,* which appeared in Arabic in 1977 and in English in 1980 as *The Hidden Face of Eve: Women in the Arab World.* Three years later, her novel *Imra'a 'ind nuqtat al-sifr* (1979) was published in English as *Woman at Point Zero* (1983). For a decade and a half now, a constant stream of El Saadawi's work, mostly fiction, has been appearing in British and American bookstores, making her one of the most translated Arab writers, male or female. At present, fourteen of her books have been translated into English and are in print.

The translation of El Saadawi's books over the past decade and a half chronicles her rising star in the English-speaking world. While her books made their imprint on the Arab world in the early to mid-1970s, they were not recognized in the Western literary market until the 1980s. Sometimes a decade or two separates the date of Arabic publication from that of its English translation.[2] But the gap has been narrowing. Now El Saadawi's books are translated promptly, with the English version appearing shortly after the Arabic if not simultaneously with it. For instance, *Memoirs from the Women's Prison* appeared in Arabic in 1983 as *Mudhakkirati fi sijn al-nisa'* and in English in 1986. *The Fall of the Imam* was published in Arabic in 1987 and in English in 1988. Her latest novel, *The Innocence of the Devil,* appeared in Arabic in 1992 (as *Jannat wa-Iblis*) and in English in 1994. El Saadawi's memoirs, *A Daughter of Isis,* (1999) were published in English almost simultaneously with the Arabic edition. At times, more than one of her books have appeared in English in the same year, an honor few writers in any other language can boast of.[3]

There is also a noticeable shift in the kind of publishing houses that are bringing her works out. The press that introduced El Saadawi to the English-speaking world was Zed Books of London, which has since published several of her novels, an anthology of her works, and her autobiography. El Saadawi made her American debut through the small, left-leaning Beacon Press in Boston, which published *The Hidden Face of Eve* in 1982. Saqi Books in London and City Lights of San Francisco, both small publishers, brought out *Memoirs of a Woman Doctor* in 1988 and 1989, respectively. However, the new edition of *Memoirs from the Women's Prison,* first published by the Women's Press in London in 1986, was picked up by the University of California Press, a large, prestigious academic publisher, which also brought out *The Innocence of the Devil* in 1994. Obviously, the pro-

2. For example, *Imra'atani fi-mra'a* and *Mawt al-rajul al-wahid 'ala al-ard* appeared in Arabic in 1968 and 1974 respectively and in English in 1985 as *Two Women in One* and *God Dies by the Nile. Searching* appeared in English translation in 1991, more than twenty years after it first appeared in Arabic in 1965 under the title *al-Gha'ib* (The absent one). Similarly, El Saadawi's first novel, *Mudhakkirat tabiba,* was published in Egypt in 1958 but was translated in 1988 as *Memoirs of a Woman Doctor.*

3. The following pairs of books appeared in the same year: *She Has No Place in Paradise* and *Death of an Ex-Minister* (1987); *Memoirs of a Woman Doctor* and *The Fall of the Imam* (1988); and *The Innocence of the Devil* and a new edition of *Memoirs from the Women's Prison* (1994).

duction of El Saadawi's books for the English-speaking consumer has been shifting from England to the United States, and from small, activist-oriented presses to more mainstream academic ones.

The shift to major American presses is consistent with El Saadawi's growing status within the U.S. academy, where she has been inscribed as both a celebrity and a representative Arab writer. The institutionalization of women's studies and, more recently, of postcolonial and multicultural studies has helped make a space for El Saadawi's work on the syllabi of a variety of courses. Her books are assigned in both graduate and undergraduate classes on women's writing in general, African and Middle Eastern postcolonial literature, world literature, biography and autobiography, politics, and feminist theory. El Saadawi herself has taught in the United States, at the University of Washington, Duke University, and Florida State University.[4] Her work also makes a strong appearance in that most canonizing of publications, the anthology. She is ubiquitous in anthologies about Arab and Middle Eastern women.[5] Moreover, she is often the only Arab writer featured in anthologies not specializing in the Middle East: her essays appear in global collections such as *Sisterhood Is Global: The International Women's Movement Anthology* (Morgan 1984) and the *Heinemann Book of African Women's Writing* (Bruner 1993). She is the only Arab woman writer who has an entry in *The Feminist Companion to Literature in English: Women from the Middle Ages to the Present* (Blain, Clements, and Grundy 1990), and she is the only Arab writer, male or female, in the *Contemporary Authors Autobiography Series* (El Saadawi 1990b). An anthology of El Saadawi's nonfiction writing, *The Nawal El Saadawi Reader* (1997), was published (by Zed as part of its women's

4. This information is based on a limited, informal survey I conducted while writing this chapter. The survey took the form of questions I posted on various online lists (women's studies, African literature, Arabic literature, postcolonial studies). I asked those who taught El Saadawi to mention the name of the course in which she was taught, the names of her books that were assigned, and something about the response of the students. I thank all those who responded to my questions; the information they gave was very helpful.

5. See, for example, Fernea 1985; al-Hibri 1982; Badran and cooke 1990; Bowen and Early 1993.

studies list), also a first for an Arab author. More than ones that address Middle East specialists, these anthologies play a crucial role in establishing El Saadawi in the Western academy as a celebrity and a representative Arab writer.

El Saadawi's inclusion in these anthologies highlights one of her most salient characteristics, her mobility across international borders, which accounts for her high visibility outside the Arab world. In addition to her trips outside Egypt (partially documented in her book *My Travels Around the World* [1991a]) and her participation in international conferences, El Saadawi worked for the United Nations for some years. After being dismissed from her job as director of Egypt's Ministry of Health following the publication of her controversial book *al-Mar'a wal-jins* (Woman and sex) (1971), she took charge of the UN program for African women in Addis Ababa for one year; then she was responsible for the women's program of the UN Economic Commission for West Asia in Beirut. The large number of English-language interviews with El Saadawi and her visibility in the mass media in England and North America further attest to her mobility and her accessibility to Westerners.[6] El Saadawi's books are reviewed by mainstream print media, which often recommend them for a general audience; news of her movements and affairs are consistently reported; and prominent writers review and acknowledge her on the pages of such prestigious newspapers as the *New York Times* and the *Los Angeles Times* (for example, Mukherjee 1986; Sontag 1994).

All of this makes El Saadawi an interesting subject for a reception study. Much has been written in response to Gayatri Spivak's question "Can the Subaltern Speak?" (1988), but less attention has been given to figures like El Saadawi, who is not a subaltern, either in her society or in the West. Not only is she not the stereotypical silent woman of the Third

6. Interviews with El Saadawi include El Saadawi 1980a, 1981, 1990a, 1992b, 1993a, 1993b, 1994a, 1995a. Reviews of her books have appeared in newspapers such as the *New York Times*, the *Washington Post*, the *Christian Science Monitor*, the *Financial Times*, the *Toronto Star*, the *Guardian*, and *Publishers Weekly*. Articles about her appeared in the *Washington Post*, the *San Francisco Chronicle*, the *Chicago Tribune*, the *Atlanta Journal and Constitution*, the *Sunday Telegraph*, the *Guardian*, *Canadian Dimension*, the *Seattle Times*, and the *Gazette* [Montreal].

World, but also she speaks for herself and has direct access to her international audience. However, for El Saadawi, as for other Arab and Third World intellectuals who cross national boundaries and occupy multiple locations, it is a struggle to address the divergent assumptions, expectations, and interests of both Arab and Western audiences. Consequently, these writers, El Saadawi among them, are inevitably caught in the net of power relations that govern interactions between the First and Third World.

The Hidden Face of Eve in a Western Context

Despite her high visibility, her strong presence in the American academy, and her access to a Western audience, El Saadawi is not always in control of either her voice or her image. The history of her reception in the West shows El Saadawi struggling against misappropriation, but it also shows her accommodating the West's reading of her. It is a story of both resistance and complicity, and it begins with the reception of *The Hidden Face of Eve*, which marked El Saadawi's official crossover to the West. It became one of her most influential books, often hailed as a "classic." In what follows, I will discuss the context in which the book was read in England and America, show how it was received by reviewers, and point out the differences between the English and the Arabic editions. The reception history of this book illustrates, I believe, the way an Arab woman writer's text is transformed through translation, editing, and reviewing once it crosses cultural and national borders.

El Saadawi's visibility in the West coincided with two major international events: the United Nations international decade of women and the Iranian Revolution and its aftermath. While these contexts facilitated her entrance into the First World, they also defined and framed her for a Western audience. The United Nations' declaration of the period from 1975 to 1985 as the decade of women signaled official international interest in the lives of Third World women, provided them a forum in which to speak, and gave an impetus to global feminism. One issue of central interest to Western women was clitoridectomy, a topic addressed at the UN-sponsored Copenhagen conference of 1980. The coverage of this event in the U.S. media linked clitoridectomy and El Saadawi and gave both a prominent position. Under the headline "Female Circumcision a Topic at UN Parley," a *New York Times* article (Dullea 1980) begins by recounting El Saadawi's own excision, the same story that opens *The Hidden Face of Eve*. Another article credits El Saadawi with bringing clitoridectomy to the attention of the international community and its health organizations. It concludes: "Dr. Saadawi's campaign against this practice was rewarded when the conference recommended adopting national policies and, if necessary, laws against it, and when UNICEF declared itself 'seriously committed' to its eradication" (Slade and Ferrell 1980). Although this article mentions that El Saadawi discussed other issues relating to Third World women, such as education, health, and employment, it is clitoridectomy that was singled out and highlighted.

El Saadawi's own accounts of the treatment of excision during the conference and of the role she played are markedly different. In one interview soon after the conference, she criticizes Western feminist attendees for their ignorance of Third World women's concerns and for their focus on issues of sexuality and patriarchy in isolation from issues of class and colonialism. She denounces their treatment of clitoridectomy, making it clear that she resents the "sensationalizing of marginal issues in Copenhagen" and the use of female circumcision to emphasize differences between First World and Third World women. She insists, rather, that similarity should be underscored, declaring that all women are circumcised, if not physically, then "psychologically and educationally" (El Saadawi 1980a, 177). El Saadawi had expressed these ideas even before Copenhagen, writing in her preface to the British edition of *The Hidden Face of Eve*: "But I disagree with those women in America and Europe who concentrate on issues such as female circumcision and depict them as proof of the unusual and barbaric oppression to which women are exposed only in African and Arab countries. I oppose all attempts to deal with such problems in isolation" (1980c, xiv). She argues that Western feminists' concentration on female circumcision diverts attention from "the real issues of social and economic change," replacing "effective action" by "a feeling of superior humanity" (xiv). In both the preface and the interview, El Saadawi presents herself as one Third World woman among many, all of whom are breaking with Western feminists' limited agenda and struggling for the advancement of women in the Third World on several fronts, and she uses "we" to emphasize her collective identity (1980a, 177; 1980c, xv). In contrast, the American media cast El Saadawi in Copenhagen as an isolated victim of excision fighting a lone campaign against it (Dullea 1980; Slade and Ferrell 1980). This is the image of El Saadawi that eventually prevailed, a one-dimensional simplification both of her far-reaching feminism and of the various issues facing Third World women.

El Saadawi's entrance into the Western public sphere also coincided with an event that rekindled the Western fears of Islam, the Iranian Revolution of 1978–79. The deposition of the pro-Western Shah and his replacement by an Islamic government opposed to the United States demonstrated that Islam posed a real threat to Western political and economic interests in the Middle East. In this highly charged political atmosphere, interest in Islam was revived and heightened, and the reception of El Saadawi's *The Hidden Face of Eve*, which appeared in English on the heels of the Iranian Revolution, was conditioned by the Western interest in and hostility to Islam.

In the preface to the British edition (dated 1979 and absent from the Arabic edition), El Saadawi explicitly connects the aims of her book with those of the Iranian Revolution. Devoting half of her introduction to this momentous event, she celebrates it as a great anti-imperialist blow to the West, especially the United States, defends it against its critics and against Islam's detractors, and exposes the real motives of its enemies, particularly the United States and the Egyptian regime of Anwar Sadat (El Saadawi 1980c, vi-vii). She defines the Iranian Revolution as "in its essence political and economic. It is a popular explosion which seeks to emancipate the people of Iran, both men and women, and not to send women back to the prison of the veil, the kitchen and the bedroom" (iii). Her celebration of the Iranian Revolution is also a celebration of Islam and its anti-imperialist impulse (iii-iv). She affirms that her own project is continuous with that of the Islamic revolution since in her view the liberation of women is not separate from their political, economic, and national liberation. She emphasizes that "the Iranian Revolution of today . . . is a natural heritage of the historical struggle for freedom and social equality among Arab peoples, who have continued to fight under the banner of Islam and to draw their inspiration from the teachings of the Koran and the Prophet Mahomet" (iv).

El Saadawi's preface to the first English edition is an attempt to exert some control over her feminist critique of her culture, which she locates within an uncompromising critique of imperialism. In doing so, she anticipates the way Western audiences will read her book, realizing that they may try to use her criticism of her culture to further distance the Third World and to reaffirm stereotypes of it as underdeveloped and backward. If nothing else, her preface shows El Saadawi's awareness that she is addressing a different audience, with assumptions and expectations different from those of the book's original Arab audience.

But El Saadawi's introduction irked even her new readers. Two reviewers writing for feminist journals in England and America expressed their disappointment with the introduction, especially its celebration of the Iranian Revolution, Islam, and nationalism. Leila Ahmed admires El Saadawi's feminist critique of her culture and of its view of sexuality but dismisses the introduction as mere rhetoric that does not offer a forceful or clear argument. According to her, it is written in anger: "Out of such anger women are driven to support, as El Saadawi does here, revolutionary movements that have nothing to recommend them except that they are indigenous to the Third World and are opposed to the West" (Ahmed 1981, 751). She particularly faults El Saadawi for her celebration of the Iranian Revolution. Magda Salman, reviewing the book for the leftist magazine *Khamsin,* was even harsher on El Saadawi's positions on the Iranian Revolution and also on Islam and nationalism in general. She sees El Saadawi as "an Arab feminist who has fallen into the deep trap of nationalist justification and defensive reactions designed to prettify reality for the benefit of critical 'foreigners'." She concludes that El Saadawi "has failed to go an inch beyond the Arab-Muslim nationalism of the Nasserites, B'thists, and their ilk." Particularly troubling for her is El Saadawi's view that "all women's struggles must be subordinated to the battle for national liberation" (Salman 1981, 122). Both Ahmed and Salman indirectly recognize that El Saadawi's problems in that introduction are the result of her attempt to address a Western audience, not the Arab audience originally intended for the book. But neither of them appreciates fully El Saadawi's difficulties with this new audience, and they perhaps dismiss her too hastily. Not recognizing the complexity of the situation that El Saadawi was struggling to see in its totality, these reviewers implicitly fault her for not being feminist enough, at least in her introduction.

Defending El Saadawi, Irene Gendzier shows a better understanding of the writer's dilemma. In her foreword to the U.S. edition of *The Hidden Face of Eve,* Gendzier makes clear that one of the first encounters between Western and non-Western feminists was over the Iranian Revolution (El Saadawi 1982, viii) and locates El Saadawi's position within this charged context. With El Saadawi's preface to the British edition in mind, she justifies El Saadawi's defense of the Iranian Revolution: "In what was sometimes a defensive tone, she argued against Western feminists as well as the reactionary clergy. Saadawi's intention was to undermine the notion of a monolithic Islam while criticizing a policy which she regarded as regressive and a deprivation of women's civil rights" (viii). Gendzier anticipates how the book will be regarded by Westerners, and, like El Saadawi herself, she attempts to control this response by telling her audience how to read the book: "For those feminists who have long lamented the deprived status of Middle Eastern Arab women, Saadawi's book will confirm their fears. But it will also require that they re-examine the bases of their strategies vis-à-vis Third World women and women's movements" (viii). While Gendzier was accurate in anticipating the Western readers' response to El Saadawi's book, she, predictably, could not influence the way it would be read.

The early response to *The Hidden Face of Eve* seems to have caused El Saadawi to rethink how she should frame her book for a Western audience. The passionate defense and celebration of the Iranian Revolution disappears from the new introduction she wrote for the U.S. edition in 1982, an omission probably reflecting her experience with the British edition and perhaps tacitly conceding that American audiences would be even less tolerant of open denunciation of American foreign policy. The anti-imperialist rhetoric is also gone.[7] The focus in the new introduction is

---

7. One could also argue that at this point El Saadawi was disappointed in the Iranian Revolution and so changed her rhetoric. While this may be partially the case, the absence of

more on the way religion is used as an instrument of oppression by political institutions in the Third World (El Saadawi 1982, 3–4). She still rejects the Western paradigm, inspired by hostility to Islam, that sees religion as the primary reason for the inferior status of Arab women, and she insists that "any serious study of comparative religion will show clearly that in the very essence of Islam, as such, the status of women is no worse than it is in Judaism or in Christianity. In fact the oppression of women is much more glaring in the ideology of Christianity and Judaism. The veil was a product of Judaism long before Islam came into being" (4). El Saadawi continues to defend Islam against Western misrepresentations, but the tone of her defense here is more subdued and less militant than in the earlier version. Although she is still trying to exert some control over how her book will be received, she has apparently decided to adjust her rhetoric to accommodate the expectations of her new audience. This accommodation takes the form of appeasement when the issue of clitoridectomy is discussed. In the introduction to the British edition El Saadawi denounced those who exploit female circumcision for its sensational value and dwell on this so-called "barbaric" practice to the exclusion of other serious issues. In the U.S. introduction, however, not only does she neglect to provide such a caution, but also she herself calls the practice "barbaric" (1982, 5). The reception of the earlier British edition clearly influenced her decisions about how to present her project here. In order to be heard, El Saadawi seems to have felt that she had to compromise, yielding at least partly to her audience's expectations.

But these differences between the British and the U.S. introductions are only part of the story. In crossing from Egypt to Europe and then to

---

all anti-imperialist rhetoric from this introduction indicates that other factors were at work. Moreover, when asked in a 1992 interview if she still saw the Iranian Revolution in the same positive terms as an anticolonialist movement for change, El Saadawi responded that the original Iranian Revolution has totally failed because it was aborted by colonial powers that "played a role to shift it from a political and economic revolution to a religious revolution" (1992b, 35). Speaking to the leftist readers of the *Progressive*, El Saadawi still defends the original anti-imperialist and socialist nature of the revolution. In another interview given during the Gulf War, she mentions again the anti-imperialist nature of the Khomeini regime (1991d, 24).

the United States, the book itself underwent major alterations in both content and form. *Al-Wajh al-'ari lil-mar'a al-'arabiyyah* (literally, The naked face of the Arab woman) becomes *The Hidden Face of Eve*. Entire chapters in the Arabic edition disappear from the English translation. Two chapters in particular, "Woman's work at home" and "Arab woman and socialism," in which El Saadawi critiques capitalism's exploitation of women and argues for a socialist economic and political system, are not in *The Hidden Face of Eve*. These are significant omissions since the critique of capitalism in favor of socialism was central to El Saadawi's project, written at the height of the implementation of Sadat's pro-capitalist "open door" policy, to which she was vehemently opposed.[8] Also absent are passages that assert Arab women to be ahead of American and European women in demanding equality for their sex, that celebrate the progress Arab women have made, and that exhort them to see wars of liberation as empowering to them. One missing passage reads: "It is important that Arab women should not feel inferior to Western women, or think that the Arabic tradition and culture are more oppressive of women than Western culture" (El Saadawi 1977, 166, my translation).[9]

8. The open-door policy adopted by Anwar al-Sadat's regime in the mid-1970s opened the Egyptian economy for foreign investments and multinational corporations. The policy was opposed by several political groups and many intellectuals.

9. In the Arabic edition, the chapter "Positive origins of the Arab woman" begins with the following paragraph, which is absent from the same chapter in the British and U.S. editions: "The Arab woman was ahead of the European and American woman in resisting the patriarchal class system. The American woman did not realize till the last years of the twentieth century that the dominant language is that of Man, and that the word 'man' means human or all humanity, and that the masculine case includes both men and women. Some women's liberation movements in America and Europe try now to change the language. But the Arab woman did this fourteen centuries ago." Then El Saadawi mentions the incident when Muslim women objected to the Prophet that the Quran addresses only men, an objection that resulted in new verses mentioning both men and women (1977, 39). A tamer version of this passage appears in the afterword to the British edition: "Arab women preceded the women of the world in resisting the patriarchal system based on male domination" (1980c, 212). In another instance, she informs her readers in a footnote in the Arabic edition that, while attending a conference in the United States, she criticized the stereotypical representation of Arab women in U.S. movies (53). This footnote is absent

Even more significant than the translation's omissions are its additions. *The Hidden Face of Eve* has sections that do not exist in *al-Wajh al-ʿari lil-marʾa al-ʿarabiyyah,* including the chapter suggestively titled "The Grandfather with Bad Manners." While both the Arabic and the English editions open with the story of El Saadawi's excision as a six-year-old, only the translation has a chapter called "Circumcision of Girls." The only time El Saadawi mentions circumcision in the original edition is in the flashback to her childhood described in the opening paragraphs. No complete chapter devoted to circumcision appears in any of her other theoretical books either, not even in the most controversial one, *al-Marʾa wal-jins.* Although the chapter "Circumcision of Girls" is adapted from her book *al-Marʾa wal-siraʿ al-nafsi* (Woman and psychological conflict) (El Saadawi 1976a), even there it does not exist as an independent chapter; it is part of a larger section that discusses several aspects of women's lives, such as early or loveless marriages or the hardships faced by peasant and factory women. This much-quoted chapter, the one usually assigned in courses in U.S. universities, has been added to the English translation, and, to emphasize this chapter and the theme of circumcision even more, the whole first section of *The Hidden Face of Eve* is given the dramatic title "The Mutilated Half," which, again, is not in the Arabic edition.

In addition to these differences at the level of content, the English edition reverses the organization of the chapters as they first appeared. Sections dealing with sexuality, which were originally placed in the last third of the Arabic edition, are put first, while the exposition of Arab women's history is relegated to the end of the book. The earlier parts of the Arabic edition explain the processes that subjugated *all* women in order to show that woman's inferior status was not a natural one but the result of particular social and historical conditions. Referring to the history of Arab and Muslim women in particular, El Saadawi illustrates that these women used to be stronger than they are now and that their present disempowerment and degradation are not caused by Islam, with the implication that true

---

from the English edition. In both of these cases, she is trying to distance herself from Western feminists in front of her Arab audience, but then removes these passages from the English-language editions so as not to alienate her Western audience.

Islam empowers women. The reorganization, however, emphasizes issues of sexuality and underplays the historical context of these issues. It is an arrangement more suitable for a Western audience less interested in history than in satisfying an insatiable appetite for an exotic and oppressed "other."

The new title, too, seems to invite the English-speaking reader to experience the book as a glimpse behind the veil. While the Arabic title, "the naked face of the Arab woman," emphasizes the baring of the face, a metaphor suited to the political aim of the book, which is to speak the truth about Arab women's lives in the hope of changing them, the English title foregrounds the covered face.[10] By employing one of the main, and most stagnant, metaphors in hegemonic Western discourse about Arab and Muslim women, the new title confirms rather than unsettles its readers' assumptions. Moreover, the "Arab woman" of the Arabic title disappears, giving way to Eve, which further moves the book away from history into the realm of myth.

It is a very different book, then, that appeared in American bookstores in 1982. Predictably, reviewers emphasized some sections and ignored others, influenced, of course, by changes to the text. For instance, one reviewer, Vivian Gornick, titled her review "About the Mutilated Half" and focused her discussion on the twin issues of circumcision and Islam. She declares the book "a curious work . . . written in a country and for a people that require an educated introduction to the idea of equality for women" (Gornick 1982, 3). Her one-paragraph summary stresses only the aspects of the book that discuss Arab women as victims. She portrays El Saadawi herself as a victim by dwelling on her circumcision and her imprisonment, which she claims resulted from El Saadawi's speaking about taboo sexual matters. In fact, El Saadawi was not a lone victim of patriarchal society, persecuted for her feminist views, but rather a political activist, imprisoned along with 1,500 other Egyptians for her opposition to the Camp David agreement. As

10. This original aim is made clear in El Saadawi's dedication, which reads: "To my daughters and sons, the youth of the Arab world, including my daughter Mona and son 'Atif, with the hope that the future be more truthful and enlightened than the past or the present" (1977, my translation).

for El Saadawi's defense of Islam, the reviewer easily dismisses it by declaring that "no culture as religion-dominated as Arabic culture can ever accomplish social or political equality for women. . . . Western feminists do have reason to think Islamic law will never grant women full recognition. It may be possible to abolish the practice of circumcision, but it will not be so easy to abolish the idea of woman as an instrument of man's honor or dishonor." She condescendingly concludes, *"The Hidden Face of Eve* reminds us of where we have all come from" (Gornick 1982, 3). El Saadawi's book, then, becomes a testament to the progress that American women have achieved in contrast to their oppressed Arab sisters, supposedly still groaning under the shackles of Islam.[11]

This review is typical of the way that all of El Saadawi's other works have been received in the United States. She is almost always mentioned in the context of circumcision and fundamentalist Islam, as simultaneously a victim and an authority on both. By 1991 one writer could only remember that "Saadawi's most famous book, *The Hidden Face of Eve,* [is] about her experience of undergoing a clitoridectomy in her native Delta village" (Roth 1991, 10). Articles by and about her appear under charged headings such as "Betrayed by Blind Faith" (Mukherjee 1986), "Egyptian Pens Terrorised by Islam's Sword" (La Guardia 1992), and "Challenging a Taboo: Going to Jail for Politics, Sex and Religion" (El Saadawi 1985a). El Saadawi is almost always figured as a campaigner "stand[ing] alone in the fight for increased justice and democracy for women" (Roth 1991, 10). Since receiving death threats in Egypt, like so many other secular intellectuals, she has been seen in the United States as the ultimate victim of Islam, declared by Susan Sontag (1994) to be an Arab Taslima Nasreen, who, according to another writer, "creates an anthem for all those nameless millions who died the outer or the inner death, sentenced by fundamentalist Islam's cruel and unjustified repression of women" (Roberts 1993). El Saadawi's story of persecution is told and retold every time her name is mentioned, on cover blurbs, in newspapers, and in articles in academic journals.

11. For a response to this review, see Basu 1982.

This representation of El Saadawi erases important aspects of her political identity and distorts others. For example, Western commentators often claim that her feminist views on female sexuality led Sadat to imprison her and Mubarak to close down the Arab Women's Solidarity Association.[12] In fact, it was actually her opposition to Camp David in 1981 and to the Gulf War in 1991—not her feminism per se—that brought these reprisals. If mentioned, El Saadawi's political views are usually dismissed as irrelevant and "far left," as some reviewers put it (Jacoby 1994). Moreover, since El Saadawi is seen as writing of "a way of life that in many aspects has not changed for centuries," the specific historical context of her works is systematically erased ("The Innocence" 1994). Thus different accounts merge, and her books, experiences, and arguments become indistinguishable from one another. According to one report (Fullerton 1989), for instance, while El Saadawi was in prison in 1981, she met Firdaus, about whom she then wrote her novel *Woman at Point Zero* (which was actually published well before El Saadawi's imprisonment). According to another (Werner 1991), *The Fall of the Imam,* a novel immediately connected to the assassination of Sadat, is said to be a critique of Ayatollah Khomeini and the Iranian Revolution. El Saadawi's voice and image, then, are framed by the Western discourse about her in a way that fits First World agendas and assumptions: the socialist feminist is rewritten as a liberal individualist and the anti-imperialist as a native informant. This framing often discredits El Saadawi with her Arab audiences.

Although she makes some efforts to resist the West's misrepresentation of her, El Saadawi, I argue, also invites it in some ways, allowing her works to be used to confirm the prevailing prejudices about Arab and Muslim culture. Furthermore, her self-representation to her Western readers encourages and confirms their readings of her. For instance, she does not show herself as part of a feminist movement, as someone learning from the experiences and building on the achievements of other women,

12. El Saadawi sometimes encourages this understanding. See, for example, El Saadawi 1991b, 156.

but rather as exceptional and a pioneer.[13] She underscores her difference from other intellectuals by emphasizing that, unlike them, she does not belong to any particular political party (El Saadawi 1980b, 170).[14] While she admits that her prison experience taught her the value of "collective political work" (1992b, 35), her representation of that experience in *Memoirs from the Women's Prison* (1994c) confirms the superiority of her political independence. One of the main objects of satire in that book is Marxist and Muslim fundamentalist women prisoners, whom El Saadawi represents as fanatic and ideologically dogmatic.[15] At the same time, she casts herself as the leader of the women prisoners, the one making decisions and initiating action.[16] Most importantly, El Saadawi distinguishes her feminism by claiming for it an authenticity lacking in that of her Arab feminist critics, whom she pronounces "Western" and therefore inauthentic (1993b, 175). In addition to being essentialist (describing an

---

13. One obvious example of this self-representation is the obituary El Saadawi wrote for Amina al-Said in the *Guardian* (El Saadawi 1995b), in which she dismisses al-Said's feminism by showing that al-Said was conventional in her views of women and compromising in her dealings with the powers that be, and in which she hardly mentions any of al-Said's long feminist history. For readers' angered responses to this obituary and its omissions, see Croucher 1995; Gindi 1995.

14. See also El Saadawi 1985a; 1992b, 35; 1994a, 25; 1994c, 30, 126, 159.

15. See, for example, her caricatures of Bodoor, the Muslim woman, and Fawqiyya, the Marxist woman (El Saadawi 1994c, especially 38, 115, 126, 130). Much of the humor in the book is at their expense, even at the level of making puns on their names ("Bodoor," meaning "the one with the beautiful face," is given to the prisoner who completely covers her face; "Fawqiyya," meaning the "pedantic one," is given to the Marxist prisoner. It is significant that when El Saadawi decided on an excerpt from the book to be published (1985a), she chose the episode that makes fun of Bodoor, "the Muslim fundamentalist," thus catering to her Western audience's appetite for stereotypes of Islam.

16. It is interesting to compare El Saadawi's representations with those of Latifa al-Zayyat in her prison memoir *The Search: Personal Papers* (1996). Two things stand out: first, while al-Zayyat mentions El Saadawi, along with other women prisoners, she does not portray either of them as a leader. Second, at no point does al-Zayyat put down her fellow prisoners, including the Muslim fundamentalists who stand at the opposite end of the political and ideological spectrum from her. On the contrary, her solidarity with them as women comes through with poignancy.

Arab/Eastern thought that is untouched by the West and opposed to it), this claim is also inaccurate, for as we shall see later, El Saadawi's feminism synthesizes concepts and frameworks from disparate origins. But by disqualifying other Arab women's feminism, El Saadawi offers herself to the West as the true representative of Arab feminism. To complete this picture, she narrates her life story as either a success story of the rise to prominence of a rural, Third World woman or a persecution story about a feminist harassed by a patriarchy intent on subduing her. The two narrative lines often merge, and the organizing principle of both is individualism—one of the most cherished ideological concepts of her middle-class Western audience.

The Arab Context of Reception

A different view of El Saadawi emerges if we consider her within the original Arab context of her books. In Egypt and the Arab world, El Saadawi is neither a victim nor a lone campaigner for women's rights, but rather a product of a specific historical moment that puts her squarely within her culture, not outside it. Although by the early 1970s she had published some fiction, it was her nonfiction—particularly *al-Mar'a wal-jins* in 1971—that brought El Saadawi to the attention of Egyptian and Arab readers. This book was followed by *al-Untha hiya al asl* (Female is the origin, 1974b), *al-Rajul wal jins* (Man and sex, 1976b), and *al-Mar'a wa-l-sira' al-nafsi* (Woman and psychological conflict, 1976a), all published before *al-Wajh al-'ari lil-mar'a al-'arabiyyah* (1977). These influential books appeared in the specific context of the post-1967 Arab/Egyptian defeat by Israel. This defeat was a turning point for many intellectuals, who, as a result, directed their critical gaze inward toward themselves and their society. They believed that the unexpected and crushing military blow and the ensuing loss of land were caused as much by a corrupt Arab society as by Israel's military might. Not merely directed at leaders and their corrupt regimes, this approach attempted to scrutinize and expose the roots of the problem as these writers saw it, not its outward manifestations. Their critiques were part of a radical project that aimed at questioning and undermining the various structures of power governing both the individual and the group.[17]

El Saadawi's early writing participates in this cultural project as she herself acknowledges in her introduction to the U.S. edition of *The Hidden Face of Eve:* "During the past years a number of serious studies have been published, and have contributed to the unmasking of many social ills that require a radical cure if Arab society is to attain real freedom in all fields of endeavor whether economic, political, human, or moral" (1982, 2). In looking for a "radical cure" for Arab society's ills, El Saadawi and other Arab radical cultural critics both diagnosed the disease and prescribed the treatment. A full recovery, they believe, will be attained only by rejecting Western paradigms, perspectives, and scholarship, on the one hand, and religious obscurantism and modernizing Arab neopatriarchy, on the other (Sharabi 1990, 21). This is a crucial point if we are to understand El Saadawi's writing for it explains both her eclecticism and her attitude toward the West and Islam. Readers of her nonfiction encounter Freud, Marx, and the Prophet Mohammad all on the same page, where she also mixes genres and employs various concepts from different philosophies. In being eclectic, El Saadawi is actually asserting her independence. Moreover, while she rejects Islamic obscurantism and the use of religion as a tool of oppression, she also fights against the Western (mis)understanding of Islam. What might appear as inconsistency in her work is, in fact, an expression of the dual project of the post-1967 Arab cultural critic, whose long-term goal was "to subvert simultaneously the existing social and political (neo)patriarchal system and the West's cultural hegemony" (Sharabi 1990, 23).[18] In *al-Wajh al-ʿari lil-marʾa al-ʿarabiyyah* in particular, El Saadawi carries out this subversive project by confronting head-on issues such as "the place and meaning of the cultural heritage (*turath*); the relation of historicity, the question of religion, identity, tradition, and modernity" (Sharabi 1990, 27).

El Saadawi, then, is not "something of an anomaly in Egyptian cultural life," as one American critic has called her (Hitchcock 1993,

17. See, for example, al-ʿAzm 1968; Adonis 1974; Sharabi 1975; Zayour 1977.
18. See Boullata 1990, 129–30, on what he calls her "ambiguity" toward Islam.

34).[19] That she was writing not in isolation but as part of an emergent, progressive, secular, cultural critique cannot be overemphasized. Her attack on patriarchy, for instance, was echoed by Hisham Sharabi's (1975) study of the patriarchal Arab family and how it socializes its children into submission, conformity, and dependency. Like El Saadawi, the Lebanese psychologist Ali Zayour (1977) approaches Arab society as an analyst, employing psychoanalysis to study the anxiety and disequilibrium produced in the Arab personality by a changing and contradictory society. However, El Saadawi's original contribution to this radical critique is her foregrounding of sexuality and gender. While the Arab critics mentioned above talk for the most part of a nongendered individual, El Saadawi takes the radical step of gendering her Arab subject.[20] Moreover, El Saadawi's feminist critique was instrumental in *popularizing* the discourse about sexuality and about women's rights. Unlike the more academic writings of radical feminists such as Fatima Mernissi and Khalida Said, hers are written in an accessible language that is neither literary nor technical. Her simple diction, crisp sentences, and short paragraphs give her books a journalistic flavor and appeal to a wide reading public. Her nonfiction mixes genres, juxtaposing critical analysis, scientific discourse, polemic, case histories, personal anecdotes, and autobiography. She addresses readers with the confidence of a physician, the passion of an activist, the credibility of an eyewitness, and the pathos of an injured woman.

El Saadawi's nonfictional writing differed from the prevailing Egyptian feminist discourse in that it focused on poor women, emphasizing their oppression and exploitation. While this emphasis fell within the parameters of the general leftist intellectual discourse, it was subversive in the context of Egyptian feminism, which expressed the interests of middle-

19. Hitchcock justifies this view of El Saadawi as follows: "She is educated but from the countryside; she is a feminist, but one who emphasizes class struggle in relation to questions of women's oppressed position; she questions the proscriptions of religion, but she is a strong proponent of Islam" (34). But as I argue in this essay, the attributes enumerated by Hitchcock place El Saadawi squarely within, not outside, post-1967 Egyptian cultural life.

20. Other women writers who engaged in a similar kind of critique around the same time are Fatima Mernissi (1975) and Khalida Said (1970).

and upper-class women and was articulated by members of these classes such as Qasim Amin, Huda Shaarawi, Durriyya Shafik, Caisa Nabrawi, and Amina al-Said, among others. In the 1970s, one must not forget, the self-appointed head of the women's movement in Egypt was none other than Jihan el-Sadat, the Egyptian president's wife. While "establishment" feminists like Jihan al-Sadat and Amina al-Said advocated women's rights and acknowledged the need to improve women's condition, they adopted a reformist agenda to effect change. El Saadawi rejected their limited liberal agenda and challenged their strategies for liberation, demanding not reform but a socialist restructuring of the whole society. In other words, her polemical writing was as much a response to this feminist tradition as it was a critique of patriarchal society generally.[21]

El Saadawi as Novelist

Few Arab critics would question the important contribution that El Saadawi's theoretical/polemical writing has made to oppositional Arab thought.[22] More contested, though, is her status as a novelist. Arab critics and readers are generally surprised at the accolades heaped on El Saadawi's fiction in the West, and some have concluded that the popularity of her novels has less to do with their literary merit than with their fulfillment of Western readers' assumptions about Arab men and women (Hafez 1989). This response to El Saadawi's fiction is usually dismissed in the West as the result of Arab male hostility toward her as a feminist writer.[23] To go beyond these rather reductionist explanations, we need to consider El

21. For an indication of the rift between El Saadawi and this liberal feminism, see her obituary of al-Said (1995b).

22. For instance, Sharabi (1988, 32–33) singles out *Woman and Sex* for its radical impact, as do Joseph Zeidan (1995, 125) and Afif Faraj (1985, 346), among others.

23. See, for example, Malti-Douglas's 1995a, 1995b. Hitchcock also simplifies El Saadawi's relation to her critics when he writes, "She is one of Egypt's foremost writers, and yet most of her works were initially published and indeed were best known outside Egypt. She is unpopular with Egyptian officialdom and with Islamic scholars, including many of her Arab sisters who see their concerns being represented or reduced through the voice of a renegade from Kafr Tahla" (1993, 34). I do not deny, however, that there is some truth to

Saadawi's fiction in the context of the modern Arabic literary tradition within which it is read and judged.

As critics of Arabic literature have noted, the Egyptian novel, although mostly written by men, was from its beginning a "woman-centered" genre. Women were main characters or main problems, as is clear from some of the early titles, such as *Zaynab* (Haykal 1914) and *Sarah* (al-Aqqad 1938). The theme of love and the question of woman's position in society were central to these novels and to other early examples of the genre, including Ibrahim Abd al-Qadir al-Mazini's *Ibrahim al-katib* (1931) (*Ibrahim the Writer*), Taha Husayn's *Du'a' al-karawan* (1934) (*The Call of the Curlew*), and Mahmud Tahir Lashin's *Hawwa bila Adam* (1934) (*Eve Without Adam*). In the works of the popular romantics of the 1950s and 1960s, women continued to be central characters. Some of these writers, such as Ihsan Abdul Quddus, for instance, attempted "to break down the taboos concerning what can be mentioned in literature." This was done by telling in a sensational and titillating way the story of the "struggles of young girls from good families to liberate themselves, chiefly on the emotional and sexual plane" (Kilpatrick 1992, 246). Alongside this literature, and partly in opposition to it, was the "committed literature" of the 1950s and 1960s, influenced by socialist realism. According to the proponents of this school, the real artist is an active agent with a responsibility to give voice to the oppressed of his or her society. Writing soon after the revolution of 1952, at the height of a period of decolonization in the Arab world, the first generation of "committed" writers was optimistic, confident that the struggle for liberation and justice would be inevitably victorious. This generation includes, for example, Abd al-Rahman al-Sharqawi, whose novel *al-Ard* (1953, translated as *Egyptian Earth* in 1962) depicts peasants' resistance to oppressive landlords, and Latifa al-Zayyat, whose *al-Bab al-maftuh* (1960) (The open door) tells the story of one woman's successful struggle for emancipation.

---

the notion that El Saadawi's popularity in the West does have something to do with her telling the West what it wants to hear about Arabs, or that there are sexist Arab critics who are hostile to El Saadawi's feminism. However, these explanations do not suffice to explain her critical reception in either the West or the Arab world.

The "revolutionary optimism" (Kilpatrick 1992, 252) of writers like al-Sharqawi and al-Zayyat could not be sustained after 1967, for the defeat by Israel affected novelists the same way it did other Arab intellectuals. Post-1967 writers, "the Gallery 68 generation" in particular, had a more pessimistic view of their society and its future and wrote against an establishment that, they felt, betrayed the promises of the revolution. In *al-Hidad* (1969), Muhammad Yusuf al-Qa'id condemns oppressive patriarchal authority, and in his later novels he targets al-Sadat's Egypt. Yahya Taher Abdullah likewise critiques patriarchy in his *al-Tawq wa'l-iswirah* (1975) (The choker and the bracelet), in which he traces the lives of three generations of women. And Jamal al-Ghitani in his historical novel *al-Zayni Barakat* (1971) dissects the workings of the authoritarian state. As a novelist, El Saadawi belongs to this generation of leftist writers, sharing with them their belief in committed literature and their hostility to the establishment in its various oppressive forms.[24] The hopeful tone of her first novel, *Mudhakkirat tabiba* (*Memoirs of a Woman Doctor*) (1958), gives way to the pessimism, or, at best, the strained optimism, of her later novels, written at what she would describe as a time of counterrevolution.

El Saadawi's literary achievement, however, lies not so much in her social criticism as in the forward push she gave to Arabic feminist narrative. While she was not the first to write "feminist novels," she stands out as the one who made the Arabic feminist novel recognizable as a genre.[25] Other writers of what we might call feminist novels chose not to become full-time novelists: Amina al-Said, who wrote *al-Jamiha* (The defiant) in 1950

24. In a review of *Woman at Point Zero* and *The Circling Song*, Wen-Chin Ouyang (1996) places El Saadawi's fiction within the tradition of the "novel of ideas" in particular. I would like to thank Ouyang for allowing me to read her review before it appeared in print.

25. Both al-Said's *al-Jamiha* and al-Zayyat's *The Open Door* portray the struggle of one young woman for self-actualization. The similarities between al-Zayyat's novel and El Saadawi's *Two Women in One* in terms of themes and plot are considerable. Other writers of feminist novels before El Saadawi include Colette al-Khuri, who wrote *Ayyam ma'ahu* (Days with him) (1959) and Layla Baalbakki, who in *Ana ahya* (I am alive) (1958) writes of one woman's search for emancipation and in *al-Alihah al-mamsukhah* (The disfigured gods) (1960) of Arabs' obsession with the hymen. See Zeidan's study for a useful survey of Arab women writers.

(the first "Arab feminist novel" according to the Egyptian critic Raga' al-Naqqash [1995]), pursued a pioneering and successful career in journalism, and Latifa al-Zayyat, after the defeat of 1967, stopped publishing fiction for twenty-five years, devoting herself instead to teaching and to literary criticism (see, for example, al-Zayyat 1994). El Saadawi was also writing at a more opportune moment than the Lebanese Layla Baalbakki, who was tried for the explicit sexual passages in her 1963 book *Safinat hanan ila l-qamar* (Spaceship of tenderness to the moon). More importantly, El Saadawi succeeded in building on the momentum and name recognition she had acquired through her nonfiction, writing unambiguously radical, angry works that secured for the feminist novel a place on the literary map of modern Arabic literature.

Arab commentators have recognized this achievement. The Syrian literary critic George Tarabishi has devoted a whole book to El Saadawi's fiction because, in his opinion, she is "the principal exponent of the Arabic feminist novel" (1988, 9). Literary historians of the Arabic novel, Arab and non-Arab alike (for example, Roger Allen, Joseph Zeidan, and Trevor Le Gassick), give El Saadawi a place in their histories specifically as a proponent of the radical feminist novel. However, while these critics appreciate her contributions, they also point out what they see as the weaknesses of her fiction. Tarabishi, for instance, criticizes El Saadawi for abstracting her men and women in *Woman at Point Zero* and reducing them to "one dimensional" characters. Such characterizations, he argues, fail to illuminate complex human relations and therefore "do not make for good literature" (1988, 17–18).[26] Afif Faraj, a more conservative critic than Tarabishi, faults El Saadawi for imposing an ideological discourse on the world of literature, for shifting between the polemical essay and narrative, and for presenting

---

26. Roger Allen, however, reserves judgment on El Saadawi's literary merit. He writes: "Fiction at the hands of Nawal al-Saadawi becomes an alternative and powerful means of forwarding her opinions concerning the rights of women in Middle Eastern society. The voice of her narrators is strident, and the message unequivocal. It remains to be seen what position her works will retain in the history of modern Arabic fiction, but there can be little doubt that she will be numbered among the most prominent fighters for her cause in the latter half of the twentieth century" (1995, 107–8).

her opinion through self-evident statements rather than layers of events (1985, 331). He concludes that "character in El Saadawi's novels is almost an empty board except of the ideological statements written in large type. . . . The Saadawian heroine remains a captive of the rigid ideological text, and this text controls the narrative, plot and the fate of the characters. Her mechanical plot is built around an idea, like an Arab musical built around the words of the songs" (320). Zeidan concurs, pointing out that the novels' strength—their "commitment to the cause of women's liberation"—is also their weakness, for this commitment tends to "overshadow many of her stories to such a degree that, at certain points, the thoughts and statements of her characters seem forced and inappropriate" (1995, 130). In certain places in *Memoirs of a Woman Doctor,* for instance, he claims, "the novel functions as a soapbox from which al-Saadawi preaches her views in a declamatory manner unsuited to a novel" (131).

Critics have questioned not only the form of El Saadawi's fiction but also her message. Tarabishi targets what he calls her "individualistic philosophy" and "elitist attitude." In his view, Firdaus's struggle in *Woman at Point Zero* "is aimed at liberating not her female sisters, but herself" (1988, 32), and her "nihilistic asceticism" is a way to reject reality, not to change it. He concludes: "Firdaus's story is undoubtedly worth telling. However, presenting it as an individual, isolated case is one thing; and elevating it to the level of a theoretical issue is quite another" (33). In an earlier study of El Saadawi's *Two Women in One,* he contends that the main character's fears of the herd and her feelings of exceptionalism, or of difference, do not lead to "individuation" but to elitism (Tarabishi 1978, 23). Along similar lines, Ahmad Jasim Al-Hamidi contends that El Saadawi's fiction changes class struggle into gender struggle (1986, 197) and the "alienated condition" into an "elitist condition" (187). He finds the endings of her novels particularly problematic. Faraj concurs, arguing that there is no hope of liberation for the Saadawian heroine, whose consciousness and behavior are dependent on reaction and on who moves in every novel from rebellion to submission (1985, 340). The Egyptian critic Sabry Hafez admires El Saadawi's intentions, but pronounces her fiction a failure—ideologically because it "invert[s] the prevalent patriarchal order without a clear understanding of the dangers involved" and artistically because of the author's "one dimensional approach" to her material (1995, 166, 170). The Egyptian novelist Salwa Bakr criticizes El Saadawi's view that the problem of women is mainly sexual," arguing that priority should be given instead to women's inferior economic situation" (quoted in al-Ali 1994, 65).[27] Bakr is not the only woman writer to criticize El Saadawi as a novelist. The Iraqi novelist Alia Mamdouh charges her of "turning creativity, which is imagination and living memory into a lab to show sick, deformed samples which she presents as generalized social types" (1996, 12). El Saadawi is also faulted for her repetitive style, weak language, and lack of technical development (Faraj 1985, 346; Hafez 1989). The Anglo-Egyptian novelist Ahdaf Soueif, who herself writes about female sexuality, speaks for many when she remarks, "El Saadawi writes good scientific research, but she writes bad novels. It is unfair that the West thinks that what she writes represents Arab women's creative writing" (1996, 12).

As the above summary shows, El Saadawi's Arab critics are not homogeneous. Similarly, those who write about her in the West bring to her work a variety of perspectives and approaches, although at times recognizing the same issues raised by Arab critics.[28] Others have dealt with

27. Bakr says, "This does not mean that I do not view sexuality to be a problem for women, but it is not the most important one. The most important thing is that services such as health care, nurseries, etc., are very poor because of the bad economic situation" (quoted in Al-Ali 1994, 65). Similarly, Amina al-Said criticizes El Saadawi's priorities: "Nawal has the right idea. . . . But this talk of sexual revolution and legalized abortion before most women can read is absurd" (quoted in Roth 1991, 10).

28. See Emberley 1993; Ouyang 1996 and 1997. In addition, some reviewers have pointed out other "problems" in El Saadawi's fiction. For example, in her review of *The Innocence of the Devil*, Laura Cumming argues, "Her naive iconography never varies. . . . The rigid binary oppositions within which her novels operate constrict the purpose El Saadawi avows in her non-fiction, which is to campaign against patriarchy as oppressive to men as well as to women. . . . Determined to generalize centuries of female suffering, El Saadawi creates an ahistorical fiction in which women are reduced to symbols of sexual oppression and men are their interchangeable torturers" (1994, 8). Another reviewer writes, "The novel is curiously heavy going, often seeming overwrought and oversignificant. Portentous abstractions and paradoxes . . . are too frequent. . . . [It] tends to sink beneath the weight of its extranovelistic implications. One feels claustrophobically imprisoned within the author's lushly written resentments" (M. D. Allen 1995, 637–38).

the problematic of reception (for example, Hitchcock 1993; Mitra 1995). In general, however, Western critics have given El Saadawi's fiction a more positive reception than their Arab counterparts. This difference can be accounted for in part by the very different frameworks within which they situate her fiction, often discussing it in terms of "resistance literature" (Harlow 1987), "Third World women's texts" (Saliba 1995), "testimonial literature" (Hitchcock 1993), or even more general categories such as "the picaresque novel" (Payne 1992) or "feminist writings" (Accad 1987; Salti 1994; Lionnet 1995). However, while these categories and contexts illuminate some aspects of El Saadawi's novels, they overlook others. As several recent postcolonial critics have pointed out, postcolonial and feminist frameworks can be so generalizing as to be misleading (Mohanty 1991; Ahmad 1992; Donnell 1995). Because the Arab context is largely absent, these works tend to exaggerate the subversiveness and exceptionalism of El Saadawi's fiction. Thus while Malti-Douglas in her monograph on El Saadawi declares that, "of all living Arabic writers, none more than Nawal El Saadawi has his or her finger so firmly on the pulse of Arab culture and the contemporary Middle East" (1995a, 2), she treats El Saadawi in isolation from other Arab women writers. As I have pointed out elsewhere, "the few passing references to the contemporary scene seek to show not how El Saadawi emerges from and engages with her culture but how she transcends it" (Amireh 1996a, 231). Sometimes El Saadawi's fiction is placed within an Arab context existing at such a comfortable distance from the actual moment of production as to make the connection between text and context tenuous at best.

More pertinent for the present discussion than what Western critics say about El Saadawi's fiction is the way their criticism is framed. Critics writing in the West seem to assume that they are more reliable, fair, and disinterested, and therefore more qualified to judge El Saadawi's fiction than their Arab counterparts. El Saadawi herself encourages this assumption. In a recent interview she praises her Western critics for being "objective" and declares that she is not interested in what her Arab critics have to say because they are not qualified to appreciate her personality, which is different from anything they are accustomed to.[29] In another interview she makes clear that she no longer writes for an exclusively Arab audience: "Before, I didn't have the pleasure or the freedom to experiment. But now I want to go beyond that, to experiment with the language, to experiment with ideas, to have more freedom. Even if the book is not published in the Arab world. At first, I wrote for the Arab people, men and women. And I had to consider my audience. I was not writing for angels in the sky. My audience was the Arab people. So, if I spoke about something they would totally reject, it would not be there at all. But now I don't care" (El Saadawi 1990c, 404).

Some Arab readers have picked up on the fact that El Saadawi is not speaking to them anymore. One female reader views with suspicion El Saadawi's popularity in the West: "She's not really fighting for a cause. She is fighting for her own cause. . . . I don't feel she's worth following. She's made her name outside of Egypt, rather than inside Egypt" (Gauch 1991, 1). According to the Egyptian novelist Jamal al-Ghitani, El Saadawi "is living in America because she wants a Nobel Prize. She is writing for the West, she cannot feel the true problems of women" (quoted in Lennon 1994, 29). In using El Saadawi's dislocation to dismiss her writing, these critics assume "that identities are to space, and that a pure and authentic standpoint can be developed only if one remains rooted firmly within the territory of one's origin" (Michel 1995, 87). Ironically, El Saadawi herself has used a similar argument to discredit those who disagree with her, claiming that many of the feminists who criticize her live in the West and therefore are Western in their feminism (1993b, 175), and, according to one interviewer, she calls Edward Said "an arrogant intellectual who has a Westernized interpretation of the Middle East" (Winokur 1994, 12).

When critics' "authenticity" cannot be called into question, El Saadawi invokes another strategy. In response to Tarabishi's criticism of her in *Woman Against Her Sex* (a response that appears as an appendix in the English translation of the book), El Saadawi declares the book "a per-

---

29. Al-'Uwayt, 'Aql. "La ahtamm bi-maqalat al-nuqqad, al-qurra' hum alladhin Sana'uni." *al-Anwar,* 18 July 1992, 9. This reference is given in Zeidan 1995, 301–2, 348.

sonal attack." She objects, among other things, to Tarabishi's argument that there is autobiographical material in her novels and that she seems to identify psychologically with her heroines. She ridicules Tarabishi for using elaborate theory (Freudian psychoanalysis) to read what she calls "a simple novel" (Tarabishi 1988, 189–211). However, other critics have written about the autobiographical elements in El Saadawi's writing and about her identification with her heroines or have used elaborate theoretical approaches to read her novels, and neither El Saadawi nor anyone else has objected to their readings.[30] But Tarabishi is more critical of El Saadawi. Many critics in the West have adopted El Saadawi's attitude toward Tarabishi and defend her against his supposedly personal attack motivated by misogyny and opposition to feminism. They express outrage and amazement that such a book has been written at all, and, for them, the mere fact that it has been translated into English proves that there is a conspiracy to defame El Saadawi.[31]

These sorts of responses to Tarabishi and to other Arab critics of El Saadawi illustrate the imbalance in power relations between Western-based intellectuals and their Arab-based counterparts. They seem to say that it is acceptable for the Third World to supply primary texts but that criticism of these texts is more ably done in the First World (see Mitchell 1995, 475). These defenders of El Saadawi generally view Arab male critics with suspicion and hostility. Thus, for instance, a passing remark like Edward Said's that El Saadawi is "overexposed" and "overcited" in the West (1990a, 280) is blown out of all proportion and offered as representative of "one of the negative consensus positions on the Egyptian feminist" (Malti-Douglas, 1995b, 283). These defenders often conflate El

---

30. See, for example, Harlow 1987; Badran and cooke 1990, 203; Hitchcock 1993; Lionnet 1995.

31. Hitchcock, for example, expresses his "frustration with the fact that the first book-length work on Nawal El Saadawi available in English happens to be an extended antifeminist diatribe by a Freudian" and hopes that the work in progress of another critic more sympathetic to El Saadawi will "displace Tarabishi's efforts" (1993, 207–8). Similarly, although she does not directly engage Tarabishi's argument itself, Malti-Douglas laments that "the book is the only extended work on El Saadawi in a European language. Such a situation is most extraordinary for a Middle Eastern intellectual" (1995a, 10).

Saadawi's critics: official state censors, conservative critics who reject the feminism of her nonfiction, and literary critics of her fiction are rolled into one persecuting entity called "Arab male critics." [32] This supposed gap between Arab and Western critics is central to the construction of El Saadawi's identity as a persecuted feminist who is not appreciated in the Arab world she criticizes.

However, this defense of El Saadawi ignores the context of critiques such as Tarabishi's. They never mention, for instance, that he is not really singling out El Saadawi for his Freudian analysis; in fact, this book is the third in a series of books using psychoanalysis to read Arabic literature. In the first (1982), Tarabishi studies the works of feminist Amina al-Said along with male writers, and, in the second (1983), he analyzes the ideology of manhood in Mahmoud Dib's and Hannah Minah's works. [33] Knowledge of Tarabishi's other criticism would show that he is not an antifeminist. In his criticism of Minah, for instance, he points to the misogyny and sexism in the Syrian writer's novels. He underscores the contradictions existing between Minah's statements in support of women's liberation, to which Tarabishi is sympathetic, and his misogynist representations of them in his fiction (1983, 87). Tarabishi offers intelligent readings of women's characters that many feminists, including El Saadawi herself, would find illuminating. Discussing the stereotypes of women in Minah's work (1983, 115, 117), for example, he shows how Minah attaches negative values to "femininity" and then opposes it to "manhood," with all its positive connotations (79). But even beyond Tarabishi's individual readings, his critical project as a whole is, in my view, not opposed to El Saadawi's. His writing foregrounds sex and gender as important categories of analysis, and his readings bring to Arabic literary criticism the same vocabulary that El

32. See for instance Malti-Douglas 1995b, 283–85, where El Saadawi's "detractors" are all lumped together and given the same motive. Thus Edward Said, Islamic Fundamentalists, the Sadat and the Mubarak governments, and George Tarabishi all become equivalent "detractors" out to "silence" the feminist writer.

33. The fact that only his book on El Saadawi has been translated into English has to do with the obvious fact that El Saadawi is a known figure in the West while writers treated in his other books, though prominent in their own countries, are virtually unknown outside the Arab World. No American publisher would be interested in a book about them.

Saadawi uses in her theoretical feminist writings. Rejecting taboos, both believe that sexuality and gender are legitimate subjects for analysis and study. Although Tarabishi is not a feminist critic and does not claim to be one, neither is he an antifeminist, and his work does not deserve the wholesale dismissal it has received in the United States. One does not need to agree with his readings of individual texts or to embrace his Freudian theoretical framework to recognize that his analysis raises worthwhile questions about El Saadawi's fiction and feminist fiction in general.

Teaching El Saadawi

The reservations of critics like Tarabishi and Sabry Hafez about El Saadawi's fiction are particularly relevant in light of its popularity in college courses in the West. Arguably the most important site of reception, the Western classroom often assumes that "fiction can do the job that history, geography, economics, sociology, etc., are supposed to" (Bahri 1995, 74). Often the only Arab texts that students encounter, El Saadawi's novels "inform" them about Arab women and Arab society. What complicates matters even more is that fiction and fact get confused both in the novels (as in *Woman at Point Zero,* for instance) and in El Saadawi's biography. It is not surprising that students, like reviewers and critics, tend to see the novels as windows onto a timeless Islam instead of literary works governed by certain conventions and produced within a specific historical context.[34] According to one student, *The Fall of the Imam* depicts what "time and history must seem like for freedom-seeking women in Islam: an endless repetition of the same event with only slight variations. This kind of narrative structure . . . captures what I imagine to be Islamic women's ex-

---

34. For example, in their written comments on *The Fall of the Imam,* graduate students taking a seminar on the postcolonial literature of North Africa and the Middle East at the University of Alberta (taught by Lahoucine Ouzgane and Nasrin Rahimieh) did not mention at any point the relationship between the novel and the assassination of al-Sadat. Would they have read it differently if that immediate context were emphasized? I believe so. It is interesting that Malti-Douglas refuses to put the novel in that immediate context (see 1995a, 92). Not so the Egyptian critic Sabri Hafez. My deepest gratitude to Lahoucine Ouzgane for making student responses available to me.

tremely limited sense of agency. And the huge question Saadawi presents is: what can women, oppressed by the historically justified patriarchy of Islam, do? How to break out of the endless repetition?"

Several instructors who teach *Woman at Point Zero,* the most popular of El Saadawi's books, indicate that they have to work hard to prevent their students from using it merely to confirm their stereotypes. In the words of one teacher, "Western students tend to get fixated on clitoridectomy and the veil" (Sagar 1995). Anticipating this problem, some teachers provide background material on colonialism to help establish a historical context (Mitra and Mitra 1991; Sagar 1995; Saliba 1995, 143), to encourage students to break with essentialist and ethnocentric theoretical perspectives, and to remind them of similar abuses that women undergo in Western cultures (Gingell 1995).[35] These efforts and "reminders," however, are not always sufficient (Gingell 1995). One typical reaction, especially to defloration and female genital mutilation, is for students to feel "awed into silence" (Sagar 1995).[36] In addition to the above contexualizing methods, I believe that it is important to draw the students' attention to the politics of reception itself and to make this issue an object of study as a way to further historicize El Saadawi's work. Students should be encouraged to question their location as readers and to

35. Despite their call to read El Saadawi's novel in context, Mitra and Mitra (1991) make the same mistake as the Western critics they criticize: they read El Saadawi's novel as if it were a sociological text without much attention to its sociopolitical and literary contexts.

36. Hitchcock writes that "El Saadawi's novelization of the psychic horrors of clitoridectomy is no less significant in translation, nor indeed is Firdaus's brutalizing experience as a prostitute. For the hegemonic 'Western' consciousness conditioned to a phantasm of the Arab woman as veiled, submissive, or secluded, none of El Saadawi's major characters . . . seems to fit. If nothing else, El Saadawi's fiction would bear testimony to a conscious undermining of Orientalist preconceptions even if such forms of oppression are still significant factors in the lives of many Arab women" (1993, 51). This, however, does not seem to be the experience of other teachers who responded to my inquiry. One wrote that the novel "stunned" her students—"they were either entranced by it, or didn't know what to say" (Loflin 1995). Another wrote that she had "to fight [her students'] tendency to do the 'oh those women over there have it worse' imperialistic view when addressing concerns of women in other non-US societies"(Kensinger 1995).

examine the mediating processes connected with translation, editing, reviewing, and academic canonization that make El Saadawi's books available to the Western student.

I first read El Saadawi in the mid-1970s as a teenager living in a small West Bank town under Israeli military occupation. With a mischievous smile, the librarian in our two-room public library slipped me a copy of *al-Mar'a wal-jins* (Woman and sex). That smile was familiar, for I had seen it before on his face whenever he recommended a book he thought proper young women were not supposed to read (the list was long and included such works as *Anna Karenina, The Communist Manifesto, A Doll's House, Uncle Tom's Cabin,* and the complete annotated works of Lenin). That night I could not put the book down, and the next day I went back for more. By the end of the week, I had read three of El Saadawi's polemical books. The influence these books had on me, and on the friends I shared them with, was profound. They literally gave us voice. Imitating El Saadawi's militant tone, we found in them plenty of ammunition to counter the arguments of reactionaries, whether Islamists or secularists, whom we energetically debated inside the classroom and outside.

My El Saadawi phase lasted for a year or so. I read a couple of her novels, but their effect was by then tame, and I went on to other stimulating books by both Arab and foreign authors, many of which were then banned by the Israeli military authorities. Years later, while attending graduate school in the United States, I encountered El Saadawi again, on the pages of newspapers and journals and in presentations and conversations at academic conferences. But this encounter was very different from the earlier one. Like some American students, I too was awed into silence. For in both the popular and academic whirlwind of discourses about El Saadawi and Arab women, I hardly recognized the author I knew. Even more disturbingly, I hardly recognized myself.

This essay is the result of a personal attempt by an Arab feminist who writes for a largely Western audience to relocate El Saadawi. Through my search I have learned that in order to undo silences—mine and those of others—in order to bridge the gap between the reception of El Saadawi in the West and in the Arab world, and in order to partially redress the asymmetry of power between those of us who are situated in the First World and those who are not,[37] we need to adopt a different way of reading El Saadawi and other Arab women writers. It is imperative that we always historicize not only the writer and her work but also the reader. We must take into account both the *original* context of production and reception and the *current* moment of consumption. Our role as critics and teachers and our relationship to the texts and authors we study at a particular historical moment should become objects of inquiry as much as the books themselves.

37. From 1997 to 2000 I worked in areas under the Palestinian National Authority in the West Bank.

3 Reenvisioning National Community in Salwa Bakr's *Golden Chariot*

MAGDA M. AL-NOWAIHI

Salwa Bakr. *Courtesy of Salwa Bakr*

Salwa Bakr was born in Cairo in 1949 and began writing short stories in the 1970s. Her first collection, Zeinat fi janazat al-ra'is *(Zeinat at the president's funeral), was published in 1986. To date, she has published four novels and six collections of novellas and short stories; she was also co-editor of the feminist journal* Hagar. *Two of her collections of short stories have been translated into English:* The Wiles of Men *(1992) and* Such a Beautiful Voice *(1992). Her novel* The Golden Chariot *(1991) has been translated into German and Dutch as well as English (1995), and was the basis of a 1994 film entitled* Kart Ahmar *(Red card).*

State Discourse and the Novel

In Egypt, one of the hallmarks of post-1960s literary production has been a doubled anxiety not simply over the reality that authors have been attempting to represent, but also over the very order of representation. The general postmodern skepticism about the adequacy and relevance of the literary forms and genres available for interrogating the world has been compounded by a deteriorating state of affairs, not only in the

68

economic and political spheres, but also in the public arena of discourse and exchange of ideas. The Sadatist regime (1970–81) allowed a degree of liberty in publication and loosened the reins of censorship, but this was accompanied by a strong drive to map out a certain morality of speech and even thought under the guise of civility; a drive epitomized in Sadat's infamous laws of "shame," "the Egyptian family," and "the morals of the village" (qanun al-'ayb, al-'a'ila al-misriyya, akhlaq al-qariya), the village in this scenario supposedly being the repository of "traditional values." On the one hand, the government was moving away from a philosophy of accountability for the welfare of its citizens by privatizing the economy and espousing policies of global market economy and of "opening up" to the West. At the same time, it expected from those citizens private and "traditional" norms of behavior in the public discursive arena, such as respectful heeding of the father's words and rules—with Sadat naturally filling in for the father.[1] Writers found themselves in a position where their work might not be considered dangerous to internal stability or to the nation's security as it had been under the previous regime of Nasser, but they were harshly subjected to a different kind of scrutiny and a different order of "morality" that deemed them envious, spiteful, covetous, shameless, and immoral if they dared to question or object.[2]

Moreover, because the government had taken the moral high ground and was incessantly involved in loud sermonizing, I believe there was, and still is, a strong need on the part of the authors to distance themselves from this official high moralizing tone, but to do so without abdicating their own moral responsibility. They are unwilling, each in his or her own way, to abandon the imperative to warn, criticize, and guide, and to do so

1. For a somewhat similar situation in South America, see Mary Beth Tierney-Tello 1996, especially 24–27.

2. For some of the authors' own statements on issues of freedom in writing and publication, see *Fusul* 1992, special issues on "Al-Adab wa al-Hurriya" (Literature and freedom), and *An-Naqid* 1991, 41–79. These authors display a keen awareness of the multiple guises that censorship can assume. Writers have sometimes retold their experiences with various forms of censorship in their novels, with the best-known case being that of Son'allah Ibrahim. See Samia Mehrez 1994.

on the basis of a firm set of beliefs, yet do so in a tone not too loud or brash; one that is distinctly different from the authoritarian official discourse prescribing "right" and "wrong." Thus one of the defining characteristics of the post-1960s writers is this balance they have created, ensuring that their writings be in a style, or styles, that are muted yet radiating with justifiable anger, equally subtle and hard-hitting, and seeping with bitterness and sorrow without descending into nihilism or despair. Their writings, without sounding opinionated or prescriptive, remain firmly entrenched in the struggle to recreate the world on the basis of a search for justice, equality, and freedom.[3]

The forced intrusion of the family scenario and private norms of behavior on the sphere of public discourse must have presented further challenges to the authors. Mikhael Bakhtin defines the "modern historical novel" as a narrative that attempts to fuse "a time-sequence that is *historical*, serving as the channel for the life of the nation, the state, mankind" with "individual life-sequences"; "to find an historical aspect of private life, and also to represent history in its 'domestic light' " (Bakhtin 1981, 217). If we extend this definition to include most novels, and I think we can, then we see how writers needed to find new narrative and discursive modes to connect individual stories with the life of the nation in ways that could replace the government's convoluted inscription of a certain familial paradigm and communal "village morals" on the public scene. These narratives should lay bare the oppressive mechanisms of control of both the family and the state, but at the same time that they explode the myths of the benign family and the benign state with its supposed civility, they must reattach the individual life stories of their characters to the "historical time-sequence," and reintroduce the desire and dream for a communal mode of existence that is less oppressive and manipulative—that is, in fact, both civil and ethical.

In addition to these problematics of representation general to all

---

3. This is true of the folk-story-like writings of Yahya Taher Abdullah's *The Mountain of Green Tea* (1983), Jamal al-Ghitani's historical narratives such as *Zayni Barakat* (1988), the mixture of factual and fictional modes in Son'allah Ibrahim's *Dhat* (1992), and the near-poetic style of Edward Kharrat's *City of Saffron* (1989), to name just a few examples.

Egyptian writers, women writers encounter further challenges. If they choose to write about women in family settings, and most of them do choose to, they find themselves forced to justify these choices, and to answer questions regarding the relevance of their writings and whether they are representative of anything besides "women's issues." The Marxist-Feminist Literature Collective tells us that "criticism of women writers is in general divided between the extremes of gender-disavowal and gender-obsession" (Marxist-Feminist Literature Collective 1996, 332), and that is very much the case in Egypt as it is in other places. Whether they want to or not, women writers often find themselves playing trivializing semantic games and categorizing themselves as either writing "women's literature" or not, being "feminist" or not. In response to relentless questioning, they often find themselves either having to sound militantly insistent on the precedence of women's experience, including women's oppression, or humbly acceding that they only see women's oppression as one more facet of the general suffering of whatever community they are part of.

Salwa Bakr and the Poetics of Disorientation

Salwa Bakr, one of the Arab world's leading contemporary writers, has been forced to address these issues repeatedly. To give just one example, in an issue of the cultural journal *al-Hilal,* typically entitled "Women's Literature or Literary Women?" (*Adab Nisa'i Am Nisa' Adibat?*) in a piece which she entitles, significantly, "Far from his bed" (1995) ("Ba'idan 'an firashihi"), Bakr responds to the attack that she does not like men and writes against them by turning the tables.[4] She claims that the men who launch this attack against her in fact do not like her women characters because they do not fit stereotypical male representations of females, for they are neither gorgeous seductresses who expend the largest portion of their energy cavorting in the male bed, nor are they symbols, like a tree or a

---

4. Critics also get dragged into these types of arguments. Hoda El Sadda feels impelled to declare that "Salwa Bakr's stories are not directed against men, a fact which has earned her the admiration and approval of many critics" (1996, 133). Al-Ali (1994, 68–69) also addresses this issue of whether or not Bakr's writing is directed against men.

flower or the land itself, for beauty and goodness and giving. Rather, they are representative of the majority of "real" or "ordinary" women who are neither angels nor devils, but humans struggling to survive and to endow their everyday life with some meaning and beauty (Bakr 1995a, 88–91). In other words, she is not interested in perpetuating androcentric images of women and is anxious to deal with them as subjects rather than as discursive constructs. Elsewhere she talks about "the masculine literary eye" that objectifies women and their experiences, and how she feels impelled to create a new literary language to deal with the world of women as it actually is. Moreover, she claims her narratives are indeed representative of society as a whole and of its various classes, affiliations, and occupations. Her work is not limited to sexual issues, but addresses a gamut of concerns, including pollution, education, and the health-care system (Al-Ali 1994, 64–67). And Salwa Bakr is, in fact, not overestimating the representational scope of her writings, for she does succeed in facing the various challenges that I have mapped out, and in writing narratives that are women's literature, Egyptian literature, Arab literature, and world literature.

Salwa Bakr, now in her early fifties, began writing in the early seventies, and her first published work, a collection of short stories entitled *Zeinat fi janazat al-ra'is* (Zeinat at the president's funeral), came out in 1986 (Bakr 1986). To date she has published four novels and six collections of novellas and short stories, as well as numerous articles, and was co-editor of the feminist journal *Hagar.* Two collections of her short stories have appeared in English translations,[5] in addition to the novel that is the focus of this essay, *The Golden Chariot Does Not Ascend to Heaven,*[6] which also has been translated into German and Dutch and has been the basis of the 1994 film *Red Card* (*Kart Ahmar*).[7]

---

5. See Salwa Bakr 1992a and 1992b.

6. Salwa Bakr 1991; English translation by Dinah Manisty 1995b. When quoting from or referring to the novel, I will first include the page numbers from the Arabic, followed by those from the English translation by Dinah Manisty. Unless the text specifically indicates that it is my translation, the Manisty translation is being used.

7. For a more detailed biographical essay on Bakr and excerpts from an interview with her, see Al-Ali 1994, 52–69.

A plot summary of *Al-'araba al-dhahabiyya la-tas 'ad ila al-sama'* (The golden chariot does not ascend to heaven) would probably lead one who has not read the novel to the false conclusion that we are yet again in the bleak novelistic universe of tragic essentialism whose most well-known Arab representative is probably Nawal El Saadawi; a universe populated with abused victimized women, whose abuse comes at the hands of men and whose crimes are an attempt to survive in an almost immutable, relentlessly oppressive patriarchal system. *The Golden Chariot* employs the trope of a women's prison to bring together its various characters: women who have committed crimes, sometimes rather violent ones, usually against men. Moreover, we ultimately sympathize with these women, and perceive their violence as a reaction to the injustice they have suffered. And yet this narrative universe is in fact qualitatively different from that of Nawal El Sadaawi in its style, sensibility, and final impact.

Both Sabry Hafez and Hoda El-Sadda already have noted that marked difference. Using Elaine Showalter's theories, they classify Salwa Bakr as part of the third stage of women's writing: "the Female," while placing El Saadawi in the earlier second stage of the "feminist," the "feminine" being the first stage of the pioneers like Amina al-Sa'id. Both see her as breaking away from what Hélène Cixous has termed "patriarchal binary oppositions." Hafez is particularly interested in the ability of her novella *Maqam 'Attiya* "to break the male's monopoly on the divine and provide the sacred with a feminine aspect" (Hafez 1995, 171), while El-Sadda briefly reviews her entire oeuvre and identifies some of the distinguishing aesthetic features as breaking the binary oppositions between private and public, classical Arabic and colloquial Egyptian, and not singling man as the primary oppressor of women, but instead laying bare "the social norms and beliefs enforced by both men and women" (El-Sadda 1996, 140). I would add that Salwa Bakr breaks down various categories that are traditionally seen as binary oppositions through her use of what I will call the poetics of disorientation. In the most refreshingly funny and simultaneously heartbreaking manner, Bakr's narrative moves back and forth between spaces, characters, and languages that are normal and aberrant, normative and peripheral, centered and marginal, ridiculous and serious. By juxtaposing and dislocating both thematic and stylistic spaces, her narratives disorient readers in order to challenge their expectations, thereby presenting a powerful critique of that which has become normative in Egyptian life and redefining the concept of community. In this project, not least of her targets are the very ways in which we apprehend, make sense of, and represent our world. Under the guise of humor, Bakr is constantly pushing her readers to rethink almost all their categories of thought and speech: political, literary, and religious, among others. She is invested in exposing the superficiality and hypocrisy of the various languages we have become accustomed to, and she divests these languages of their value by humorously ripping away their mantle of respectability and seriousness. In their place, she does not offer us another serious moral language, but instead a humorous topsy-turvy world that disorients to reorient, pushing us to voyage under the surface of her style in search of meaning and value.

Spaces Normal and Aberrant

Four primary locations compete for dominance in the narrative space of *The Golden Chariot Does Not Ascend to Heaven,* and each serves to shed light on as well as to complicate the others. The present moment takes place within the peripheral space of an Egyptian women's prison where all the main characters, including Aziza, whose story frames the work, are "criminals" who exist on the borderlines of society, for their actions have marked them as abnormal and/or unethical, and most are also said to be on the borders between sanity and madness. Yet most of the events recollected and narrated occur outside the prison walls, primarily in Egypt of the 1970s and 1980s, though they also go back all the way to the 1940s of the twentieth century. The third and fourth spaces are the sky or heaven of the title (missing in the English translation), which Aziza dreams of as the ultimate horizon of escape, and the golden chariot that will carry her there. These two later spaces serve as the first layer of connective tissue that brings together characters and events difficult to assemble under one rubric, for the women whose stories are told are ostensibly the ones selected by Aziza to accompany her on her journey to heaven. Moreover,

Aziza has to reach a certain stage of understanding and sympathy for these women, in spite of their crimes and petty behavior, before she allows them a seat on the chariot.

It is important to remember that the story which Salwa Bakr is telling us is very different from the one that either Aziza, the women, or even that other nameless narrator are telling us, and is a result of the intersections and divergences between these many voices. This is a polyphonic narrative, in which Aziza's voice is almost constantly disorienting of and disoriented by not only the voices of the other women as they tell their stories, but also by another narrating voice; one that seems more rational and balanced, and that is also more biting and distancing.[8] The author makes critical choices regarding the material that she will allocate to each narrator. Ascribing the desire for the golden chariot to mad Aziza allows Bakr to present a sympathetic view of the women without risking that an overly sentimental or cloyingly noble forgiving tone pervades the novel. Thus it is Aziza's voice that describes these thieves, drug dealers, and murderers as "most distinguished and noble women . . . really angels without wings" (Bakr 1991, 32/1995b, 24), and the prison warden as one "whose pure spirit and body was that of a true saint who could only be venerated in heaven" (156/134). But while Aziza is busy thinking of an inmate's "angelic face," the other narrating voice brings us down a few notches by insisting on including details of that same inmate scratching herself (129/110), or finding a piece of grit in her bread and shifting it to the front of her mouth with her tongue, then spitting it out while proposing to change her profession from pickpocket to the more lucrative and "historically authentic" one of prostitute (119/102). The humor resulting from these often clashing perspectives on the women allows us to sympa-

8. Several indications point to the double-voiced quality of narration in the novel. For example, Aziza is unaware of the name of the pharonic goddess whose statue she saw and whom she compares to Umm El-Khayr, but the reader is made aware that the name is Hathur. Similarly, Aziza does not know the real name of the silent woman whom the inmates call Shafiqa, but the readers know that it is Taghrid and can therefore interpret the full significance of the title of the chapter "Grief of the Sparrows," since Taghrid means the chanting of birds.

thize without suspending our critical faculties, to understand without necessarily accepting, and to evaluate without harshly judging.[9]

Ascribing the dream of heaven to mad Aziza also allows Bakr to simultaneously normalize and decenter the desire for "that beautiful place in heaven where there is grace and favour, everlasting, supreme happiness and true, deep love between human beings" (1991, 217/1995b, 191). That desire is not an inherently ludicrous one, for after all it resembles the aspired utopia of more than one political ideology and is not dissimilar to the afterlife proposed by the three main monotheistic religions. Yet Aziza's vision, which allows for the accumulation of trivial, largely irrelevant details side by side with lofty aspirations and sublime goals, will neither allow the reader to seriously embrace this dream nor to easily dismiss it. It is difficult to suppress irreverent giggles when we are told that the chariot would have "magic, white, winged horses, which would take off to the sound of rousing melodies provided by the god of music and entertainment, like those she heard an army band play long ago in the city" (64/52), or when Aziza spends page after page describing the dresses and hairstyles the women would wear on their heavenly journey, and the dinner-dance at a five-star hotel that will precede the ascent (212–19/188–92). And yet how can we fail to be touched by Aziza's fervent desire to offer these women a second chance and to insure that they have access to justice and compassion in this other world? I believe that it is precisely the otherworldliness of this dream that Bakr is attempting to undermine, and instead to doggedly insist that the focus of desire must be "to achieve justice and mercy on earth" (156/134). Several factors lead me to this conclusion. There is more than one place in the narrative when an intense anger, laced with disappointment, is hurled in the face of God, who is found lacking when it comes to managing human affairs. The following

9. But often it is the voice that is not Aziza's that moves the tone upwards toward the pretentious, through spouting sociological and psychological babble that is then suddenly contrasted with a shift downwards toward the colloquial, which we can identify with the women's voices. See, for example, 27/20 and 68/55. These tone shifts are not as pronounced in the English translation. Latifa al-Zayyat has commented on the fact that Aziza is not the only or even the main source of values in the novel. See al-Zayyat 1992b, 273–77.

quotation is close to the conclusion of the fourth chapter, immediately preceding the chapter entitled "Mercy Before Justice":

> This line of thought not only made Aziza sad but extremely angry as well. She lifted her head and fixed her eyes on the iron bars of the window and let out a cry of protest directed towards an undefined and supreme force which she considered responsible for all that had happened and would happen in the future to this decent, lovely girl with her pure heart and childlike innocence. All the while she peered upwards at a chink of blue sky, cloaked by dark gray clouds, sadly saying: "Can you hear? Can you see? Things have gone too far to be ignored any longer." (128/110)

This "chink of blue sky" appears at different moments in the text, almost always associated with failed dreams, unrealized desires, and a deep sense of bitterness and despair at ever receiving mercy or justice (for example, Bakr 1991, 157/1995b, 135). It may be ironic that Aziza's remedy for her disappointment in God is to dream of going up to heaven, but there is one important shift: as Aziza dreams, she focuses more and more on the chariot itself. And if we add up the information that is interspersed throughout the novel, we realize that together with the rather ridiculous details of dresses and hairstyles, Aziza is also concerned with selecting women who will contribute to the safety and well-being of all the riders, whether by singing and entertaining them, or by offering medical care if they fall sick, or simply by loving and comforting their fellow travelers. There are also those whom it is best to exclude from this interdependent community, and this detail is equally telling. After considering the inclusion of a Communist, Aziza decides it is wiser not to, for the girl would talk of politics, incite the passengers, and enrage the government, which would send its planes to abort the ascent (117/101).

Indeed it is governmental officials, in the guise of the prison bureaucrats and guards, who almost succeed in stopping the mission according to Aziza's last deliriums. But while "not a solitary star looked down on Aziza" in the throes of death, she sees the women themselves rush off the chariot to battle the prison officials, and then triumphantly return to their seats and start their ascent (Bakr 1991, 219–20/1995b, 193). Thus the chariot that starts out as a ludicrous fantasy of a half-mad woman gradually achieves the stature of a crucial oppositional space; one that is not juxtaposed simply to the prison, but also to the outside world where justice has failed, to the utopia of "these politically-minded people (who) lived in another world and knew absolutely nothing about the poor they were always talking about" (116/100), and to the heaven that Bakr and the readers, if not Aziza, know it will not ascend to, as the proscriptive title of the novel indicates. The golden chariot is not one that can be found in already existing conditions, ideologies, or beliefs, but must be created from the dreams and hallucinations of the angry and disappointed, as they rebel against the government, expel ideologues, and rage against God.

And what about those earthly spaces? The prison, not surprisingly, is a space that has made its appearance in a number of important narratives recently, and it has also been the object of significant critical attention.[10] As a chronotope, this very limited and circumscribed space can function both as a microcosm of and an oppositional space to the nation. On the one hand, it allows the narrative to bring together a variety of people from different social classes, educational backgrounds, occupations, and interests, and to have them actually interact with one another on a daily basis. The novel can roam widely between different times and places, as the characters recollect and tell one another their life stories. This results in a heteroglossia that is not limited to the multiple languages crossing and playing off of one another, but also includes various narrating voices and many different forms of storytelling. *The Golden Chariot* includes stories that follow modernist narrative conventions, but these are interspersed with more popular literary forms like fairy tales and fables, as well as oral stories that follow the rhythm of everyday speech, depend on the workings of memory, and preclude in-depth psychological analysis (for example, Bakr 1991, 58/1995b, 47; 1991, 94–97/1995b, 80–83).[11] This variety is

10. In Egypt, two of the most interesting recent narratives in which the prison occupies a central space are those by al-Zayyat 1992a and Son'allah Ibrahim 1997.

11. Bakr sometimes gives a brief analysis of the different styles she uses within the novel. See, for example, 1991, 84/1995a, 72.

evident simply by perusing the titles of the different chapters, which self-consciously mimic a multiplicity of storytelling languages, ranging from a medieval philosophical treatise ("Fasl al-Khitab fi Ta'akhi al-Addad" [The heart of the matter: the meeting of opposites]), to a Pharonic fable ("al-Baqara Hathur" [The cow goddess Hathur]), to the lilt of a light popular song ("Fi al-'Araba al-Dhahabiyya, Dhalika Afdal Jiddan" [It's so much better in the golden chariot] [translation mine]) to a historical narrative ("Kanat Dhata Marra Zenobia" [There once lived a queen called Zenobia]), and so on. The book ultimately becomes a communal performance in which many voices chime in. I will come back to this multiplicity of styles.

Yet the prison as space, although in some ways representative of the variety of people, interests, and languages that make up the nation, is also of course markedly different from it. At first glance, it may seem that the prison is the aberrant space, while the outside world is the "normal" one, but Bakr is determined to dissociate "normal" from "normative," with only the latter serving as the true distinction between the prison and the outside world. For one thing, the fact that citizens from various classes and affiliations can only come together and hear one another in prison is already a harsh criticism of this normative outside world, of the very foundation of Egypt as an "imagined community" with uniform and collective interests and ambitions. The prison becomes a space that, to borrow Homi Bhabha's words, represents "the cutting edge between the totalizing powers of the 'social' as homogenous, consensual community, and the forces that signify the more specific address to contentious, unequal interests and identities within the population" (Bhabha 1994, 146). Moreover, the madness of the prison inmates is pronounced by psychiatrists and wardens to be not especially different from the madness symptomatic of the rest of society, and is often caused by that society rather than by the prison (Bakr 1991, 168/1995b, 146). Even the state's psychiatric ward is the "stopping place for those who could not bear the inconsistencies and futility of life" (185/163 and 31/23, 94/80, 100/84). Thus it is reality that is problematic and inadequate, and madness becomes a symptom of political impotence and cultural alienation. Madness ceases to be the opposite of sanity, and they become a continuum that destabilizes the boundaries between these two worlds.[12]

In addition, Bakr gently but persistently chips away at the expectation that freedom and agency belong to that outside world. *The Golden Chariot* is organized according to two primary time sequences: a linear one that characterizes the individual stories told by the inmates about their lives in the outside world, stories that have a beginning, middle, and end, with events moving forward and building up to a certain conclusion. In contrast, the communal time sequence of life in prison is static, or at least cyclically repetitive, with a reflective, backward-looking quality and no goals in sight. The normal expectation would be that the external time sequence of spatial and temporal mobility would be the one associated with a sense of freedom and agency, where choices and actions translate into tangible results that are of the characters' own making, whereas the static time sequence of the prison would be one in which characters' actions are limited and bear no consequence to the conditions they find themselves in. But although the prison world, with few exceptions, is indeed one of limited movement and choices,[13] it ultimately comes out as the kinder and gentler of the two worlds, for most individuals are shown to have very little control over their conditions or the results of their actions in the outside world. The individual stories are peppered with phrases that border on the fatalistic, and once or twice we may find ourselves uncomfortably close to an essentially nonchanging and unchangeable world of oppression and injustice, on which the characters' struggles leave not the slightest

---

12. What Barbara Harlow observes regarding the literary memoirs of political detainees, that is, that they "contest the social order which supports the prison apparatus and its repressive structures," is equally true here. "Michel Foucault too discussed the techniques and ideology of social control represented in the prison system in *Discipline and Punish: The Birth of the Prison,* where he examined the connections through modern European history between prison, monastic cell, workshop, and hospital." See Harlow 1987, 123.

13. For example, the inmates' propensity to live in the past is "due to the absence of their will to realize and act, similar in that respect to a dying person trying to hold on to life through memories, which is not quite as apparent in the imagination of someone living his/her usual days in society, and not losing hope in life" (89/76, translation mine).

mark. Thus Hinna, for example, considers her conditions to be "her or-
dained fate, which had been inscribed on a tablet in heaven, even before
the seed had been deposited in her mother's womb" (Bakr 1991,
52/1995b, 42), while "it seemed as if fate had lain in wait for Safiyya, in
the same way that it maintains its grip on all human affairs, despite the efforts individuals make to control their destiny" (150/129), and "despite
the years of hardship and toil, using her bare hands to move rocks which
stood in her way, Bahiga could only mark time and was unable to move up
the ladder" (167/146).

A Nation Gone Awry

But Salwa Bakr is not trying to argue that human agency, individual
and collective, is unrealizable, and that it is useless to strive for change, for
ultimately the responsibility for inequality and injustice lies primarily on
the norms and institutions that allow these conditions to remain firmly entrenched and even perpetuate them. It may be that "illness and good
health are in God's hands and that He, in His wisdom, decides who is des-
tined to have one or the other" (Bakr 1991, 134/1995b, 116), but this
situation is not helped any by a health-care system that is only accessible to
the wealthy and powerful, and that considers the lives of the less privileged
quite dispensable (for example, 9/6, 11/7, 160/140). Indeed, Bakr exposes the very institutions over which the premise of the Egyptian state is
built, and unmasks their claims to serve and protect the people as mere
fabrications, and by extension the loyalty and trust that its so-called leaders demand from citizens as undeserved at the very least. The "sense of an
absence of justice in life" that most of the characters harbor (141/122) is
in large part due to their realization of the abysmal failure of the three
major institutions of any modern nation: the police, the army, and the ju-
diciary. Far from the official slogan "police in the service of the people"
(*al-shurta fi khidmat al-sha'b*), we see police officers who think nothing of
slapping citizens around by way of interrogating them (79–80/65,
150/128), falsifying official documents when it suits their own purposes,
and trafficking in drugs (126/108). Even when they do manage to catch
the right person, it is clear that this is serendipitous rather than a result of

any premeditated strategy (*bi-tariqat al-sudfa al-qadariyya*) (41/31). The army officers whose duty it is to protect citizens from external enemies are themselves miserable and oppressed, and in their turn are involved in gang-raping helpless women (140/121). As for the judge who quite typically rushes through his cases without due deliberation because he has an important lunch date (179/155), surely he must have misunderstood the dictum "the legal system above all." (*al-qada' fawqa al-jami'*).

There is ample evidence to support the characters' conviction that the government never understands nor gets to the bottom of any problem (Bakr 1991, 125/1995b, 107), particularly in its economic plans that are inept at best (198/174–75), flip-flopping often (190/167), and uncaring of the most vulnerable members of society (76/62). These economic policies promote an atmosphere of rampant consumerism and lack of meaningful productivity that makes this the era of the middleman, or so-called businessman (138/119, 152/131). The possession of nonessential consumer goods becomes a sign not only of power, but also of "modernity" and "civilization" (41/31, 101/85–86, 150–51/129–30, 148/127), and since the unfair educational system and hiring practices dash any hopes of upward mobility for most people, and simply allow an elite minority to maintain its position in society (162/143), then any aspirations to become a "modern civilized" individual are doomed to failure. The resulting despair and self-hatred are intensified by the "small pyramid" carried secretly inside most people, acting "as the gauge by which the individual defines his identity, seeking the esteem and respect of all those above him in the pyramid and scorning all those beneath him" (168/147). This is made especially clear by the presence of at least one character, Zaynab, who "always triumphed at whatever cost, as princess of her own destiny, making her own life choices just as Zenobia Palmeira did in ancient times" (181/157). Zaynab, or Queen Zenobia, has all the qualities favored by this value system: wealth, good family and connections, and beauty, with the only thing working against her being her gender, and as a result her privileged status extends from the outside into the prison world, with a much shorter sentence than usual, and with the other poorer inmates cleaning, washing, and cooking for her, and appointing her to rule in their disputes (173/150). Thus many of the injustices in prison are an extension and reflection of the unjust hierarchies that exist in the outside world. The frequent arguments and disagreements that sometimes deteriorate into physical violence between the inmates are a direct result of the tensions and divisions that plague the Egyptian nation.

The Prison-House of Family

But while prison life is not glamorized or sentimentalized, this is a space where at least some of the horrors of the outside world can be overcome. Ultimately, this is a community with strong ties of friendship and genuine caring, where many of the interactions are characterized by a gentleness and devotion hard to find in descriptions of the outside world. Thus an inmate may stay up all night nursing her sick friend, making sure she gets her medicine on time (Bakr 1991, 8/1995b, 5–6), while a younger woman carries a sick older one to the bathroom and cleans her up like a daughter (81–82/66–67), and so on. Two important qualities characterize these interactions: they often are described as and come to replace familial ties, and they cross along class lines that would have been insurmountable in the outside world. In prison, it is possible for a pampered aristocrat and a common pickpocket "to be like two sisters from the same womb, showing the same degree of sympathy and human understanding for each other" (119/108), and for an inmate to cuddle and nurse the warden's infant daughter as if she were her own (86/73–74).

Not only are these interactions an outlet for feelings that cannot be expressed due to separation from biological families, but also the inmates seem to become better sisters and daughters and mothers in prison. Thus Umm el-Khayr, who, before coming to prison, actually considered it her maternal duty to return her daughters back to "the chicken coop of the husband" (translation mine) whenever they came complaining about these husbands (Bakr 1991, 86/1995b, 74), is in total sympathy with Aida and asks her "to lean on her as a mother" (99/84), for she is outraged to learn that Aida's own mother did not respond to her complaints about her abusive husband and forced her to stay in the marriage, thereby precipitating a catastrophic turn of events (98–113/83–96). Umm el-Khayr is unaware of the irony in this, but the suggestion is that the indifference and cruelty of Aida's mother are not a result of any innate pathology, but of the oppressive conditions of her world in upper Egypt, and similarly that Umm el-Khayr can afford to be as loving and sympathetic as she is because she is outside of that world and its pressures. In fact, it is the prison's ability to disrupt the status quo and function beyond societal impositions and regulations that allows an alternative familial model to flourish among these women: one that is more respectful of each member's needs; that is based on negotiation rather than manipulation, and compassion rather than rigid adherence to prior rules.

Indeed, of all the normative institutions that Bakr is determined to strip bare, the family gets a major share of criticism. The public/private space of prison allows for the infiltration of intimate stories, linking "the law of the family" and "shame" (al 'ayb) in horrifying new ways; exposing the interconnections between exploitation inside the family, the state, and equally important, the world of representation, which are no longer seen as discrete spaces. Bakr presents us with stories of women for whom the family turns out to be the reversal of its almost mythical representation as a unit that supports and protects its more vulnerable members. The law of the family decrees that the father should be honored and obeyed because he is the guardian who preserves it, shielding his dependents from harm and doing his utmost to safeguard their well-being. But just as government authorities demanding their citizens' loyalty are exposed as undeservingly inefficient and corrupt, the fathers in these stories are also unmasked as men whose pleasure or interest is in direct conflict with that of their daughters and wives. Bakr significantly begins and ends her narrative by breaking two of the most sacrosanct taboos: with Aziza's story, she scrapes away at the incest taboo, and with Shafiqa's, she demolishes that of infanticide. Shafiqa's sister, a gentle, generous soul and mother not only of her three orphaned children but also to her younger siblings after her own mother's death, is killed according to her father's and brother's arrangement because she sinned against the rules of honor when she fell in love with a man of a different religion.[14] The dishonor is all theirs, however, particularly when we learn that the father was contentedly fast asleep and snoring heavily on the very night of the murder (Bakr 1991, 197/1995b, 173).[15]

In the case of Aziza, Bakr softens the blow of incest by having a step-father rather than the biological father seduce the thirteen-year-old girl, but emphasizes the incestuousness of the setup by including details of this man's caring for Aziza as a father from her early childhood: bathing her, brushing and braiding her hair, and telling her bedtime stories while she was cuddled up in his lap (Bakr 1991, 28/1995b, 20–21). His seduction of Aziza is facilitated by her confusion and reconciliation of these two roles of daughter and mistress, almost as if the lingerie and perfume he buys her as a teenager are the natural extension of the toys and candies he brought home for her as a child. This confusion continues up until Aziza's death, for she alternates between thinking of him as her wonderful lover and de-scribing their sexual encounters as violation or rape. Aziza's sense of guilt, or the lack of it, is even more confused and confusing. While she displays no guilt whatsoever over killing her stepfather, she is thoroughly ashamed of herself for once being attracted and even considering marriage to a young eligible bachelor (22/16), and although she only occasionally al-lows herself to acknowledge that she may have betrayed her mother by sleeping with her husband, she deeply regrets not having shared with her mother this lover's gifts to her (18/13). This confusion mirrors the dis-

14. Shafiqa's story, or that of her sister, violates more than one expectation. As I men-tioned above, Shafiqa's real name is Taghrid, and there is a play on that in the title of the chapter. But the name Shafiqa is also significant, since its most famous holder in this century is Shafiqa al-Qibtiyya (the Copt), about whom a quite popular movie was made sometime in the early 1970s. The historical Shafiqa was a Christian who fell in love with a Muslim, and fi-nally became a nun and took a vow of silence. It would therefore be natural for the reader also to expect this Shafiqa to be a Christian, and it is in fact not easy to determine her reli-gion, except for one detail that Bakr strategically lets slip by: that Shafiqa's sister was a veiled woman.

15. This is actually one instance where I feel Bakr becomes too heavy-handed in her depiction of male cruelty and unfeelingness.

orientation Aziza feels about ascribing blame, since she never feels certain as to whose responsibility her affair was. Should she be held accountable for that relationship, since she obviously derived pleasure from it, or was she the helpless prey of an accomplished predator who used his position in the family to ensnare her, and does her mother share part of the blame, either for being so oblivious to what was happening (her mother is literally blind), or for guessing but ignoring the reality of the relationship so as not to violently disrupt the family? Or is it a mixture of all of the above?

Subversive Humor and the Dislocation of Representational Modes

This confusion, and the confused sense of guilt of the other inmates, is in fact a result of the discrepancy between the lived reality of family life and its religious, legal, and mainstream official as well as popular cultural representations; the wide rift between the material conditions of male/female relationships and its idealized version that is instilled in women from early on. Aziza is able to kill her lover and yet continue to adore him (Bakr 1991, 11/1995b, 7–8), Azima to have hers professionally castrated but continue to cling to their happy love memories (79/64, 81/66), and Hinna to believe that "one's husband should be respected" (58/47) and yet feel no shame or guilt over killing him (45/38), because of the unbridgeable gap between the actualities of these relationships and the expectations and hopes that have been cultivated in these women through the languages of love and passion that inundate them.

The disorientation bordering on madness that Aziza, Azima, Shafiqa, and the others suffer from is due to the fact that the myths of love, marriage, and family life have exploded in their faces, and nothing will heal the scars. Their lives have turned out so differently from the love songs of Fayza Ahmad and Abd el-Halim Hafiz, from the happy ending of every fairy tale that concludes with, "and they married, and lived in everlasting happiness, and had sons and daughters" (*w-itgawwizu, w-'ashu fi tabat w-nabat, w-khalliffu subyan w-banat*.) Sexual interactions between husbands and wives bear no resemblance to the expression of love and intimacy that they are drawn out to be, but are rather symptoms of exploitative power relations (for example, Bakr 1991, 103/1995b, 87; 1991, 134/1995b, 116), and the reality of the wedding night, which necessitates that Hinna spend "a whole hour sitting in a tub filled with warm water, with half a spoonful of salt added to it, until the pain had subsided a little" (47/39), is far removed from the decorous door that closes on the newlywed lovebirds kissing passionately that concludes many an Egyptian film. Nor does Mahrusa's struggle to feed her children while her husband is busy gambling and selling off the few prized possessions purchased with her hard-earned money bear any resemblance to the stereotypical role of boisterous mother-in-law torturing her henpecked son-in-law and encouraging her daughter to do the same, a role that she plays in the popular Qaraquz, or Punch and Judy show; this while the proprietor, playing the role of the poor oppressed husband, is busy sexually harassing Mahrusa and coercing her into a life of prostitution.

But Bakr is not content to reveal these various popular cultural productions for the malicious, albeit unintentional, fabrications that they really are, for she is almost equally invested in unmasking not only the romance, but also the more respectable literary genre of the bildungsroman, and in exposing it as the middle-class construction that it ultimately is. While the romance can be described as a journey toward successful integration into the family, in the bildungsroman the movement is from the inside to the outside, away from the family as ideological representative of the social order. But the sorrow over separating from the family is often mitigated by a heightened sense of self and an ability to articulate nonconformist views and take pride in this newly found independence. It is a triumph of individuation, even though the triumph is oftentimes laced with nostalgia for a more communal mode of living.[16] But for the majority of the women of *The Golden Chariot,* the collapse of the myths of love and family results in confusion, madness, and silence. Aside from a general lack of or a misplaced sense of guilt, these women cannot consciously articulate their oppression or proudly celebrate their ability to individuate. When they give vent to their feelings, it is not in the introspective or deeply self-analytical language of modern narrative. That is left for Bakr's readers and

16. For a more detailed discussion of this tension, see Al-Nowaihi 1999.

critics; her characters, however, must remain representative of their class, education, and indoctrination: they must remain disoriented, driven "to the point of breakdown and to the brink of madness" (Bakr 1991, 100/1995b, 84).

The women of *The Golden Chariot* cannot speak their sorrow because they are bombarded with languages and forms of representation—political, religious, scientific, and literary—that are irrelevant or meaningless, and "isn't silence in a world raging with nonsense a sign of ultimate sanity rather than madness?" (Bakr 1991, 186/1995b, 164). But while the women themselves may resort to silence, Salwa Bakr cannot. In fact, her very depiction of their disorientation is part of the battle she wages against this cheapening and abuse of language, for it allows the readers to interpret the political significance of these women's silence even while they themselves cannot.[17] Sometimes she confronts the issue directly, as in the following diatribe against the various strands of contemporary poetry:

> Lately these ceremonies [Azima's lamentations] had become more popular for reasons she never knew, but she suspected they responded to a need for something which had been lost through the empty words sung by the poets which inundated the public day and night on the radio and television. Equally, those obscure poems written by poets who fancied themselves as avant-garde writers and which were occasionally published in magazines and newspapers did not in any way address the issues and sentiments which preoccupy the public. Nor did poems by the other outmoded poets who insisted on writing in the old Amudi style, weaving their poetry from worn threads of a chivalry which no longer existed, for the values of the noble knight were no longer suited to the trials of daily life and the bitter struggle for survival. (Bakr 1991, 69–70/1995b, 56–57)

But this type of direct criticism is in fact rare in the novel, for even when Bakr executes a direct hit, it is often a quick blow that is swiftly replaced with a new target, as in the following dismissive jab that does not

17. For a discussion of silence as an aesthetic site of resistance, see Al-Nowaihi 2001.

linger very long: "Before that Zaynab lived a life full of excitement and joy, worthy of becoming the subject for a film, except for the Egyptian film-industry of course, lest it become ugly and vulgar" (Bakr 1991, 173/1995b, 150, translation mine). Moreover, the heavy-handed approach usually gives way to a more subtle one: a sly humor that both tempers and strengthens her criticism. Comic dislocation pervades the text through violating generic rules by means of ludicrous exaggeration, deliberate misuse of words or phrases, and mixing of vocabulary and/or styles from very different contexts or genres. This comic dislocation is a perfect antidote to the language of newspapers that is replete with outright lies (154/132), to television and magazines that not only are irrelevant but also implant impossible dreams for more consumer goods in people's minds (136/117, 97/83), and to "authentic" cultural productions that have themselves become commodities on display to wealthy tourists on their trysts in Haram Street nightclubs (73/59), or stuck on stages by the government to appease its sense of guilt (72/58). This sly humor, with its ability to give voice to the discontent of the voiceless and to write a working-class narrative that avoids some of the pitfalls of the typically middle-class novel, which is in fact one of Salwa Bakr's strongest assets,[18] also is unfortunately almost totally lost in the English translation.

It is by now a truism that comedy and humor do not translate as well as tragedy, for, as Umberto Eco explains it, although both modes depend on the breaking of rules and frames for their effect, comedy does not make explicit within it the frame that it is violating, whereas tragedy does. Consider the case of parody, for example, which Bakr's text is rich in. The humor of the imitation is entirely dependent on the audience's *prior knowledge* of the style and conventions of the genre that is being parodied, of the typical content that is being displaced. If the audience has not previously assimilated those norms and now takes them for granted, if it needs to be told about them within the text, then it is highly unlikely that they will find the parody funny. The rules of genre must be presupposed and

---

18. Ferial Ghazoul calls this the "eloquence of the oppressed." See Ghazoul 1990, 107–24.

considered inviolable before its disruption can be humorous (Eco 1983, 269–78). Moreover, Bakr's novel is rich with the cultural codes of everyday life that are unfamiliar to an English-speaking reader, and the humor is often at the expense of these cultural codes, so that it is not surprising that this humor is much diminished in the English translation. With this proviso, let me just give a few examples. The incongruity between the base, mercenary motives and the passionate, exaggeratedly romantic language of many a suitor, which the women all too often accept as sincere, is detectable in the intrusion of seemingly irrelevant details of Azima's nails and neck in the following instance: "He told her, as he fondled her long fingers with filed nails, painted with light red varnish, that his love for her knew no bounds and that he was passionate about every bit of her beautiful body, especially her long white neck which was plump as a silver jar" (Bakr 1991, 74/1995b, 60). As he intently watches her face and mouth, we realize that what he is admiring are her golden molars, indicative of the wealth he has every intention of enjoying, without falling into the trap of these "Jaws" (translation mine. *Al-fakk al-Muftaris*" is the Egyptian rendition of the popular movie *Jaws*) (75/61). Instead of the customary "marriage nest" for which the lovebirds of songs and movies accumulate straw upon straw, Bakr offers us a "marriage cage, for which the two will collect one bar after the other with their mutual toil and sweat" (165/144, translation mine). The language of love is often mixed with that of commerce as well as war, so that fancy wallpaper greatly enhances a bridegroom's sexiness, a vacuum cleaner ensures the newlyweds a lovely life of everlasting marital bliss (101/86), and passionate love songs are tear-gas bombs that prevent a peaceful resolution, and when the lover is tired of the no war/no peace situation, he breaks the cease-fire and starts a campaign of innuendo (76/62).

This sly humor often appears at some of the most tragic moments in the text, so that in a funeral "there were enough tears to cause another death by drowning" (Bakr 1991, 67/1995b, 54);[19] abused, abandoned

---

19. Although not a literal translation from Arabic, this is one of Manisty's more successful renditions of the humor in the original.

Aida shed tears that "surpassed all the weeping performed by the First Lady of Tears, Amina Rizq, in all her films" (99/84, translation mine); and Azima's failed suicide attempt is diverted into a description of the damage sustained by the vehicle on which she landed (66/53). Is Salwa Bakr being as cruel to her creations as the God some of her characters rage against when she deliberately evokes smiles and giggles at their most traumatic experiences? A clue to an answer is offered by Bakr herself in the following passage describing the allure of Azima's voice: "that voice with a sad rasp that flirts with the feeling, deeply entrenched in the psyche, of weakness, oppression, and hopelessness, as an eternal fate decried by God, and unrelated to the existing misery in which these masses (the audience) lived" (71/57, translation mine). This easy appeal to feelings of fatalistic hopelessness and mournful self-pity is exactly what Bakr is avoiding, and satirizing, through her comic dislocations. She refuses to allow us to wallow in tears that might momentarily purge us but ultimately leave us just as defeated and powerless. She insists on violating representational modes that perpetuate our victimization, just as she attacks the norms and practices on which they depend. And in their place what she offers is a genuine, deep, and heart-wrenching pathos. When we smile at Mahrusa's bitter tears mourning her beloved washer (137/117), or at Umm Ragab's three pounds that "represented a glorious conquest" (40/30, translation mine), or at the poor beggar who was "deprived of his dearest possession, a woman's double-breasted jacket" (34/26, translation mine), we are recognizing that the loss of a washer for an impoverished overworked mother with many children is in fact cause for deep mourning, that possessing the three measly pounds is a most momentous event in the life of someone like Umm Ragab, and that it is a warm jacket, and not any romanticized notion of honor, let alone style, that is a poor man's dearest possession.

Without even realizing it, we are performing the opposite of what usually happens in parody, for we are no longer amused at the irrelevance of the subject matter, but rather at the vehicle of representation that has traditionally considered such subject matter beneath its dignity. We are in a world of inverted parody, where the inferiority of the subject matter is not only tempered but also reversed. The result is a pathos of a specific quality: It is the pathos of a poor traffic policeman, probably an underpaid draftee, away from village home and family, who leaves the Cairo traffic to just sort itself out while he enjoys a couple of falafel sandwiches (Bakr 1991, 67/1995b, 54). It is the pathos of three orphaned children waiting for their mother, who will never return, to come home with their favorite fruit juice (196/172): children for whom the hunger for love and the hunger for food will probably remain inextricably bound—and forever unsatisfied. This is the tragic pathos of Egyptian daily life.

Conclusion: Dreaming of New Communities

The Golden Chariot is thus a working-class novel that sharply criticizes contemporary Egypt through utilizing and violating both popular and elite forms of representation, for where texts, deliberately or not, collude with ideology, Bakr, with deliberate humor, instigates a collision. Just as societal norms and institutions responsible for oppression, madness, and silence must be demolished, languages and narrative and discursive modes that, consciously or not, reinforce these societal norms must also be toppled. Through transforming private spheres into public, political issues, and marginal spaces into "representative" ones, new communities are constructed, and a band of mad, criminal women becomes the collective protagonist and the true products and representatives of the Egyptian nation. As we move from one story to the other, almost in a parody of sequence and causality, we realize that the real connections between these women are not, as the narrator or Aziza tells us, the optimum seating arrangement in the golden chariot. Rather, these stories become manifestations of the general condition of a nation that has lost its sense of purpose and seems to no longer care. The real connective tissue between these stories, then, is misery—but it is also laughter. This confusing laughter, or disorienting humor, is a sure sign that Salwa Bakr has not given up on this nation, and still deeply cares. By forcing her readers to make sense of her topsy-turvy world, and to unravel the disorientations in order to locate the true connections and the real object of satire, she is making out of the reading itself a "strategy of affiliation" and an invitation to rebuild at least the desire for community. For Bakr's community of readers, the words of Wayne Booth are apt indeed: "Total strangers, we had just performed an intricate intellectual dance together, and we knew that we were somehow akin."[20]

20. See Booth 1974, 31. Booth's book has been instrumental in my thinking through Bakr's uses of humor.

4 *The Sixth Day* of Compassion
The Im/Possible Communities of Life Toward Death

MARY N. LAYOUN _____

> Qui partage le malheur des autres?
> (Who can share/allot the misfortune of others?)
> —Andrée Chedid, *Le Sixième jour* [1]

Andrée Chedid. *Courtesy of Andrée Chedid*

Andrée Chedid is a tremendously prolific writer of poetry, prose fiction, drama, essays, and children's books, for which she has won numerous prizes and awards. Her works have been translated into nine languages. Born in Egypt in 1920, Andrée Chedid was educated in Paris and Cairo, resided from 1942 to 1945 in Lebanon, and has since lived in France. Though a first book of poetry, On the Trails, *was published in English, Chedid writes almost exclusively in French. She situates her work predominantly, although not exclusively, in the Middle East of both the modern period and, less frequently, the ancient past. Her location as an Arab woman and a Francophone writer*

1. Although I have consulted the excellent translations of Chedid's work with interest and pleasure, the translated passages here are my own, rendered rather more literally and less elegantly in the interest of understanding the "impossible communities of life toward death" to which Chedid's fiction points.

poses complex and crucial questions about the function of ethnicity, lang-
uage, place of birth, and place of residence in situating writers and their
texts.

Of Chedid's substantial oeuvre, only four novels have been translated
into English: Le Sommeil délivré *(1952), translated as* From Sleep Un-
bound *(1983);* Le Sixième jour *(1960), translated as* The Sixth Day
(1987) and translated into Arabic in 1979; La Maison sans racines *(1985),*
translated as The Return to Beirut *(1989); and, more recently,* L'Enfant
Multiple *(1989), translated as* The Multiple Child *(1995). A collection of*
short stories, essays, and selected poems, The Prose and Poetry of Andrée
Chedid *(1990), was also published in English. A selection of her poetry is in-*
cluded in the anthology Women of the Fertile Crescent: Modern Poetry by
Arab Women *(edited by Kamal Boullata 1978). Chedid's numerous prizes*
for her poetry and prose include the Prix Louise Labé (1966), L'Aigle d'Or
(1975), the Prix de l'Académie Mallarmé (1976), Bourse Goncourt de la
Nouvelle (1979), the Grand Prix de la Société des Gens de Lettres (1990), the
Prix des Quatre Jurys (1994), the Prix Albert Camus (1996), the Prix Paul
Morand, and the Grand Prix des Poètes (1999).

S aleh's harsh question to his aunt, Umm Hassan, in Andrée Chedid's
Le Sixième jour (1960) is a persistent challenge to the possibility of
community, of understanding or compassion, that resonates not only
throughout that novel but throughout much of Chedid's work. "Qui
partage le malheur des autres?" (Who can share/allot the misfortune of
others?) (Chedid 1960, 18). It is precisely to such a challenge that much
of Chedid's fiction addresses itself.[2] In this brusque rejoinder of the weary
and probably cholera-stricken young man to his dead mother's sister as
she seeks to console him is a marker for the always present possibility of
*mis*understanding and *lack* of compassion. Yet there is certainly no moral
imperative to compassion in Chedid's work. Rather, compassion or the acceptance of a shared misfortune is compelling in Chedid's fiction because

2. For some of Chedid's prose fiction in French, please see Chedid 1952a, 1952b,
1960, 1963, 1969, 1972, 1974, 1981, 1982, 1983, 1985, 1987, 1989a, 1989b, 1990,
1992, 1995, 1998, and 2000. For selected critical commentary on her work, see Accad
1982, Germain 1985, Izoard 1977, Knapp 1984, and Levis-Mano 1974.

of the irrefutable imperative of death. It is in this context that both this earlier work and her later novel set in the context of the Lebanese Civil War, *La Maison sans racines* (see Chedid 1985), are a testimonial of sorts to the power of the inevitability of death and also to human compassion in the face of that inevitability.

Compassion in both novels is an often halting and tentative recognition of and acceptance of a share in "the misfortune of others"—misfortune that is, ultimately, death. Its "sharing" is also an allotment or a dividing up—*partager*—that has, of course, always already occurred in the indisputable fact of human mortality. But from that *partager* in both senses of the word, a kind of community of shared and allotted misfortune is possible in Chedid's fiction. That such a community born of the recognition of the shared/allotted misfortune of death is fragile is an understatement. It is a compassion and a community of a very particular sort. And it is one into which some of the novel's characters must be insistently drawn—Okassione, the initially opportunistic street performer in *Le Sixième jour* most notably. Others, as Umm Hassan and the boatman Abou Nawass, seem already in possession of that compassion.[3]

And compassion in Chedid's novels is further distinguished by a fervent longing. In the citation from the poet Badr Shakir al-Sayyab that opens *La Maison sans racines,* that longing is, in what is already a familiar articulation, "to share the burden borne by mankind." But further, and as

---

3. There are numerous instances of the old woman's compassionate generosity in spite of her own poverty and her grief at the illness of her grandson. As Umm Hassan crosses the various districts of Cairo, making her way to the Nile and, ultimately, she hopes, to the sea, she hides her critically ill grandson by day and travels on foot by night, pushing the boy in a little hand cart. In spite of her own troubles, she notices a little beggar girl, sucking hungrily on a melon rind, crouched underneath the cart in which the old woman pushes her grandson. Umm Hassan takes the little girl to the grocer and buys her something to eat. (And, in the delight on the little girl's face at having something to eat, Umm Hassan subsequently sees a horrific vision of the little girl rotting away, dying, before her eyes.) Later, passing through another district of Cairo, she gives away a plate of food that she's been given to "the most tattered of the street urchins." In each instance though, the thought (or reality) of death accompanies the old woman's compassion as it does that of Abou Nawass. This does not diminish their acts so much as it contextualizes them.

suggestively, it is to "resurrect life" (Chedid 1985, 7). If we read this later novel against the earlier one, the literal deaths of Hassan and his grand-mother, Umm Hassan, in *Le Sixième Jour* precipitate the figural resurrec-tion of the young boy for the community of survivors, of the yet-to-die. The "resurrect[ion of] life" to which the fragment from Es-Sayyâb's poem refers is far more explicitly figured in the earlier novel:

> Never had Abou Nawass felt so intensely what a child is. "He's alive," he repeated to himself. "Tomorrow is alive" . . .
> "The child will see the sea, Umm Hassan!" . . .
> The child was everywhere, the child existed; near her, in front of her, in the voice, in the heart of these men. He was not dead, he could not die. It seemed as if they were singing, those voices. Between the earth and tomorrow, between the earth and the horizon the song was uninterrupted.
> "Life, the sea . . ." she murmured. "Finally the sea." (Chedid 1960, 186–88)

The response of Chedid's fiction—as of Umm Hassan and her story—to Saleh's question of the possibility of shared misfortune is a positive one, if one also paradoxical and limited. For compassion does not—cannot—forestall death. Rather, death is that toward which human life, compas-sionate or not, inexorably moves. More properly, death is that in which life is always already imbricated. This is the allotted *malheur* or misfortune that is shared in the recognition of that allotment. On the one hand, this is obvious if often purposefully "forgotten": everyone dies. Yet the sugges-tion of Chedid's fiction is not some simple or casual acceptance of an in-evitable death. If in conclusion the dying old woman and the three men on board the boat are drawn together by the dead/living boy, the terror of death is nonetheless fiercely felt: "Death is with us, boatman. Let's return at once" (Chedid 1960, 149).

This is the frantic cry of the somewhat less-than-compassionate Okas-sione, the street performer in *Le Sixième jour,* as he discovers that Umm Hassan's young grandson is dying of (a highly contagious) cholera on board the boat. To his shrill fear, the boatman Abou Nawass responds calmly and firmly. *"La mort est toujours avec nous"* (Death is always with us) (Chedid 1960, 149). And, indeed, death has consistently registered its presence from the opening lines of the novel. *Le Sixième jour* begins with Umm Hassan on the road from the impoverished district of Cairo, where she lives with her husband and grandson, to her natal village of Barwat. Egypt is engulfed by a cholera plague that has just taken the life of Umm Hassan's sister. When she returns to the cholera-devastated village to attend to her sister's burial, Umm Hassan is struck by the fierce toll the plague has taken on the village. Her effort to console her family is met with resistance and even hostility. She is an outsider, someone figuratively "dead" to the concerns of the village. "It's been many years since you were one of us." "You're too far away; you understand nothing of us" (14). This accusation on Umm Hassan's return to the village could have a particularly ominous undertone. Not simply because Umm Hassan might "understand nothing" of her family in the village. But also because her very return to them might have contributed to or have been the cause of her grandson's subsequent illness. Yet, suggestively, this possibility is of lesser significance in the novel. The way in which Umm Hassan's young grandson contracts cholera is never made absolutely clear. Cholera is, in any event, highly contagious. And as the young boy's cholera-stricken schoolteacher is taken off to the hospital, he warns Umm Hassan to watch Hassan for signs of the disease because the two of them have spent a great deal of time together. Illness and death could be the result of Hassan's and Umm Hassan's very eagerness for his betterment, of Hassan's own brightness (and hence the schoolteacher's special concern for and extra time spent with him), or of Umm Hassan's determination to educate her grandson. Or Hassan's cholera could equally be the result of Umm Hassan's contact with her family in cholera-devastated Barwat. In other words, the plague and, finally, death could have been carried to Hassan by those who love him most in the world. For the schoolteacher is hardly less committed to or fond of the young Hassan than Umm Hassan herself. But, more importantly for this novel than the literal source of death or its actual cause, death is not simply someone's "fault"; *"la mort est toujours avec nous."* Death is always already everywhere; it is already "always with us." The literal source of the disease that causes the young boy's death is secondary.

◎⦿◎

But of course, as a sweeping general pronouncement, this suggestion of Chedid's novels that death is everywhere and without a single culpable source could be considered profoundly troubling. In spite of the anonymous and indiscriminate plague and the equally anonymous and apparently indiscriminate sniper in *La Maison sans racines*, death and war and illness are not simply the way of the world or the inevitable situation of human existence. Or, at least, in better moments, we might like to argue that the latter two—war and illness—are not. Death, if only in Chedid's novels, *is* the way of the world; it *is* the inevitable situation of human existence. The inevitability of death is such a commonplace as to be utterly unremarkable. Yet there is something else suggested in Chedid's fiction, to which we will return, that points beyond the commonplace inevitability.

Even the fictional citation of the historical events of a devastating plague in Egypt (or an even more devastating civil war in Lebanon) as the setting for Chedid's novel complicates a simplistic effort to locate singular culpability or inculpability for either the literal deaths those historical events caused or the literary deaths the fictional narrative relates. Surely, ignorance and fear of "modern science" in *Le Sixième jour* contribute to the spread of the cholera epidemic. So, however, does the ignorance and fear of the practitioners of modern science figured in the characters of the two Egyptian nurses who charge into Umm Hassan's shack or in the public health officials who can't be bothered to explain what they're doing or why to residents of rural villages like Barwat. And so does the fear and ignorance that underlie even a benevolent desire to render assistance, as in the person of the young European nurse, Dana, who accompanies the two government nurses to Umm Hassan's house in the first part of the novel. But most of all, the poverty of both the district of Cairo in which Umm Hassan and her family live and of the rural village from which she comes, the lack of clean water, of an adequate sanitation system, of decent housing—these things contribute most significantly to the spread of cholera that is the cause of the deaths in the novel, as they were undoubtedly the causes of the cholera plague itself in Egypt of the 1940s. But duly registering the weight of these factors and noting the unequal ability of differently classed characters to seek to escape from death, Chedid's novels nonetheless foreground death as finally inescapable. Simultaneously her novels foreground the question of what fictional characters do in the meantime, how they interact with one another in the face of the "malheur" of death.

In this context, the opening citation in *Le Sixième jour,* drawn from the closing of Plato's *Gorgias,* is suggestive. For in that dialogue Socrates seeks to explain to his interlocutors, enamored as they are with a particular opportunistic conception of rhetoric, how life should be lived and how a different conception of rhetoric is linked to a good life. And in conclusion, Socrates links the living of a good or just life to the absence of fear in the face of death, to dying a good death. Just prior to the passage quoted in the opening of *Le Sixième jour,* Socrates states: "No one who is not an absolute fool or coward can fear death itself; it is committing injustice that men fear. For if the soul arrives in Hades burdened with a load of inequities, that is the worst and last of all evils" (Plato 1971, 102).[4] In order to make his point clearer to the resistant Callicles, Socrates tells him "a story to show you that this is true." The subsequent passage is quoted in the opening of Chedid's novel: "Then listen well, as they say, to a very fine story which you may consider a myth but I regard as true; for I want you to take everything I say as the strict truth" (1960, 9). The story that Socrates proceeds to relate is one that he has modified from Homer concerning Zeus's more just revision of the process by which the gods render judgment on mortals after their death. In death, Socrates points out, body and soul are separated but both bear the marks of the life they have lived. And both appear anonymously and without artifice to be judged by the gods. Socrates concludes his story to Callicles of the gods' rendering of "utmost justice" to mortals with the invocation to Callicles and his cohorts to join him as he seeks, "in cultivating the truth, to be as good as I am able during my life and when I die in my dying" (Plato 1971, 106).

Umm Hassan's life *and* her death—given over to her passionate love

---

4. Translation modified.

for and desire to save her grandson; her compassion for the poor and hungry children she encounters in the streets of Cairo even as she herself is weighed down with sorrow and worry; her compassion and willingness to listen and tell stories even to Okassione at his moments of most self-interested fear and greed; her ability to evoke in those around her a recognition, even if initially reluctant, of "what a boy really is," of a shared misfortune in the allotment (*partager*) of death (*malheur*)—is another story like that of Socrates (a fiction but "true") of a life toward death and the im/possible community it creates.

⚜

If Saleh indicts his aunt, Umm Hassan, for her long absence from and consequent lack of understanding about their village, a very similar accusation of lack of understanding, of inability to comprehend the local situation—and by implication of culpability for her own death as well as that of her granddaughter Sybil— is addressed to Kalya on her return to Lebanon in Chedid's *La Maison sans racines*. She too is indicted as an outsider, one who does not or cannot understand what is happening around her. And, like the possibility that Umm Hassan's ignorance and fear caused her grandson's death, the indictment of Kalya's ignorance and *lack of* fear as at last partly responsible for the deaths that occur in the novel is not utterly untenable.

Various characters in both novels register the notion of one's personal responsibility for the events that occur around them or at least for their location in the midst of those events. And this notion of individual responsibility is not simply dismissed in either *Le Sixième jour* or *La Maison sans racines*. In fact a comparison of the careful narrative description of each novel points to the immense class differences and consequent differences in the ability of the two grandmothers, Umm Hassan and Kalya, to be personally mobile, to shape personal surroundings.

But, understanding the situation is not simply what Saleh, in the passage from *Le Sixième jour* cited in the opening, assumes it to be. It is not simply holding the perspective on or reading of the situation as the local residents do—even if both Kalya and Umm Hassan are simultaneously local residents of a sort *and* outsiders. And Umm Hassan remembers as she returns to her impoverished village all the reasons why she left it for the capital city—the hope of making a living for herself, of doing better for her children, of educating her grandson. In spite of her husband's longing to return to the social relations and open landscape of the countryside, the old woman understands some things about her village only too well. Yet and simultaneously, after many years in the city, she *is* an outsider; she does not unequivocally share the perspective of her village folk any longer. Kalya too is, but is not, a local resident of Lebanon. By virtue of birth to Lebanese parents and of summers spent with her grandmother in Lebanon, she is "Lebanese." Raised and educated in Egypt and later a resident of Paris, Kalya is not simply "Lebanese." Infinitely more privileged, more mobile, more affluent than Umm Hassan, Kalya returns to a home that is not exactly hers, the markers of which she reads differently than those around her.

But as in *La Maison sans racines* so too in the earlier novel, there are multiple markers of what is happening. There is more than one way to read the situation that surrounds the novel's main characters. And it is not always clear which is the more acute reading. The cholera that kills Umm Hassan's sister also strikes Oustaz Selim, the young teacher in the school where the old woman sends her grandson. But the responses, the readings, of the teacher and of Umm Hassan are distinctly different. It is from the young schoolteacher's assurances to Umm Hassan, as he insists that the young boy go off to call an ambulance, that the title of *Le Sixième jour* is taken. In contrast to the suspicion of the villagers of Barwat (and of Umm Hassan) about modern medicine's ability to cure cholera, the young schoolteacher assures Umm Hassan as he is taken away to a hospital that he will return in six days. For on the sixth day, the outcome of the illness is clear. The novel is, then, configured in three parts of six sections each. On the sixth day, in the sixth section of part three, Umm Hassan and her young grandson die. And on the same sixth day, the young boy lives. The outcome of the illness is clear. "Le sixième jour . . . [the schoolteacher] ajouta-t-il se remémorant les termes du journal, 'c'est une vé-ri-ta-ble ré-sur-rec-tion!' " (Chedid 1960, 35)

And on the sixth day, there *is* a "veritable resurrection," as in the phrase from a journal that the schoolteacher struggles to remember. But of course Hassan is dead and so is his grandmother. What "lives" is something else. What lives is "tomorrow" and what Abou Nawass recognizes as "what a boy really is." And he recognizes it precisely because of his acceptance of *"partage le malheur des autres"*—his sharing *and* allotment of the misfortune of others. Even the initially self-centered and opportunistic Okassione, who makes money for himself by turning in cholera victims to the authorities, finally recognizes his "sharing and allotment of the misfortune of others." As the old woman lies dying on the deck of the boat on the dawn of the sixth day, waiting to hear that her grandson has recovered, Okassione kneels down and takes Umm Hassan in his arms. "Caressing her moist temples, gently stroking her wrinkled cheeks. . . . Never had the street performer felt such anguish. One day you fall from your rope, you lose your balance, you find yourself back in the midst of others, in the midst of their suffering, you don't play or take things lightly any longer [*on ne joue plus*]. You can't continue to play. 'My heart bleeds, it is the first time' " (Chedid 1960, 185).

Both *Le Sixième jour* and *La Maison sans racines* tell the story of precisely the recognition of the death-always-with-us as what engenders compassion and community. Even the most apparently impervious character, Okassione, recognizes his implication in the suffering of Umm Hassan and joins with the other two men on the boat to testify with compassion to the continuation of something else that is not simply life-before-cholera. The death of the old woman and her grandson and his own allotment of that *malheur* bind Okassione to the dead. And it also binds him to the other two men on the small boat.

If the resultant community of shared/allotted misfortune is less explicit than in *Le Sixième jour,* a refrain very like the observation of Abou Nawass about the omnipresence of death, the recognition of which forms the basis of that community, sounds throughout *La Maison sans racines:* "La mort fascine les hommes, c'est étrange" (Death fascinates men, it's strange). "Les hommes convoitent la mort" (Men long for death) (Chedid 1985, 92, 118). To this strange call of death, another refrain in *La Maison sans racines* forms a kind of counterpoint. That is the repetition of the mundane expression, *"tout s'arrange"* or "everything is settled." The everything that is settled in the opening as in the conclusion of *La Maison sans racines* is (but not only) a misreading or misstatement of sorts. But, in another context, it is the sum total of what happens in the novel. Everything *is* settled from the beginning. But it is only in retrospect that this becomes clear. Unlike the careful linear progression of *Le Sixième jour* as it structurally follows the six-day course of cholera, *La Maison sans racines* begins and ends with almost the same moment: Kalya's momentary distraction from watching two young women walk toward one another across the open square beneath an apartment window in Beirut. A sniper fires from a rooftop and one of the young women falls. Kalya rushes out of the apartment toward the center of the square, calling out to her young granddaughter to stay inside. This italicized first section of the novel accounts for Kalya's almost slow-motion progress toward the two young women. Her movement toward the center of the square is interspersed with memories of her childhood summers in Lebanon, with her thoughts of her young granddaughter and of this most recent summer in her natal homeland. Everything *is* settled already in the opening of the novel, though neither the readers nor the characters realize it quite yet. Although narrative time here does not follow the linear progression of a developing disease, the nonlinear progression of Kalya's memories as the narrative of her death develops almost as inexorably as the progression of cholera in *Le Sixième jour*. The repetition in the closing of *La Maison sans racines* of Kalya's response to the sniper's first shot is echoed as well in the repetition of the phrase "everything is settled." And again, only in retrospect and for the not-yet-dead does the actual weight of that mundane phrase—as mundane as the inevitability of death—become clear.

After a fiery exchange with another cabdriver with whom he narrowly avoids colliding, Tewfik assures Kalya and Sybil that "everything is settled"—*"tout s'arrange"*—as he drives them into Beirut from the airport on their arrival in Lebanon. "Kalya will remember those words later on" (Chedid 1985, 27), the narrator notes ominously. And of course with the benefit of hindsight, at least in the most literal sense, everything is not settled at all. The violence that flares up in the foreground of the novel or echoes in the distance is precisely the beginning of a long and devastating war. Everything is *not* settled. Quite the contrary. To underscore the point, in conclusion as Kalya lies dying of a sniper's bullet in the square, having seen Sybil shot down as well, her brother Mario repeats the same phrase to her. " '*Tout s'arrange,*' he insisted, he lied. He hoped that his words reached her. . . . '*Tout s'arrange*' branches out, multiplies, echoes. Kalya would like to shake her head but the phrase persists" (247).

Like *Le Sixième jour, La Maison sans racines* too opens and closes with the omnipresence of death. And here too a grandmother, Kalya, and her grandchild, Sybil, die in the conclusion. In fact and even more explicitly than in *Le Sixième jour*, we are already at the end of *La Maison sans racines* from its first lines, with the sound of the sniper's first shot fired into the square. That shot strikes one (or both?) of the two young women, Myriam and Ammal, who enter it from opposite directions to meet—"to re-unite"[5]—in the center of the square as a demonstration of intercommunal solidarity. As the two women lay in the center of the square, entwined and bleeding (a community of blood in potential death), Kalya rushes down the stairs and out into the square. Her urgent efforts to reach Myriam and Ammal are narrated in an almost dreamlike, slow-motion of crisis. "Time was short. She must rejoin the two women as quickly as she could. She must proceed to the square with the revolver clearly in view, to forestall any further threat, to prevent the next shot before the arrival of the ambulance. That too had been planned ahead of time, in case of an accident. She had to save what Myriam and Ammal shared; to maintain that hope that they wanted to bear, together, to the center of the square, where before long the diverse communities of the town would gather. To save this meeting which had been planned for days" (Chedid 1985, 17).

But it would seem that Kalya manages to save very little. In snapshot-like vignettes interspersed throughout the remainder of the novel,[6] she advances with interminable slowness toward the center of the square and the young women who lie bleeding there. Her movement toward them is interrupted by memories of her own childhood visit to Lebanon from the Egypt where she grew up. And it is interrupted by more recent memories

---

5. *Une fois rénuies.* When they reunited, events would unfold as previously planned (Chedid 1985, 13).

6. Perhaps not coincidentally for the structural organization of *La Maison sans racines,* Kalya is a photographer in Paris.

of this latest visit with her young granddaughter from the United States, Sybil, to the "land of her ancestors" from Paris where Kalya had eventually settled. Kalya's memories, however, are not delegated to the first-person narration of Kalya herself. Instead, as in *Le Sixième jour,* a third-person narrator relates events and provides almost lyric connections and interludes in the inexorable progress toward death in the novel. There are three distinct narrative times in *La Maison sans racines,* as the novel specifies in opening. They are the summer of 1932, the early summer of 1975, and the late summer of 1975. This latter time is distinguished from the earlier two by italicized print. Arabic numerals mark the passages set in July and early August of 1975. And Roman numerals mark the passages of the novel set in the summer of 1932.

So clearly, outside of the novel and with benefit of historical hindsight, though it is never explicitly named as such, the space and time to which Kalya and Sybil return is the opening of the Lebanese Civil War. Within the novel, the gesture to those events subsequent to the story times of the novel (if not necessarily of its narration) is in a long italicized passage utterly devoid of punctuation. The almost two pages of catastrophic events that will come to characterize the war in Lebanon hinge on a single preposition—"before" (*avant*). The efforts made by Ammal and Myriam and others like them must happen *before* the unfolding of what the novel's narrator, and implicitly its readers, know to be an irrevocable history of more than a decade-long civil and anti-occupation war. Yet, clearly, the novel's characters are unaware of the future anterior, of what will have been. And that ignorance or oblivion has mortal consequences. For as Kalya proceeds across the expanse of the open square, she herself is mortally wounded by a sniper's shot. And, as Sybil races toward her beloved grandmother from the doorway of the apartment where she had been watching the older woman's progress, the young girl too is fatally shot and crumples to the ground. The Sudanese servant rushes to Sybil's side and picks her up, whirling desperately around with the dead girl in his arms "like a whirling dervish" (244). The song he sings to the lifeless child, a lullaby "of his own childhood and of the land of the Nile" (244) recalls the songs of Abou Nawass and Dessouki, his Nubian shipmate, in *Le Sixième jour.* But unlike theirs, or the song that Umm Hassan hears at the end of the novel, Sliman's song of the endless coming and going of the water, "from the headwaters downstream," ends with another series of sniper's bullets that "riddle his body, interrupting the song" (245).

The title, the text, and the narrative voices of the novel suggest the catastrophic historical moment that Kalya and Sybil enter on their return. Their home or house or family is titularly identified as one without roots— *maison sans racines*. As with so much else in Chedid's novel(s), there is, but not only, a commonsense meaning to the suggestion of the title. Sybil and Kalya are benevolent interlopers, without any real ties to, "roots" in, their "home" in Lebanon. But from the opening of the novel, there is a suggestion of other kinds of ties between Kalya and Sybil and their home-that-is-not-quite-one. As he drives them into Beirut, Tewfik "studies their faces in the rear-view mirror." To his question: "Are you from here?" Kalya responds, "Not quite, my grandparents emigrated." Tewfik responds, "Even so you're from here! It's in our blood, that we're emigrants. I would have recognized you anywhere. You, and even the child" (Chedid 1985, 25). Subsequently, in one of few overt self-references, the narrator continues, contemplating the signs of identity and belonging: "Here or wherever, despite intermixing and generations, Tewfik always recognizes them, the émigrés, I don't know how: the curve of the nostril, the shape of the eye, the line of the nape of the neck, a particular clicking of the tongue, a shake of the head. He sometimes discovers them from a sign or gesture borne of these ancient regions, and which is perpetuated, like a live wire [*un fil conducteur*], mixed with other habits, with other movements" (25). It is not, then, simply that Kalya and Sybil are without roots themselves. However wishful Tewfik's recognition and reading of their faces might seem, it is not this sense of "rootless" that is primary in *La Maison sans racines*. For "roots" in this novel have less to do with language and accidents of birth or residence than with a kind of repeated choice and commitment.

The narrator significantly refocuses an exchange between Kalya and her sister-in-law Odette as they recall their departure from Egypt years earlier, one to Lebanon and the other to Paris.

"The older I get the more I put down roots. What about you Kalya?"

"I don't think I do, no."

What are they, roots? Distant ties or those [ties] that are woven through life? Those of an ancestral land rarely visited, of a neighboring land where one spent one's childhood, or are they those of a city where one has lived the longest? Hadn't Kalya chosen, on the contrary, to up-root herself? Hadn't she desired to graft those different roots and sensibilities onto one another? A hybrid, why not? She rejoiced in the crossbreeding, in the composite perspectives which didn't block the path to or turn away from other worlds.

"Why did you return now, with the child? What's the reason?" [Odette asked Kalya]. (Chedid 1985, 79)

For *La Maison sans racines,* roots are something else, a something else suggested by a passage from Khalil Gibran that is the second opening citation in the novel: "Your house [*maison*] will not be an anchor but a mast" (Chedid 1985, 7). The "rootlessness" of Sybil and Kalya's house (or family or home) is, to paraphrase Abou Nawass as he recognizes Hassan's life-in-death, "what a house really is." There are no roots that can secure a home against movement.[7] And it is to that house-as-mast blown by the winds and carried on by the currents that Kalya and Sybil return.

What is at stake is not so much a "house without roots" as it is the sometime or always residents of the house who ignore or are ignorant of the house's condition. It is in recognition of this ignorance that Kalya's niece Myriam wonders what she might say to Kalya so that she "won't leave as lightly as she came. So that she won't go back with false ideas, with false photos" (Chedid 1985, 127). Still, the impending disaster of Kalya's and Sybil's return home is only too clear. That clarity, of course, is not quite shared equally or even by all of the characters in the novel. Though the longtime inhabitants of Lebanon, like Myriam, more frequently worry about escalating dangers and tensions, the clear knowledge of impending civil war is not quite available to any one. But it is most especially not avail-

7. The constant references to flowing waters, to the sea, to the movement of the Nile can scarcely be insignificant in this context.

able to the two women—the grandmother and her granddaughter—who have come "home" from afar.

In the conclusion of *La Maison sans racines,* as Myriam and Ammal are taken in an ambulance to the hospital—they will survive, the medical attendant assures the onlookers—and as Kalya, Sliman, and Sybil lie dead or dying in the center of the square, the community of survivors is far less clearly suggested than in *Le Sixième jour.* And even then, in that novel, the nature of compassion and its potential community is an ambivalent one. *Le Sixième jour* culminates in a fragile community of men who bear witness to Umm Hassan's steadfastness and love for her cholera-stricken grandson. Together with the old grandmother, Umm Hassan, the three men on board the boat that was to take the old woman and her grandson to the sea, to health and to freedom, constitute a figural community of life-toward-death. They constitute a figural community in the face of death that they rename life. In an almost ritual iteration, each one of the three men speaks the same words to Umm Hassan as she herself lies dying of cholera. They each tell her that the cold and still child, the "icy stone" that is Hassan, is alive. And, after a fictional fashion, Hassan *is* alive.

But in *La Maison sans racines,* there is not quite such a figural community, even though Mario rushes to his sister's side to assure her of Sybil's survival. He "lies" to Kalya that the young girl will fly out of Beirut that next day: *tout s'arrange.* Although he is witness to what has occurred in the square, Mario cannot mark the possibility of a community of compassion. That possibility is even more fragile in what readers of the novel, and the novel itself, know to be the subsequent seventeen years of war in Lebanon.[8] Yet, as in *Le Sixième jour,* the potential of a community cognizant of its sharing in and allotment of *partager,* the misfortune of others, rests with the witnesses to what has happened. In this novel, one of those witnesses is, of course, Mario. A resolute non-witness is Odette, who literally and figuratively sits with her back to the window. Kalya herself is, as the novel opens, such a witness. And, in fact, the sniper fires at the two

---

8. Though published in 1985 and thus before the Taif Accords that officially ended the war in Lebanon, the narrative present of the novel is clearly cognizant of the years of war subsequent to the story present of the novel.

young women precisely at the moment that Kalya turns briefly away from her position as witness on the balcony. Her moment of inattention as witness marks the first shot. Subsequently, or perhaps simultaneously, she moves from being a witness of events in the square to being a participant. Sybil and Sliman too trace a similar trajectory. Only each of these three latter witnesses is dead in the novel's conclusion. There are only two other witnesses to the events in the square. One is introduced in the final page of the novel, a young boy "who saw it all, contemplates the square and the people [there]. In his head, things have begun to stir" (Chedid 1985, 248).

The enigmatic introduction in the novel's conclusion of a young boy who sees it all and begins to respond is a lonely marker for an as-yet-unarticulated response to the events of the square. What will his response be? What "things have begun to stir" in his head? Far less sanguine than the conclusion of the earlier novel, *La Maison sans racines* does not specify an answer to these questions. And yet, it is this novel that opens with the excerpt from Badr Shakir al-Sayyab with its longing to "share the burden of mankind" and "resurrect life" (Chedid 1985, 7). This is the implicit proposition made to the witnesses of events in the square who "see it all" and can "share/allot the misfortune of others" (Chedid 1960, 14), which is equally the misfortune of us all. There is no necessary mandate to accept that proposition. But if Chedid's two novels are situated as interlocutors to one another, the suggestion is clearly that of the potential of im/possible community in recognizing, sharing, and allotting the "misfortune" of human mortality and death. The reiteration of this suggestion leads to the final witness to the events in the square of *La Maison sans racines*. That witness is figured by the inexplicable introduction of the little boy in the last page of the novel. The unidentified and enigmatic boy-child who "sees it all" can be understood as a figure for the implied reader of Chedid's novel. That reader is the final witness to life-toward-death. And it is also to that final witness that Saleh's question is addressed: *Qui partage le malheur des autres?*

Part Two
_____

Narrating the Nation

5 Partitions and Precedents
Sahar Khalifeh and Palestinian Political Geography

BARBARA HARLOW _____

Why are we so moved by songs of loss? Are we a nation of romantics? Well, not anymore. Love lying broken at your feet makes your soul a commodity in the market of blood.

—Wild Thorns

In the first [poem] I was the mother (*al-um*), and now I am the land (*al-ard*). Tomorrow, no doubt, I will be the symbol (*al-ramz*). . . . I am not a symbol. I am a woman (*al-mar'a*).

—Bab al-saha (The courtyard's gate)

Sahar Khalifeh. *Courtesy of Sahar Khalifeh and the Sakakini Center*

Sahar Khalifeh was born in Nablus in 1941. Her arranged marriage at the age of eighteen ended in divorce, and her writing career has since taken her to the University of Iowa, where she completed a doctorate in American Studies and creative writing in 1988. She returned to Nablus during the first Palestinian intifada, where she established a Women's Resource Center that published the journal Shu'un al-Mara'a *(Women's affairs) and contributed to the documentation of Palestinian women's lives under occupation as well as under the pressures of traditional*

113

family codes. Her novels include Al-Subbar *(1976), translated into English as* Wild Thorns *(1985);* Abbad al-shams *(Sunflower, 1980);* Bab al-saha *(The courtyard's gate, 1990);* Mudhakkirat imra'a gayr waqi'iya *(Memoirs of an unrealistic woman, 1992); and* Al-Mithaq *(The inheritance, 1997). Sahar Khalifeh travels between Amman, Jordan, and Nablus in the Occupied West Bank, where she holds the position of Director of Women's Training and Research Center in Nablus with branches in Gaza and in Amman.*

In December 1994 in Jericho, as the new Palestinian Authority was continuing to negotiate its own legitimacy with the Israeli government, a Palestinian prisoner recently released from Israeli prisons was to celebrate his marriage to the woman he had been engaged to eight years previously when he had been convicted and sentenced for the slaying of a collaborator. On the wedding night, however, the bride was shot and killed. Accusations were made against the collaborator's family who, it was claimed, in seeking revenge had missed their target, the bridegroom, and murdered his bride instead. Her funeral was a public event, attended by hundreds of mourners (*Jerusalem Times,* December 16, 1994). But a few days later, following further investigation, the bridegroom was himself in the custody of the Palestinian police, charged with the death of the woman (*Al-Quds,* December 21, 1994). The former prisoner had, it seems, discovered on their wedding night that his bride was not a virgin, and had exacted his own revenge.

This incident, reported briefly in the Palestinian press at the time, betrays in its tragically related two versions—the defense of the national honor and the punishment of a woman's dishonor—a larger narrative: the still contentious place and status of women within the historic gains and losses of modern Middle Eastern polities. Women have long figured large in Western constructions of the "Orient" throughout the confrontations—military, political, and cultural—that have engaged the two social orders for centuries, from the Crusades, through colonialism and decolonization, and now in the post-cold war era. The contrasting narratives embedded in the account of the death of the Palestinian bride are emblematic of the contemporary contradictions that disturb her own social order and her people's political aspirations no less than of the earlier histories of an East-West conflict, particularly as these have been scrutinized by Western observers and documented by international reporters.

In the case of Palestine, however, that larger globalized divide has been rewritten by the more localized cultural politics of partition. The decisive partition in 1947–48 of the mandated land of Palestine on the withdrawal of its British overseers resulted in the creation of the Jewish state of Israel and an ensuing multinational contest ever since over those territories that were to have constituted an Arab Palestinian state. The Gaza Strip came under the authority of Egypt in 1949 and the West Bank was annexed by Jordan at the same time; both areas were militarily occupied by Israel following the June War in 1967. The Declaration of Principles (D.O.P), signed in September 1993 by Yasser Arafat for the PLO and Yitzhak Rabin for the government of Israel, initiated a new, albeit still conflicted, phase in the Palestinian struggle for self-determination and self-representation. But the agreement also reiterated in important ways the historically decisive terms of that longstanding contest: policing, "free trade," and partition. Two of the novels by the Palestinian novelist Sahar Khalifeh—*Al-Subbar* (*Wild Thorns,* 1976) and *Bab al-saha* (The courtyard's gate, 1990)—both set in the West Bank town of Nablus, at once review that history and remap the geographical premises that it has entailed.

Wild Thorns, Khalifeh's second novel (and the only one of her books to be translated into English), is set in the period following the June War of 1967 and the Israeli occupation of the West Bank and the Gaza Strip. The narrative imperatives of the novel form, however, are implemented in order to critique the "master narratives"—whether the Zionist dream of settling a "greater Israel" or a Western agenda of progress that inexorably enlists peoples and places in the service of its accomplishment—that have determined and suppressed Palestinian demands for a story of their own. The linear teleology of the political economy of development, for example, is reassessed by the novel's story line that traces the proletarianization of the Palestinian peasantry and the dissolution of the family farm and its traditional order. The Israeli occupation is, in turn, challenged from without, when Usama arrives to blow up the Israeli buses taking Palestinian workers to the Israeli factories inside the "green line," and from within, by Adil, one

of those workers who is attempting to organize Palestinian laborers in Israeli factories. The dispute between Usama and Adil, former childhood
friends, serves to ground and to analyze the tensions that have riddled the
Palestinian struggle itself, differences, in other words, between inside and
outside, between armed struggle and sociopolitical transformations.

Whereas women remain critically marginal to the story lines of *Wild
Thorns,* their positioning on thresholds, in doorways, at the outskirts of
the novel's scenes, indicates their emergent role as decisive agents in the
recasting of the Palestinian national narrative. But if *Wild Thorns*'s young
women occupy peripheral places in that earlier novel, their role will be
centrally elaborated in *Bab al-saha* (The courtyard's gate), a novel set
more than a decade later amid the turbulence of the *intifada* in Nablus.
The partition that divided Palestine in 1947–48 and created the state of
Israel has here been internalized within the Palestinian social order, and
the exigencies of interpretation and struggle must be renegotiated along
new lines. Those lines, as articulated by the female protagonists of the later
novel, demarcate the cultural parameters as well as the political perimeters
of another Palestinian social order—the new geographies of struggle still
to be waged against the precedents of partition that have long been writ
large across the Palestinian historical landscape.

Placed in the interim between the June War of 1967 and 1973's October War, both of which ended in an Israeli military defeat of Arab
armies, the narrative of *Wild Thorns* is riven by the combined territorial fis-
sures and sociopolitical divisions that characterized the Palestinian struggle at that critical juncture. Written against the grain of two dominant
narratives—the teleology of Palestinian nationalism on the one hand and
the imposed imperatives of developmentalism on the other—Khalifeh's
novel both vestiges the scenario of liberation and armed struggle scripted
by the resistance movement's leadership in exile and critiques the atavistic
structures of traditionalism that continue to resist social changes from
within. Representing these two historic agendas in their partitioned collision are two of the novel's protagonists—Usama and Adil respectively:
Usama, the lone *fedai* sent in from outside to frustrate violently the coercion of Palestinian peasants by Israeli labor needs; and Adil, scion of a
landed, but now impoverished, Palestinian family who has begun working

in a factory across the green line and who attempts to educate his fellow workers so that they demand their rights and resist the systemic exploitation by their employers. The agendas themselves, however, have been instantiated by the documentation of a century of international negotiation.

In November 1917, as World War I drew to its finale, Arthur James Balfour, representing the British government, conveyed to Lord Rothschild his government's "declaration of sympathy with Jewish Zionist aspirations," in what has since become known—both famously and infamously according to the disposition of its readership across the divide of conflicting national claims—as the Balfour Declaration. In that letter, Balfour quoted: " 'His Majesty's Government view with favor the establishment in Palestine of a national home for the Jewish people, and will use their best endeavors to facilitate the achievement of this project, it being clearly understood that nothing shall be done which may prejudice the civil and religious rights of existing non-Jewish communities in Palestine, or the rights and political status enjoyed by Jews in any other country.' " Just how "clearly understood," however, the declaration's terms were has been disputed throughout the twentieth century as Arabs and Jews challenged their applications to the territorial integrity of the land of Palestine. On November 29, 1947, the UN General Assembly, considering that "the present situation in Palestine is one which is likely to impair the general welfare and friendly relations among nations," presented in Resolution 181 its plan for the partition of the territory. That accomplished, twenty years later, almost to the day, and in the aftermath of the June 1967 War, the Security Council of the same body passed Resolution 242, which, while it emphasized the "inadmissibility of the acquisition of territory by war" and called for the "withdrawal of Israeli armed forces from territories occupied in the recent conflict," nonetheless redefined the question of Palestine, the "civil and religious rights" of the Balfour Declaration, as a "refugee problem," but a problem, for all that, still requiring a "just settlement." Meanwhile, the Palestinians themselves were organizing their own struggle over the determinations of such a settlement. In 1964, the Palestine Liberation Organization was established as a genuine national liberation movement that would engage in combined armed struggle and diplomatic exchanges for the right to Palestinian national self-determination. Its political body in exile, the Palestine National Council, articulated in the resolutions passed at its successive convenings over the next two decades an accompanying policy, one that, according to Muhammad Muslih, evolved from the "total liberation phase" (1964–68) to the "secular democratic state" phase (1969–73), culminating in the "two-state solution" phase begun in 1974 (Muslih 1990, viii-ix).

Against this documentary history and its chartered disposition of peoples across a continually redrawn map, the demography of *Wild Thorns* and the intersecting itineraries of Usama and Adil are organized along another axis of "inside" (*al-dakhil*) and "outside" (*al-kharaj*), occupation (*ihtilal*) and exile (*manfa*), an axis, however, whose own fixities have been repeatedly undermined following the June War, when the West Bank and Gaza Strip were brought under the purview of Israeli military control. "One of the central features of the Israeli military occupation of the West Bank and Gaza," according to Joost Hiltermann, "has been a gradual integration of the economy of the Occupied Territories into Israel's own" (1991, 30). Usama and Adil, then, as representatives of two organizing narratives, provide as well a probing critique of the conflicting strategies of resistance as these have been elaborated from the two sides of partition. What Raja Shehadeh, a Palestinian lawyer in the West Bank town of Ramallah, referred to as the "third way" of struggle, *sumud* or steadfastness, the refusal to give way (1982), had too often been read from outside as a people's capitulation, or worse still, opportunist collaboration. Usama, then the individual from outside, national liberationist in orientation, endorsing armed struggle and guerrilla incursions, has as his mission to blow up the Egged buses that transport Palestinian day laborers across the green line to work in Israeli factories. Adil, by contrast, sees his brief from within as a collective one, protosocialist, and committed to social organizing across his community—the very project that Usama has been assigned to demolish.

The question remains, however, at the end of *Wild Thorns*, as in the period in which it was written, of the reliability—for the novel's readers and for the Palestinian people more generally—of the narrators of these alternative trajectories. According to Usama:

"There's only one dimension, one reality, that of defeat and occupation. But is this occupation or disintegration? Are they both the same for my country? It's the people themselves that defeat me more than Israel. Adil, the very backbone of the whole family, he's destroyed too. What's left? Basil and his friends? They're still too young. We'll have to wait a long time for the children to grow up. We'll need the patience of Job. But how can we be sure that every single one of them won't turn out like Adil, their hearts filled with regrets, their wrists bearing shackles that bite deep? All culture gone! All integrity! Sink, Palestine." (Khalifeh 1985, 69)

For Zuhdi, however, one of Adil's coworkers, Usama's words offend, even wound:

"When I asked him one little question, it was obvious he hadn't been listening. I thought he was like you, brother Adil. But it's clear this cousin of yours wants to impose his own ideas on us. Well, we're having none of it. Tell him we've reached the end of the road. Tell him we don't need it. This is what always happens," he went on angrily, banging the cane chair with his hand. "We speak, but they don't hear us. Who can we speak to? For God's sake, who can we speak to?" (85)

Who, that is, will account now, provide the political and ideological legitimation, for international recognition? Who, in other words, will answer for the establishment of the political—and territorial—grounds for the implementation of a historical narrative of national liberation and its socioeconomic paradigms?

The novel poses that question, like Zuhdi's, against a series of occupied topographical contexts, delineating within them the political and social geographies that continue variously to underwrite the larger historical narrative. From family farm to factory and in prison, the Palestinian social structure and the attendant contest for power within it among resistance organizations, families, and trade unions are examined and submitted to the exigencies of radically critical reorderings. Political detention, a topos already long crucial to classic resistance narratives, is given five uninterrupted chapters in *Wild Thorns,* a monumental textual space testifying to its decisive place in such accounts. The young Basil has been arrested for his participation in a demonstration against the occupation and, during his sojourn within the prison walls, he is educated to a new awareness of his responsibilities. Structured by the detainees' clandestine organization, Basil participates in their political lessons, poetry competitions, the regular sessions of the "people's school" (Khalifeh 1985, 123), and evening assemblies, and observes the processes of social ostracization of suspected collaborators, the pain and anguish of family visits, and the brutalities of solitary confinement. When he is eventually released, closing behind him the novel's prison pages, Basil relates to his family the changes he has meanwhile experienced: "My God make things easy for my comrades still in prison. Oh yes, they were real comrades. They thought I was a spy when I went in, but by the time I left, I was a comrade. I got educated, not only school subjects but special evening sessions too. Proletariat, capitalism, bourgeoisie, compradorism, and all that" (176).

If prison as institutional space looms large and monolithic within *Wild Thorns,* however, the family farm is in ruins, deserted, barely standing. Usama has noticed this destitution already, on an early visit to the farm where he confronts its caretaker, Abu Shahada: "The road to the farm looked as though it hadn't been used recently. Grass grew wild over the paths. The little building once used as a reception room was locked up. He found his eyes misting over with tears as he called out, 'Is there anybody here?' " (Khalifeh 1985, 39). Its feudal patriarch (Adil's father) is living by means of a kidney dialysis machine with his family in the town, and the farmhands have begun now to cross daily into Israel to work in the factories rather than tending to the land. As Abu Shahada explains to an outraged Usama, "Better over there. . . . Nobody stands over you, making you work like a donkey from morning till night" (41). But finally it is Basil, educated by prison, who challenges his sister Nuwar with the developmental analysis: "Ah, you're all cowards, all of you. You, Adil, my mother, everyone. You use father's illness as an excuse to avoid facing facts. Adil's been working in Israel for months without telling Father. Everyone knows, including Mother, but they're all like ostriches, hiding their heads in the sand and pretending that there's no storm going on around them"

(188). And in the factory, wages are continually depressed for the Palestinian workers, documented and undocumented, a reserve army of labor for Israeli businesses across the green line, who pay income taxes, national insurance, and pension contributions (see Hiltermann 1991, 22) and are denied social benefits, health care, and compensation for injuries suffered on the job. But when Usama blows up the buses transporting those workers to their daily exploitation, the Israeli army in turn blows up the Karmi home. Two explosions, wreaking the destruction of both transport and home, of movement and place, create a sinister rendition of collective punishment and retribution, and the near-simultaneous demolition of the two narratives of nationalism and developmentalism alike.

"Yes," Adil had said at one point, "turn on the radio. Envelop me in legends, in glories of old, and in the worship of heroes" (Khalifeh 1985, 61). But the legends, like the Karmi home, the stories of Abu Zayd al-Hilali and Antar Ibn Shaddad, no more than the tales from *The Arabian Nights* (52), are no longer available as precedents to transport an enraptured audience out from under occupation. Other means of transportation—more consonant with the new modes of production—must still be devised. The buses had suggested one such accommodation for crossing the geographic barriers created by historic partition plans, but these conveyances had proved anathema to the resistance movement's own designs. Within the text itself, however, the buses, like the family farm, the factory, and the prison, had in part provided an experimental if failed movable model of social organization—constructed here around labor—for challenging the system of exploitation and the hierarchies of power created by military occupation and class differences complicated by religious and ethnic conflicts. The service taxi, in which entrance to *Wild Thorns* is made across the Allenby Bridge on the Israel-Jordan border, provides another such testing ground, with its passengers returning to the Occupied Territories from sundry visits outside: Usama determined on carrying out his mission, Abu Muhammad with remittances and gifts from the son who has been working in Kuwait, and the woman with a "plaster cast on her left forearm" (22). The service taxi, a vehicle for both social anonymity and political solidarity, instantiates from its outset a critical problematic for *Wild*

Thorns: how does one get from one place to another, from one time to the next? What options are provided by the historical narrative for elaborating new geographies of struggle—against the very precedents of partition?

Within the masculinist—if conflicting—articulations of those options that are provided by Usama and Adil, women remain largely marginal, interstitial, to the textual spaces and institutional locations of Khalifeh's novel *Wild Thorns*. Several of these women are named, women like Usama's mother, who wants to marry off her son and entrusts his fate to the beneficence of higher powers, or the wife of Adil's coworker Abu Sabir, who must contemplate the selling of her bracelets because her husband has no insurance and as an unregistered Palestinian does not qualify for workers' compensation following his factory accident. Adil's own sister Nuwar ostensibly refuses to participate in the marriage game arranged for her by her father, but her adamancy is actually owing to her romantic commitment to a prisoner with whom she is in love. And then there is Lina as well, a "boyish-looking" girl who is eventually arrested for her participation in activities against the occupation authorities. Other, as yet unnamed women, however, appear only in the background—on the sidelines and thresholds—of the narrative's corners and peripeties, their identities unknown but auguring new and emergent possibilities. On the steps of a small paved courtyard, for example, a "little girl of about four sat on the filthy ground to the right of the bucket, holding a scrap of faded cloth. This she dipped into an open drain with soap suds floating on its surface. She was pressing and wringing out the cloth with both hands, in imitation of grown women" (Khalifeh 1985, 81). But there is also the woman from the service taxi, whom Usama saw but once again following his arrival in Nablus: "A few days later, he saw her among the crowds in the old part of town. Her left forearm was no longer in a plaster cast" (25). The historical necessity of these appearances and reappearances remains unexplored within the text of *Wild Thorns*, but poses rather the urgent necessity of future historical transformations.

Usama's return across the lines of partition to the Occupied Territories had been undertaken, with no little irony, under the auspices of the "family reunification program," a program sanctioned by international standards of occupation and the enjoined proper treatment of civilians.

The program would, however, in subsequent years, be seriously hampered by the manipulations of the Israeli government and its military authorities, whose obstructionism has in turn been critiqued by the Alternative Information Center's division, Article 74.[1] The name "Article 74" refers to that article in Protocol 1 of the 1977 Additional to the Geneva Conventions of 1949; in *Punished Twice-Punished Collectively* (February 1994), one of the AIC/Article 74's ongoing bulletins, the organization particularly scrutinized the complex and discriminatory application of the statute to Jerusalem:

> In the first stage, Israeli policy regarding family reunification in Jerusalem was guided by the same principles as in the West Bank and Gaza Strip, i.e. to limit the number of new Palestinian residents as much as possible, with one significant difference: The Jerusalem Interior Ministry has practiced a policy of gender discrimination; while male Palestinian residents of Jerusalem have a good chance of being granted family reunification for their non-resident wives, applications submitted by female Palestinian residents are always refused. The Interior Ministry has cynically argued that Palestinian social and cultural norms require a married woman to go to live with her husband so that a woman's application is not justified. (1994, 4)

The issues of women and family, seemingly submerged and sidelined in *Wild Thorns,* but still foregrounded in persistent and disputed negotiations of the Palestinian question, are perhaps nonetheless writ all the larger in their very diminishment within the text: the issue of the place of women in the resolutions of that question. The conflicting narratives of nationalism and developmentalism that ground the novel's progression must yield ground to the exigencies of that other narrative tension so dramatically performed in the brutal death of the Palestinian bride: the sexualized and gendered tension between a nation's honor and its people's dishonor.

1. The Alternative Information Center is a documentation center in West Jerusalem. Its regular publications include *News from Within, Article 74,* and *The Other Front,* as well as occasional papers and briefings.

❦

Following the completion in 1988 of her Ph.D. in American Studies at the University of Iowa, Sahar Khalifeh returned to the Arab world and eventually to the Occupied Territories. In Nablus, she played a leading role in the establishment of a Women's Resource Center, an institution for training women in the work of documentation and narration of the material conditions and cultural struggles of Palestinian women under Israeli occupation. It was then too, in 1990, that *Bab al-saha* (The courtyard's gate), her fifth novel, was published. Khalifeh's return to her home in the Occupied Territories had, however, signaled a dynamics of "return" radically altered from that identified a decade and a half previously by Usama and his commando's mission, or even by the terms of the "settlement" of the "refugee problem" recommended by UN Resolution 242. The Palestinian *intifada,* that is, had already begun—in December 1987—and the translation of the focus of Palestinian resistance from outside to inside was decisive to the subsequent developments of that struggle. This shift in political priorities and geographic locales enjoined as well new imperatives of documentation and narrative—strategies such as that elaborated in Khalifeh's portrait of Umm Samih al-Saber and the killing of a collaborator. According to Penny Johnson, this short account of an elderly woman in the Old City of Nablus, confronting the combined challenges and violence of occupation and women's dispossession, reflects the writer's "literary interest in the voice and speech of ordinary people, and her feminist interest in the world of poor women" (1990, 29).

Bab al-saha narrates principally the stories of four such women as their lives intersect in the courtyard of Sakina's house in Nablus, a "house of ill-repute" (*dar al-mashbuha*) whose own local history nonetheless recapitulates the significant pressures on the social order in which it is situated. In addition to Sakina, there are as well her daughter Nuzha, who now lives alone and isolated in that house; Zakiyya, a midwife who is not afraid of the dark; and Samar, a university student researching the effects of the *intifada* on the situation of Palestinian women. Their respective personal and social trajectories cross in that forbidden terrain when the young men, the *shabbab,* of the *intifada* must seek refuge in the same house from the Israeli patrols who endeavor to regain control of the neighborhood and its byways from the demonstrating and resisting inhabitants. The storyline then no longer follows the contestation between Adil's labor organizing and Usama's commando mission, nor is the setting dispersed across the several institutional frameworks of family farm, factory, and prison. Rather it is women's exchanges, located within a women's space—popularly if disparagingly identified as a brothel, *mashbuha,* suspicious and suspect— that concentrate the textual apparatus of *Bab al-saha.* The text, in other words, poses importantly the urgent demand within a national struggle for the recognition of women's rights as human rights.

Human rights reporting, itself a genre in the contemporary world of writing and rights, entails both documentation and intervention. A recording of facts and events, of abuses of individual lives and national histories, as well as an effort to correct official records that have systematically obscured those abuses, the writing of human rights draws of necessity on conventions of narrative and auto/biography, of dramatic representation, and of discursive practices. Indeed the thirty articles of the Universal Declaration of Human Rights that was proclaimed by the General Assembly of the United Nations in December 1948 translated the standard literary paradigm of individual versus society and the narrative practices of emplotment and closure, by mapping an identification of the individual within a specifically international construction of rights and responsibilities. The Declaration, that is, can be read as recharting, for example, the trajectory and peripeties of the classic bildungsroman. While that Declaration has, since its adoption, been as much abused as used by governments throughout the world, peoples and their representatives continue to appeal to its principles. Those written appeals, the reports of human rights monitors, the documentation of international organizations such as Amnesty International, and the narratives of individuals recounting their efforts to reconstruct a human history, form the bases for rescrutiny of the relationships between the "literary" and the "political," of the place of women in politics, and of the role of the academic classroom in that examination. A new body of literature is emerging as part of the mapping of new geographies of struggle. Its narratives trace the patterns of an active and activist intersection of the cultural and the political. It is within this corpus, perhaps, that *Bab al-saha* can be seen to examine, by way of its textual displacements of locus and voice, the designs of that renewed literary critical exercise.

The novel's nine chapters and their thirty-nine subdivisions relate discursive exchanges among the women themselves, as well as between the women and their respective male interlocutors, from Israeli soldiers in the street to *shabbab* on the run. Zakiyya, for example, must explain to one military patrol that what she has in her basket are the materials she needs in her profession as a midwife. Samar attempts in turn an explanation to Nuzha about her research into women and the *intifada*. And Um Azzam, the wife of Wajih, Zakiyya's brother, who visits her sister-in-law, describes the situation of domestic violence in her own home. Many of these conversations are overheard by Hosam, one of the *shabbab* who has been wounded in an encounter with the Israeli soldiers and has taken shelter in Sakina's *dar al-mashbuha*. Women's contributions, in other words, not only determine the textual groundings of *Bab al-saha*, but establish as well the critical terms of its historic account and contemporary analysis of the question of Palestine. Whereas conventional readings of women's role within the body sociopolitic have tended significantly to emphasize (whether positively or negatively, in theory as in practice) the separation of the personal and the political,[2] the private and the public (as well as the multiple other versions of this cordoning principle), Khalifeh's novel instead collapses that distinction. *Bab al-saha* at once internalizes the public and political debate, and externalizes the otherwise privatized issues of women's lives in a compelling argument for the reciprocities of the conversations that build communities and the diplomacies that establish states.

Two topics in particular animate the women's exchanges amongst themselves and with their masculine counterparts in this Nabulsi *dar*

---

2. Discussions of these distinctions are now numerous and classic. For particularly useful analyses, see, for example, Jean Franco, "Beyond Ethnocentrism" in *Marxism and the Interpretation of Culture;* and Chandra Talpade Mohanty, "Under Western Eyes" in *Third World Women and the Politics of Feminism.*

al-mashbuha: the violence of the assault on women's bodies by the combined forces of the Israeli military occupation and the domestic brutalities
of their own men within the family and at home; and the depredations
committed against women's stories by the rehearsals of the lexicons of
love poetry and the rhetorics of nationalism. As the wounded Hosam
learns from the women who have taken him into their own protective custody: "Strange indeed is the heart of the political activist (*al-siyasi*)"
(Khalifeh 1990, 172). Or as Samar and Nuzha describe it between themselves, the heart is already "tied up" (*marbut*) (203). Samar, in any case,
had disparagingly rejected the florilegial profferings of her admirer's
poems: "In the first [poem]," she says, "I was the mother, and now I am
the land. Tomorrow, no doubt, I will be the symbol. Get it right, if you are
so clever, I am not the mother, I am not the land, and I am not the symbol.
I am a human being. I eat, drink, dream, make mistakes, get frustrated, ex-
cited, angry, I tell secrets. I am not the symbol; I am a woman" (176). And
at the end of the novel, in its very last lines, Nuzha, relentlessly resistant to
the stridencies of nationalist discourses, will take up a Molotov cocktail
against the soldiers who have killed three of the *shabbab,* including her
brother Ahmad, only to deny her own patriotic commitments: "Not because of the ghoul," she says, "but because of Ahmad" (222). "Your Palestine," Nuzha had just previously insisted, "is like a ghoul. She eats, and she
swallows, and she is never satisfied" (219).

But such declamations as these are unpopular, as reluctantly received
as had been Um Azzam's story of her husband's incorrigible practice of
beating her when she told it to Samar and Zakiyya. As Zakiyya, her sister-
in-law, responds to Um Azzam's beseeching request for a refuge of her
own against their kinsman: "What will people say?" (159), and she finally
demands of the other woman, "Lower your voice. Someone might hear
you" (163–64).

Someone might hear you. If Zuhdi, in *Wild Thorns,* had been concerned that there was no one to speak to of Palestinian nationalism, that
"they don't hear us," the words, the voices, the stories, of women and
their ordinary lives, as in *Bab al-saha,* might yet serve to breach that other
partition, the traditional and much precedented exclusion of women from
the public discourse and debates. More extraordinary still have been the

coercive efforts to extract confessions from Palestinian women political prisoners. *Making Women Talk* is the title of Theresa Thornhill's inquiry into the Israeli practices of interrogating Palestinian women detainees. Thornhill, a representative of the London-based Lawyers for Palestinian Human Rights, examined the legal framework, the methods of interrogation, the trial procedures, and finally, the question of whether Israel sanctions torture. In particular, she focused on the role played by the "confession"—both in presenting evidence against the women and as part of a systematic process of sexual harassment, the "manipulation of the Arab notion of 'female honor,' and manipulation of mothers' concern about their children" (Thornhill 1992, 16). The description, however, of her first extension of detention hearing, provided to Thornhill by Hanan Rahim, detained in December 1989, suggests through its use of verbs—their transitivity and intransitivity as well as their semantic resonance—the decisive significance of talking and of determining when to talk and when not to talk—to the Israeli interrogator's methods:

> After forty-eight hours, *I was taken* to Acre Magistrates Court for my detention to be extended. My lawyer *was present,* but I *was forbidden to speak* to her. In addition, I *was told* that I *could only address* the judge in the absence of my lawyer. I *said nothing* at all. My lawyer *asked* why the Shabak wanted to extend the detention. The *reply was,* "in order to *interrogate* her." They *said* that forty-eight hours had not been sufficient. The judge *accepted* this, and *gave* the Shabak a further seven days. (10, emphasis added)

Acted upon thus ruthlessly, Hanan Rahim's only remaining agency is through her words—or the withholding of them—and ultimately in her report of the procedure to the English human rights investigator.

If documents—from international and diplomatic agreements to UN resolutions—decided the historical precedents and geographical partitions that have long made up the question of Palestine, with the *intifada,* in particular, there emerged as well another kind of documentary, one that argued the significance of personal narrative to the elaboration of a national agenda. From human rights reports, which identified the prisoner's "confession" extracted under duress as already critical to the occupation authorities' detention of a people, or the "license to kill" that warranted "Israeli undercover operations against 'wanted' and masked Palestinians,"[3] to the portraits of Palestinians, men and women,[4] that proliferated in response to the publicity of the *intifada* in the trade presses of Western capitals, to the personal narratives of academic researchers like Samar, who have visited and studied the women of the *intifada*,[5] these documentaries tell another story. Like Samar, however, each of these inquirers was obliged to visit the *dar al-mashbuha*, to traverse partitions and cordons that have sought to locate Palestinian history and its political geography as somewhere off-limits.

Samar, however, the social sciences student who visits the other side of "the courtyard's gate," engages in a different, more and less academic, discursive strategy of question and answer. Her project, like that of many anthropologists, political scientists, and sociologists since the beginning of the *intifada* at the end of 1987, and resembling as well the work of Khalifeh's own Women's Resource Center, is to elaborate on the connections between the Palestinian uprising and Palestinian women's lives. As Samar asks Zakiyya, "What changes have taken place for women during the *intifada*?" The conversation goes on, and Zakiyya responds with her own question, "Do you want the truth?" And Samar answers, "Nothing but the truth." To which Zakiyya in turn replies once again, "Frankly, nothing has changed except their distress. There is more distress for them. . . . They have more and more worries, still the old ones and the new ones just multiply" (Khalifeh 1990, 20). And Zakiyya goes on to enumerate the in-

---

3. See, for example, the reports from Middle East Watch, *A License to Kill* (1993) and *Torture and Ill-Treatment* (1994), as well as documents from Amnesty International, Al-Haq, and the Palestine Human Rights Information Center.

4. See, for example, Orayb Aref Najjar (with Kitty Warnock), *Portraits of Palestinian Women* (1992); and John Wallach and Janet Wallach, *The New Palestinians: The Emerging Generation of Leaders* (1992).

5. See, for example, Elise G. Young, *Keepers of the History: Women and the Israeli-Palestinian Conflict* (1992); Philippa Strum, *The Women Are Marching: The Second Sex and the Palestinian Revolution* (1992); Ebba Augustin, ed., *Palestinian Women: Identity and Experience* (1993); and Sherna Gluck, *An American Feminist in Palestine* (1994).

creasing cares of the Palestinian woman under the pressures of the *intifada,* but not to the discouragement of the researcher. Samar next presses her survey's questions with Nuzha, who parries and queries for her own part, wondering what this young woman expects from her visit to the *dar al-mashbuha.* Finally, Nuzha "looked at the papers in front of the woman, the pen in her hand, and she was angry. 'Scientific research? What scientific research? Let's see what you want from me. For sure, you want to know how I got this way? You want to know how my mother got this way. And you want to know how our house got this way. Scientific research? Your scientific research sure does honor us!' " (98). But Samar's own family, her mother and her brother, also challenge her pretensions to scientific research, questioning her back and eventually accusing her of violating their traditional honor by frequenting Sakina's disreputable house and her still less respected daughter Nuzha. Samar's reply is in returning to Nuzha's side and taking her part against the biases that have surrounded and isolated her.

Bab al-saha is at once novel, documentation, and self-criticism of the *intifada* writer, a redrawing of the lines of partition that divide inside from outside. The invaders are reidentified: the Israeli military occupation, the *fedai* Usama on his way to blow up the workers' buses, the *shabbab* who take shelter in Sakina's *dar al-mashbuha*—and Samar herself, the writer-critic, the academic who would record the effects of the *intifada* on the lives of Palestinian women. The conflicting narratives here are summarized in alternative semantic fields: is it a time of *hulul* (solutions), *hilal* (legality), *ihtilal* (occupation)—or *i'jaz* (wondrous), *'ajz* (weakness), *mu'jizat* (miracles) (Khalifeh 1990, 198)? Neither of these fields, however, finally provides the parameters for a new Palestinian political geography.

Set in a brothel, Sakina's *dar al-mashbuha,* the last refuge for the *intifada's shabbab, Bab al-saha* is a radical restatement of the traditionalist constructions of women's political activism—from the popular political committees that developed during the years of the *intifada* to the minimalist representation of women within the Palestinian delegation to the peace negotiations begun at the Madrid Conference in 1991, to their underrepresentation in the post-Oslo legislative council, and their now seeming invisibility in public representations of the second *intifada*

(2000–present). Not just family farms, factories, and prisons, but broth-els, the alleged, even condemned "houses of ill-repute," the spaces of women's political and social organization, must become—if there are to be no more deaths of Palestinian brides, for example—part of the very documentation that grounds the narrative of self-determination and the agenda of state-building. Thus, according to the "Draft Document on Principles of Women's Rights," presented to complement the Palestinian document of national independence, and in tacit alliance perhaps with the woman in the service taxi, the child on the steps washing clothes in imita-tion of grown women from *Wild Thorns,* in concert with Samar and Nuzha in *Bab al-saha:*

> We, the women of Palestine, from all social categories and the various faiths, including workers, farmers, housewives, students, professionals, and politicians promulgate our determination to proceed with our strug-gle to abolish all forms of discrimination and inequality against women, which were propagated by the different forms of colonialism on our land, ending with the Israeli occupation, and which were reinforced by the conglomeration of customs and traditions prejudiced against women, embodied in a number of existing laws and legislation. (6)

Against the renewed partitionism of the Gaza-Jericho First Agree-ment, the Oslo accord, and the years of frustrated "peace process," and into the renewed violence of the second Palestinian uprising, the declara-tions of principle and draft basic laws,[6] as well as the precedents set by pre-vious documents over a century of colonization, decolonization, and recolonization, Sahar Khalifeh's *Wild Thorns* and *Bab al-saha* begin to set the terms and elaborate the grounds for an alternative analysis and a criti-cal prospectus of Palestinian political geography.

---

6. See *Declaration of Principles on Interim Self-Government Arrangements* and *Draft Basic Law for the National Authority in the Transitional Period,* available as part of the "oc-casional document series" from the Jerusalem and Media and Communication Centre, as well as Raja Shehadeh, *The Declaration of Principles and The Legal System in the West Bank* (1994).

6 A Country Beyond Reach

Liana Badr's Writings of the Palestinian Diaspora

THERESE SALIBA

> Exile is strangely compelling to think about but terrible to experience. It is the unhealable rift forced between a human being and a native place, between the self and its true home; its essential sadness can never be surmounted.
>
> —Edward Said, "Reflections on Exile"

> I feel strongly that my experience does not belong to me alone; it is an example of my people's experiences. I have nothing to hide. I have already lost everything I can lose; I have nothing to lose anymore.
>
> —Liana Badr, in Shaaban, *Both Right and Left Handed*

Liana Badr. *Courtesy of Liana Badr*

Liana Badr was born in Jerusalem and raised in Jericho until 1967, when, during the war, she fled with her father to Jordan. As a student at the University of Amman, she became involved with the Palestine Liberation Organization (PLO) and the Palestinian Women's Movement. After Black September of 1970, she escaped to Beirut,

I wish to thank S. V. Atalla, Lisa Suhair Majaj, and Souad Dajani for their insightful comments on various versions of this chapter. An earlier version of this essay was presented at the Middle East Studies Association conference in November 1994.

where she spent eleven years. In the wake of the 1982 Israeli invasion of Lebanon, she fled again, this time to Damascus, then Tunisia. In 1994, following the Israeli-Palestinian peace accord, she returned to the West Bank, where she now works within the Palestinian Ministry of Culture and is the founding editor of their periodical, Dafater Thaqafiyya *(Cultural notebooks).*

Badr's works available in English translation include two novels, A Compass for the Sunflower *(1989; Arabic edition 1979) and* The Eye of the Mirror *(1994; Arabic edition 1991), and a collection of three novellas,* A Balcony over the Fakihani *(1993a; Arabic edition 1983). Other works available in Arabic and currently undergoing translation include her latest novel,* Najoum Ariha *(Stars over Jericho, 1993b), and several short story collections. She has also published an interview/memoir of poet Fedwa Tuqan (1996), five children's books, and a poetry collection (1997).*

S ince the signing of the Oslo peace agreement the status of Palestinian refugees and exiles has remained contentious and unresolved.[1] According to one refugee in Jordan, "The deal Arafat cut with the Israelis means that people like me do not exist, that we will never go home. We have been sacrificed" (Hedges 1994). These women and men of the Palestinian diaspora are the subject of Liana Badr's *A Compass for the Sunflower* (1979), *A Balcony over the Fakihani* (1983), and *The Eye of the Mirror* (1991). Read together, these works document the history of Palestinian diasporan experience, including the "disaster" (*nakba*) of 1948, the 1967 war, Black September of 1970, the 1975–76 siege and massacre at Tel al-Zataar, and the invasion of Lebanon in 1982. From her own series of

---

1. According to Article 1 of the Basic Law, the "Palestinian people" refers only to the segment of the population living in the Gaza Strip and Jericho City and environs. "It is not certain how many of those displaced during the 1967 war and their descendents (about 800,000) and the refugees of the 1948 war and their descendents (about 3 million) will eventually qualify for inclusion in the phrase 'Palestinian people' under the Basic Law" (7). See Naseer H. Aruri and John J. Carroll (1994). The Declaration of Principles does, however, provide for a four-party committee to negotiate the return of the refugees of 1967 and defers the status of the refugees of 1948 to the final status talks, which as of this writing continue to be deferred.

exiles and others' oral histories, Badr constructs Palestinian diasporan experience as a map of discontinuous locations, wherein first Jordan and then Beirut come to represent "a piece of home," in contrast to Palestine, which remains a country "beyond reach." Badr's writings situate women's experience at the center of nationalist struggle, as they document the survival of Palestinian national identity and consciousness in the diaspora.

Nationalism, it has been argued, is articulated as a narrative (Bhabha 1990, 1; Layoun 1994, 65), and Badr's narratives construct a nationalism shaped by the exigencies of exile. As a landless people, the Palestinian nation in exile is particularly dependent on national narratives to maintain its identity and existence. Badr describes her writing process as analogous to building a house, an appropriately ironic metaphor for the dispossessed, who effectively build a nation, a "home" in exile, through both narrative and nationalist resistance. Nationalism, Edward Said writes, is "the assertion of belonging to a place, a people, a culture," and "a critical response to the ravages of exile" (1990b, 359). This dialectical relationship between nationalism and exile is captured in the 1988 Palestinian Declaration of Independence, which defines the nation as "the state of all Palestinians wherever they may be." Badr's narratives, however, expose the contradictions and inadequacies of asserting a national identity without a land base, without a country from which to struggle.

Conventional nationalist discourse positions women in two often contradictory roles, both as participants in the struggle and as preservers of cultural identity. In the first instance, war and nationalist struggle may operate as catalysts for change, breaking down traditional barriers between men and women and "undermining the operation of extant asymmetrical gender relations and exposing them to scrutiny" (Peteet 1991, 6). Yet nationalism has also historically represented a "profoundly patriarchal ideology that grants subject positions to men who fight over territory, possession, and the right to dominate" (Liu 1994, 58). In this chapter, I argue that Badr subverts gendered conceptions of nationalism, reconfiguring it, in the words of Said, as a *transnational* struggle based on a claim to homeland, human rights, and dignity (1992, 17). Said's transnational model is based on principles of justice; however, transnationalism, a concept much in vogue today, most frequently refers to the processes taking place across state borders, that is, across the borders of already sovereign states or countries (Verdery 1994, 2). The contradictions between this latter definition and that offered by Said suggest two questions: What does Palestinian nationalism mean in an age of transnationalism, when Palestinian sovereignty has been continually deferred, and when the sovereignty of the nation-state, in general, is being redefined? And how do Badr's representations of Palestinian diasporan experience transform masculinist codes of nationalism into a nationalism that may be understood in transnationalist or even feminist terms? In analyzing Badr's constructions of nationalism, I address the limits and potentials of crossing both gendered and national boundaries within the context of Palestinian transnationalism.

This transnational model, based on principles of justice and a claim to human rights rather than to a specific identity, avoids the pitfalls of nationalist consciousness, which often depends upon a static concept of cultural identity and traditional gender roles. The discourse of transnationalism may have two potentially liberating effects for Palestinian women. First, it releases them from the burdens of patriarchal nationalism. Second, it provides a space to examine the intersecting oppressions of occupation, exile, and women's subjugation. Furthermore, the transnationalism of the Palestinian diaspora, embodied in its movement across multiple borders, has created multiple modes of resistance to Palestinian dispossession. Yet exile, manifested as transnationalism, is not a choice, but rather has usually been the result of forced expulsion or war and therefore differs greatly from the more common formation of transnationalism, which depends on both territorial and political sovereignty—that is, nationalism—as a necessary component of its transborder processes. In effect, whatever transnationalism offers women theoretically, it still does not necessarily solve the problem of nation for Palestinians.

Although classical Western feminism has often defined nationalism as incompatible with women's rights, nationalism and feminism remain a mutual necessity for Palestinian women, who must contend simultaneously with national, class, and gender oppression, as well as with the conditions of exile and homelessness. As Badr explains, "My struggle for emancipation as a Palestinian is inseparable from my struggle for genuine liberation as a woman; neither of them is valid without the other" (Shaaban 1988, 164). Women's concerns must therefore be addressed within the political framework of nationalism, even as women's participation simultaneously transforms strategies of national resistance. Furthermore, because the nationalism of liberation movements can provide "a space for women's emancipation" by unsettling existing power structures (Abdo 1991, 22), the potential exists for reconfiguring masculinist forms of nationalism into a *transnational* movement still rooted in Palestinian claims to self-determination.

Liana Badr, an activist for over twenty years with the PLO, spent several years working with women's organizations in the refugee camps of Beirut. Although her stories are technically classified as "fiction," they combine narratives gathered from Palestinians in the camps, historical facts, and autobiography to chronicle the collective movement of the Palestinian diaspora. Badr's active role in the Palestinian Resistance Movement and her own experience of exile figure prominently in her writing a history of the Palestinian diaspora. Her narratives attest to the power and authenticity of histories produced by those involved in political struggle.[2]

In examining the shifting representations of gender and nationalism within Badr's narratives, we can see the processual aspects of social change over twenty years of nationalist struggle, along with the setbacks suffered by the movement and by Palestinian women. Badr portrays the interdependency of gender and nationalist revolutions, especially in *A Compass for the Sunflower* (1979), a disjointed narrative of the second wave of exile from 1967 through the early seventies. The novel reads not only as a debate with history, but also as a dialogue between genders and generations of Palestinians on questions of exile and resistance. Although themes and some characters carry through into *A Balcony over the Fakihani* (1983), three novellas of the Lebanese Civil War, this later collection is far less concerned with interrogating gender relations than with portraying the solidarity between Palestinian women and men caught within the catastrophic moments of massacre and invasion. In the context of these crises,

---

2. As Ghassan Kanafani has argued, "a researcher who does not play an active part in the resistance is not in a position to write its history." See Harlow 1992, 103.

the analytical power of gender as a category that posits power inequities between women and men appears to have reached its limits.[3] While much previous analysis of Arab women's literature has emphasized the dichotomies of gender warfare within Arab culture, Badr's stories here are concerned rather with the joint struggle of Palestinian women and men for survival against the ravages of exile and war, demonstrating how nationalist struggle strengthens their solidarity as a people even as it transforms relationships of gender. Her more recent novel, *The Eye of the Mirror* (1991), moves back in time to the siege of Tel al-Zaatar (1975–76) and includes a retrospective critique of the limitations of nationalist strategies and ideologies for Palestinian women and men facing the bloodiest incident of the civil war. Tel al-Zaatar is also a testament to the Palestinians' will to survive against overwhelming odds. By giving life to the "ordinary people who sustain the cause and suffer its setbacks" (Sayigh 1994, 9), Badr personalizes the collective trauma of dispossession and gives voice to the visions and commitments of the mass of Palestinians known as "refugees."

Rosemary Sayigh has argued that once a refugee group has been created by a particular power imbalance, this power asymmetry will be reproduced in the new environment, leading to further victimization (1988, 14). This asymmetry has been particularly true of Palestinians in Jordan and Lebanon, whose status as an excess people has haunted them through multiple exiles for more than half a century. Driven from their homeland in 1948 by Israeli forces, 800,000 Palestinians settled in neighboring Arab countries. After the 1967 war, they were joined by another 400,000 refugees from the West Bank. During the 1970 Jordanian civil war and the massacres of Black September, many refugees fled once again to Lebanon, the new headquarters of the Resistance Movement. By 1975 there were approximately 350,000 Palestinians in Lebanon, of whom one-third were still living in refugee camps. In the aftermath of exile, Palestinians consistently rejected their designation as "refugees" and redefined themselves as

---

3. In "Violence in the Other Country," Rey Chow discusses the limits of gender as a category in relation to the Tiananmen Square massacre. See *Third World Women and the Politics of Feminism*, ed. Chandra Mohanty et al. (1991, 83).

Palestinians, organizing their camps into neighborhoods that replicated the familiar neighborhoods back home. Although Palestinians who settled in Jordan were eventually granted the rights of citizenship, their status in Lebanon remains undefined, and they are often denied the right to work and other basic civil rights. Unlike other groups of refugees, Palestinians have suffered continuous attacks in their host countries, especially in Lebanon by Israeli forces and by right-wing Lebanese groups. During the 1970s under the crumbling Lebanese state, Palestinians experienced a relative level of autonomy and the support of some Lebanese political groups, namely the Lebanese Resistance Movement. However, they also became targets of anti-Palestinian groups who aligned themselves with Israel and blamed the Palestinians for their country's destruction. *"Kharabu baladna,* they have ruined our country," was a charge often leveled against the Palestinians, despite their relative weakness within the power asymmetry in Lebanon and elsewhere (Sayigh 1988, 25).

Women, War, and Nationalism

According to Badr, the subject of her work will always be "women and war, women and exile, and the plight of women facing not only the national enemy but a massed weight of inhuman traditions and a heritage of male oppression" (Buck 1992, 311). Badr's writings, however, do not conform neatly to existing literary theories on women, war, and nationalist struggle, and this may be one reason her work has been largely ignored by Western critics. On the one hand, emerging oral histories and analyses of the lives of Palestinian women have focused primarily on women within the Occupied Territories.[4] On the other hand, literary analyses of women's accounts of the Lebanese war, the topic of Badr's *A Balcony over the Fakihani* and *The Eye of the Mirror,* have given nearly exclusive atten-

---

4. Two exceptions to this are the works of Rosemary Sayigh and Julie M. Peteet. For this analysis, I have used Sayigh's oral-based history of Palestinian women in the refugee camps of Lebanon, *Too Many Enemies* (1994), and Julie M. Peteet's *Gender in Crisis* (1991), as well as their essays.

tion to Lebanese writers, leaving Palestinian diasporan women once again homeless in the literary landscape.

In *War's Other Voices,* miriam cooke describes Palestinian women writers, such as Laila al-Sayih and Hamida Nana, as "blinded to the war's real nature" because "they could only view it as a logical extension of the Palestinian struggle" (1988, 23). Cooke's argument, premised on the political disinterest of the literature of the Beirut Decentrists—Lebanese middle- and upper-class women—asserts that the Decentrists' portrayal of the war is more insightful than that of their Palestinian counterparts because they view the war as a process that resists analysis, rather than as an episode of a failing revolution (23). The Lebanese war often did have different meanings and consequences for Palestinian refugees and exiles than for the Lebanese. Yet cooke implies that Palestinian women, despite their positioning as specific targets of Israeli and Lebanese attacks and as members of a population suffering the greatest losses during the war,[5] have little to contribute to this discourse due to the "blindness" caused by nationalist consciousness. Indeed, quite often it is this problematic embrace of nationalism that is dismissed by critics concerned with specifically gendered responses to war.[6]

Evelyne Accad also analyzes Lebanese writers' accounts of the civil war in *Sexuality and War: Literary Masks of the Middle East,* positing maldeveloped gender relations as the primary cause of the war. In contrast to Badr,

5. According to Julie M. Peteet, in 1976, Palestinian women and children became specific targets of military attacks (1991, 37).

6. Cooke's contributions to the understanding of women's war narratives have been significant; in fact, in her introduction to Badr's *The Eye of the Mirror,* Fadia Faqir borrows cooke's term "Beirut Decentrist" to describe Badr, who writes of the dailiness of war (1995, vi). However, in considering gendered interpretations of war, it is significant to note that cooke states, "In many ways these Palestinian women's writings in Lebanon are like those of the Lebanese men writers . . . what matters for both is to locate and overcome the enemy" (1988, 23). In arguing against a political analysis of the war, cooke ignores the fact that for the Palestinians, at certain stages in the war, the enemies were clearly delineated. Badr's texts exemplify the complexity of Palestinian women's war narratives, which are both suffused by nationalist consciousness and critical of masculinist conceptions of nationalism.

who argues for the mutual dependency of gender and national liberation, Accad asserts that a feminist revolution must necessarily precede and inform nationalism. According to Accad, Lebanon's war is the direct result of "Islamo-Arab influences . . . [which carry] the code of honor and masculine-macho values, as well as the concomitant condition of women's oppression, to their farthest limits" (1990, 38). In her heartfelt plea against war and its destructive forces, Accad argues "that if sexuality and women's issues were dealt with from the beginning, wars might be avoided, and revolutionary struggles and movements for liberation would take a very different path" (27). In placing sexuality at the center of national liberation struggles, Accad does not reject nationalism, but rather seeks to reconcile feminism and nationalism, which she redefines as "belief in and love of one's country" (13).[7] While Accad offers some insight into the importance of dealing with sexuality as part of nationalist struggle, her exclusive focus on gender oppression exposes the problems of gender essentialism that Badr's work breaks down.

Accad's analysis, premised on the destructive sexuality of Arab culture, implicates all men as equal participants in a machismo contest of competing nationalisms,[8] whereas Badr portrays Palestinian men as victims of na-

7. Interestingly, Accad calls her form of nationalism *Lebanism,* which she defines as choosing to belong to a pluralistic culture based on the "the political notion of alterity, or acceptance of other's difference" (1990, 38). The historical roots of this term, however, hold obvious connections, as does her theory, with the Maronite ideology *Lebanism,* which includes "an emphasis on individualism and self-sufficiency, rejection of Islam and the Arab world, identification with the West and some Western values, and insistence on the survival of Lebanon as a Christian and democratic heartland in the Middle East." See Gilmour (1983, 80). Although Accad redefines *Lebanism* as pluralistic in its foundation, her critique of Arabo-Islamic culture and her unquestioning embrace of the tenets of mainstream Western feminism exemplify elements of Maronite ideology and its identification with Western values.

8. In focusing exclusively on gender relations, Accad further fails to address the links in transnational power structures. She ignores not only the asymmetry in power among the competing political organizations inside Lebanon's civil war, but also the incongruous violence committed by the intervention of outside forces—namely Israel with the backing of the United States—countries that Badr directly implicates in her narratives. Significantly Accad fails to mention Israel's 1982 invasion of Lebanon to destroy the PLO, and its decimation of over 20,000 civilians.

tional oppression with no other option but to defend their people's very existence. Badr's writing further resists the dichotomy of gender roles and gender-specific forms of resistance to account for Palestinian women involved in or supportive of armed resistance (particularly in the 1970s) as a necessary response to their domination and exile, much as they also participate in *sumud* (steadfastness), the nonviolent resistance of everyday life. Accad's conceptualization of a "reformed nationalism stripped of its male chauvinism, war, and violence" (26) often parallels the transnationalist concepts discussed earlier in this chapter. However, her own forms of cultural chauvinism and gender essentialism undermine her argument and ultimately reproduce Orientalist discourse on gender relations in Arab societies that have stereotyped the Palestinian struggle for independence as a masculinist movement.

Emergent Nationalism in *A Compass for the Sunflower*

In *A Compass for the Sunflower*, a narrative of siege and exile during the late 1960s and early 1970s, the dialogue between genders figures as a critical aspect of the emergent Palestinian nationalist discourse. This novel charts the stories of three women, Jinan, Shahd, and Thurraya, and their experiences of exile, love, and loss. The narrator, Jinan, given the name *ʿabbad al-shams* (sunflower) by her lover, Shaher, is in need of a metaphorical compass to navigate a course for the future direction of her people. The compass points to the division of East and West, the forces of the colonial divide responsible for Palestinian exile, as well as to the geographical dispersion of a group of friends driven apart by the diaspora. For the Palestinians, the revolution holds the promise not only of national liberation, but of gender and class equality as well. As Jinan states, "Everyone talked about revolution and women's liberation and about transforming the balance of class forces which had erupted in the old society" (Badr 1989, 20). However, Badr's narrative challenges romantic notions of Palestinian revolution, and Jinan's belief in this "beautiful revolution" is ultimately met with disillusionment as she contends with the realities of gender and class oppression within the Resistance Movement and repeated siege from the outside.

A Compass for the Sunflower reflects the gender and nationalist politics of the late sixties and early seventies when new positions were opening up for women as fighters, activists, leaders, and workers. In this context, the conversations and letters between Jinan and her friends take on charged political significance as they question the false value of virginity, the problems faced by women involved in political activity, and the ways in which women are taught to fear men. Male dominance is one of the many "old idols" these characters attempt to dismantle, as they try to construct a new world and simultaneously to reconstruct their lives from the fragments of exile.

Amer, Jinan's cousin and childhood playmate, exemplifies the Manichean logic of patriarchal nationalism, which views "East and West [as] two sides of an equation" (Badr 1989, 3). When Jinan sees Amer's picture splattered across the headlines for hijacking a jumbo jet, she describes his actions as representing the desperation and futility of those Palestinians who, in an act of self-protection, lash out, "stabbing at the face of the world" (39). Despite the "terrorist" image portrayed in the media, Jinan's sympathies lie with Amer, whom she sees not as an "executioner" but as "the sacrificial ram" to the conflict (39–40). Significantly, Amer's desperate "resolution" is rooted in his masculinist conception of nationalism, for in debates with Jinan, he critiques the failures of Arab nationalism in fiercely gendered terms: "Civilization's a whore between the thighs of history, and she switches around from nation to nation, and continent to continent. Why the hell did the Arabs emerge from their encounter with civilization without so much as a camel?" (39). While successful nationalism has consistently been configured as possession of the prized female territory, failed nationalism is configured here as the attempted conquest of the debased female body, a corrupted, impure woman who, in her transnational sexual encounters, refuses to be conquered. This obviously misogynist image is merely an inversion of the former and suggests the "violently gendered proscription of social agency and power" that circumscribes nationalists' ideology (Layoun 1994, 72). The metaphor further connects men's political defeat with the desire to control women in order to reassert the power of the Arab male/nation.

Given Amer's desperate impotence, it is not surprising that he resolves his debate with history through the hijacking, a futile attempt to gain power.

In contrast, Shaher represents the nationalist ideology of the *fedai* (resistance fighter), who finds meaning in action and warns against romantic views of revolution and nostalgia for the past. Shaher advocates a new culture of resistance, a redefinition of national identity as part of a complete social transformation. His criticism of existing social structures extends beyond the Manichean logic of East and West to critique worn cultural traditions and the corruption of Arab rulers. While Shaher engages in military operations, both Jinan and Shahd become active in the Resistance on other levels: they work in the camp hospitals with victims of the war; they open literacy centers to raise the personal status of refugee women; they participate in military training; and Jinan also resists the ravages of exile by writing the memories of the past. In this process of rewriting history, she receives support from the older generation of women whose stories of the 1948 exodus strengthen confidence in the Resistance among the younger generation of exiles. For women involved in the movement, resistance strategies take multiple forms and extend across many levels of society.

Although idealism often lent force to the revolutionary tide during the early years of the struggle, *A Compass for the Sunflower* also challenges romantic notions of Palestinian revolution and exile. Badr eloquently captures the horrors, poverty, and violence of the struggle, as camps are raided, women and children rounded up, and men and youth massacred. Only Jinan's friend Thurayya rejects revolutionary struggle when her fiancé is killed in a suicide operation across the border. After his death, Thurayya retreats into silence and renounces all violence, "even our revolutionary violence" (Badr 1989, 86). However, after a few years of living under the extreme conditions of Israeli occupation, she joins again in life and in the struggle, "realizing the death of a martyr had not canceled out her existence" (113). For Badr, resistance revitalizes the lives of the oppressed, and life and the struggle become one, even as her characters struggle into an unknown future. The novel concludes with the repeated refrain "Where is it leading?" (117) as Amer's aircraft is stormed and the operation ends in a fiery explosion. The narrative's compass needle seems to waver as it points to Amer's desperate "plunge toward infinity" (118), then to Shahd's return to traditional femininity. Yet Jinan concludes with an affirmation of life and of survival in some new future for her people.

Another romantic myth challenged by the novel is that of women's equal participation in the nationalist movement. Although women's participation in armed struggle signifies changing gender roles within the Resistance, it does not guarantee their equality with men. As a cadre in the camp, Jinan carries a weapon, but when she attempts to protect herself from snipers, she demonstrates her lack of technical skills by attempting to load her already loaded gun (Badr 1989, 43). This scene suggests that women's theoretical skills are of little practical use in battle. However, in other instances, women participate alongside men in military operations and suffer the consequences of prison. One woman confides to Jinan her fiancé's response to women fighters: He says that "arms have never been an ornament for women" (46) and argues that if women are armed, "there [would be] no place for men in the world anymore" (47). The participation of armed women such as Jinan and Shahd, who carry their weapons proudly, poses an obvious threat to the traditional role of men as the protectors of women and disrupts gender roles within the larger society.

After 1970, however, with the consolidation of resistance groups in Lebanon, women were gradually displaced from armed struggle and given positions in Resistance and PLO offices (Sayigh 1993, 176). As a cadre in one such office, Jinan asserts that "the particular circumstances of the female comrades called for more careful thought and study" (Badr 1989, 80). In this specifically feminist analysis, she attributes the shortage of women cadres to two factors: the social pressures of tradition—"father's pigheaded attitudes or narrow-minded relatives" who marry off young women early (80)—and the exhausting nature of the work, the "considerable losses and disappointments" that lead women to seek refuge in marriage or to work in positions other than the clinics, where they encounter daily the wounded victims of war (81). Significantly, in an interview conducted in the early 1980s, Badr herself attributes the loss of women cadres within the PLO to the organization's failure to address women's issues (Shaaban 1988, 158).

In *Gender in Crisis*, Julie M. Peteet argues that women's political activism has not "substantially distinguished itself from traditional gender ideologies," so that although gender roles have been altered within the Resistance, women continue to play a subordinate role to men (1991, 6). Furthermore, the class distinctions have been maintained, so that mainly middle-class cadres, like Jinan, hold higher positions than poor refugee women. While masculinist ideology often held up women comrades as signs of national progress, Jinan rejects her symbolic role and questions the false dichotomy of tradition/progress pervasive in the rhetoric of national liberation. When a male comrade questions her as to why she is wearing a headscarf (which she wears in fact because her hair is dirty), she responds that women's attire does not affect their work. However, she would have liked to respond, "You ultra-progressive man, would you prefer us to wear either khaki uniforms or eastern dress so that you could easily distinguish between us and categorize us and give us pluses and minuses?" (Badr 1989, 105). She points to the hypocrisy of such revolutionary men, "liberated souls in the thick of revolution" (105), who watch women scrub the floor under their feet without offering to fetch clean water. Examining the complexities of class and gender oppression, Jinan uncovers slow and inconclusive answers about the setbacks for women in the Resistance Movement, but her work in the camps among refugee women gives her solace, meaning, and some hope for "return."

Al-Awda (The return) figures prominently in Badr's stories as a tortured dream,[9] emerging against the backdrop of banished nightmares of exile, massacres, and war. The impulse to narrate the tragedies of dispossession becomes "a way of dealing with horror by turning it into narrative, absorbing it in all its detail rather than suppressing it, unassimilated and

---

9. The refugees in the camps in Lebanon refer to the Resistance Movement as *al-Thawra* (The revolution), *al Muaqawwineh* (The resistance), and *al-Awda* (The return). See Sayigh 1994, 115, n. 1. However, as the methods of resistance have changed over time, so has the language used to represent these methods. *Haq al-Awda,* The Right of Return, guaranteed to the Palestinians in numerous UN resolutions, remains a foundational principle of the Resistance, along with *Taqrir al-Maseer,* Self-Determination. The vast majority of Palestinians have agreed that these rights are not to be compromised, and yet the current agreement includes compromises on both principles.

unshared into the unconscious" (Sayigh 1994, 199). The curative quality of narrative simultaneously transforms suffering into resistance and family stories into part of the collective definition of the nation continually constructing itself in exile. "Return" is multiply configured as return to Palestine, which represents the pure homeland and place of security, return to the innocence and comfort of an untroubled past, or even return to the contaminated diasporic location (Beirut, Jordan, or the camps), which represents, at least, a "piece of home." *Haq al-Awda* ("The Right of Return") has been guaranteed the Palestinians in numerous unenforced UN resolutions. However, in diasporan literature, as in reality, "Return" occurs only in flights of memory, in stories passed on through generations of exile, and in dreams of the future.

Jinan's fragmented narrative and dislocated memories chart the discontinuity between past and present, and the uncertain future of the exile. She writes, "Exile. Nothing is as painful as exile; it stretches ahead into the future, and back into the past, and bursts through on every side at the places we've dammed up with the dry straw of memories" (Badr 1989, 74). Shaher, too, draws a clear connection between exile and the importance of collective memory and history: "The exile has left firm, clear footprints. We mustn't forget them or . . . we'll become gypsies roaming the earth in permanent exile" (5). The rewriting of history from the exile's perspective becomes a means of fending off permanent exile, an act of resisting the distortions of history. The older generation of Palestinians passes on stories of "home" to the younger generation born in exile. Past and present exiles are violently fused when Jinan recounts her family's escape from Jericho during the 1967 war, as fire from Israeli aircraft spills out of the skies: "I knew very well that we would never return. I'd rushed all round our house, confused and upset, and they'd shouted at me, 'Quickly! All you need is nightclothes. In two or three days we'll be back.' I felt sickened, thinking that this story of coming back in a couple of days was a pathetic re-enactment of what we'd always heard from those who'd left in the first disaster in 1948" (32).

This experience of exile, the repetition of loss and the false promise of return, stands in dialectical relation to the nationalist aspirations articulated by Shaher: "The one certainty is Palestine. That's the word which is real, first and last" (Badr 1989, 69). Jinan also articulates her nationalism in terms of reclaiming that which rightfully belongs to her people: "all the things I own but can't see," those pieces of the sky over Jericho, pebbles on the Dead Sea shore, the things that would allow her to be "one with the moment" from which she has been severed as a result of dispossession (118). Yet even in this early novel of emergent nationalist ideals and dreams, Badr confronts the gender and class limitations of the nationalist movement, the romantic myths of nationalist struggle, while still embracing nationalist ideology as the only means of liberation.

"Home" and the Homefront in *A Balcony over the Fakihani*

In *A Balcony over the Fakihani,* the nightmarish fragmentation of Badr's narrative of exile is further complicated by multiple voices, male and female, recounting the decimation of Palestinian camps and neighborhoods in Lebanon from 1975 to 1982. In the context of massacre and invasion, the solidarity between Palestinian women and men is evident in the ways women define their relationships to fathers, husbands, brothers; to the struggle; and to each other. The balcony over Fakihani, one of the headquarters of the Resistance Movement before 1982, comes alive with laughter, friendship, and joking, until it is destroyed in the invasion. The balcony is simultaneously a place to view the bustling life in the street and a "safe house" or haven for the community. Symbolically, it extends domestic life into public space and connects the home with the larger community.

The narration of Palestinian struggle for a homeland has often been materially symbolized by houses. As Barbara Harlow argues, the home "symbolizes the connection between women and the land and their mutual subjection to masculinist authority" (1992, 207). In these novellas, Badr's constructions of "home" are less concerned with a critique of female domesticity and sexuality than with the systematic assault on domestic stability, the transgression of private, domestic space by both Israeli and right-wing Lebanese forces (Harlow 1992, 209). Home represents the base of the resistance, a retreat and refuge, wherein personal and political agency become fused (216). In the Palestinian struggle, violence has directly targeted homes through bombings of civilian dwellings and camps, thereby erasing the distinctions between the battlefront and the home front (Sayigh 1993). In *A Balcony over the Fakihani*, "home" signifies both the Palestinian homeland and the dreary makeshift homes in exile, marked by impermanence. In their flight from Tel al-Zaatar to Damour, the refugees find dismal "homes": burnt-out, eerie shells of houses abandoned by their previous owners under similar siege. Later, when they flee to Beirut, they again occupy apartments abandoned by their former inhabitants. Repeatedly, Palestinian families move into these empty houses and attempt to transform them into homes, places of normality. Meanwhile, shelling continues outside, or "the Fascists" (Phalangists) break into these makeshift shelters, often slaughtering the inhabitants. These nightmarish images of "home," which provide no security, stand in contrast to memories of the hills of thyme reminiscent of the Palestinian homeland left behind. By configuring the nation as "home," these stories transform the traditional battle over territory into a claim for basic human rights. In this sense, they become transnational narratives.

In "The Land of Rock and Thyme," Badr juxtaposes the dark realities of homelessness and the squalor of the camps to fleeting snapshot memories of happiness in the abundant home in Palestine. Yusra tells the story of the exodus of her family and community from Tel al-Zaatar after a nine-month siege by Maronite forces from 1975 to 1976 in a retrospective of unraveling memories as she awaits the birth of her child and dreams of her husband, who lies in the Martyr's Cemetery. "Land of Rock and Thyme" is a story not only about survival, but about the "need to keep the collective memory from forgetting" (Renee Epelbaum, quoted in Harlow 1992, 245). In a section entitled "Water Has a Memory," Yusra describes how she and her sister have been waiting in line at the well for nearly thirteen hours when they receive news that their father has died from gunfire several hours earlier, and that on his deathbed, he refused to send for his daughters so that they could bring water to their brothers and sisters (Badr 1993, 10). Like his father, who was killed at age forty-six by a stray bullet during the 1948 exodus, Yusra's father is a victim of senseless killing; his experience represents a repetition of Palestine's ill-fated history. When Yusra hears of her father's death, she recalls a time when she carried water under sniper fire and fell, spilling the water and weeping for its loss.[10] Water becomes an image of memory, a fluid, unifying element that connects scattered images and broken lives; an image of life and death, of landlessness. Yusra's brother Jamal yearns for the sea; but in the exodus, he is killed by a quick bullet to the head for giving his identity as "Palestinian." Later, all of the men and youth who have escaped the siege are rounded up by the Phalangists and executed in the museum. These are the consequences of Palestinian identity that Yusra contemplates when she thinks about the birth of her fatherless child: "It would be a Palestinian, from its first moment in the world" (25).

For exiles, "home" has multiple meanings, gradations of isolation and alienation. As Yusra remembers her husband, Ahmad, a *fedai* who has studied in India, she recalls his hopefulness that "the 1980's would see us return" (Badr 1993a, 22). Although Yusra and Ahmed are both refugees, they have different experiences of home. When he asks her, "do you know what it means to be away from home, there, in a remote part of the world?" (21), he refers to India and considers Lebanon a piece of home, even as he describes for Yusra the beauties of Palestine, which she has never seen. He pulls out a map of the region that reads: "Remember. This must be turned into reality" (21). One of the means of creating this reality is through memory, and the word "remember" echoes in refrain throughout Yusra's story. Born in exile herself, Yusra envies Ahmad because he has at least seen the town he came from and can recall its almond and olive trees. Before his death, Yusra has an ominous dream of them sleeping in a house atop a rock that is about to fall and crush them. "You're anxious about getting a house," Ahmad replies. "We'll soon find one to live in" (28). This home, secure from disaster, is both an image of their domestic unity as a family and one of the collective dreams of return, to a house, a protection against the persistent violation of domestic spaces by siege, displacement, and massacre at the hands of Israeli and Lebanese forces.

---

10. Badr here undoubtedly refers to documented attacks on women in Tel al-Zaatar. In 1976 during the nine-month siege of the camp, "hundreds of women were killed attempting to bring water to their dehydrated children under heavy artillery fire and sniping." See Peteet 1991, 37.

Women's loss of their husbands to the struggle, as signified by the tender relationship between Yusra and Ahmad, represents another violation and disruption of domestic space. In interviews with Palestinian refugee women in Lebanon, Peteet notes that women described the first decade of exile in terms that evoke death and a state of mourning. As one refugee explained, "Losing Palestine, our homes, was like losing a husband or a son" (1991, 26). In the 1948 war, and after 1964, as men joined the Resistance Movement, the loss of husbands and sons became a reality. The recurring trope of the lost husband, however, subverts the conventional metaphor of the nation as woman, the homeland as the female body. In regendering the nation as male, these women's narratives emphasize the steadfast solidarity between women and men of the Resistance.

"A Balcony over the Fakihani," the story for which the collection is named, depicts a similar story of compassion and solidarity between Palestinian women and men. Set in the Fakihani quarter of Beirut, one of the centers of the Resistance Movement, this narrative is told through the shifting perspectives of Su'ad, her husband, Umar, and their friend Jinan (the same Jinan of *A Compass for the Sunflower,* who here plays a less significant role). Su'ad and Jinan sit on the balcony every afternoon, looking out over the quarter, recalling their life in Amman before Black September, as Umar and neighbors congregate on the balcony to join in "the kind of talk that refreshed the soul" (Badr 1993a, 45). Su'ad, however, describes the balcony as being overtaken by a flourishing carpet plant with heart-shaped leaves covered with blood-red spots, a foreboding image of death.

Su'ad's relationship with Umar and their life together are shaped by the conditions of their shared exile, suffering, and commitment to the Resistance. When they plan to marry, Su'ad's father warns her against marrying a *fedai,* who, although Tunisian, also is exiled from his homeland because of his political activity. Together they endure the indignities of exile: Su'ad, for example, cannot get work when they are desperate for money because, like all Palestinians in Lebanon, she is denied a work permit; and Umar is arrested and jailed for storing arms, even though he holds the required permit. Because of their growing poverty, they move from Beirut to Shatila, where Su'ad is struck by the temporariness of the makeshift homes of the camp (Badr 1993a, 44). Although Umar's activities in the Resistance keep him always coming and going, Su'ad feels that everything is fine as long as they are together, for when Umar is home, he shares the responsibilities for their two children and lightens Su'ad's anxieties. When they finally return to Beirut, to that "piece of home," Su'ad sees each balcony as a "part of the other houses," an extension of "home" that connects them to an entire community (47). The balcony then symbolizes the extension of domestic solidarity between men and women to the political community.

Under the constant threat of loss, gender relations are not so much relations of power, but rather relations in which men and women find solidarity and solace from the ravages of their lives. Central to the story is Umar's illness and his treatment and recovery in a sanitarium in Germany. At this point, the story shifts to Umar's voice, and we hear his deep affection and appreciation for his wife upon leaving her: "I felt like someone discovering for the first time that this woman was a woman before she was my wife, that she was something molded from the clay of life just as the springtime soil is planted with seedlings. Was this just a poetic fancy? Perhaps" (Badr 1993a, 51). Umar, however, remains months away from home in the sanitarium; eventually he falls in love with his doctor, Louisa, who listens to stories about his wife and children and to the minute details of life back home. Umar's conflict of living between two worlds—between the comforts of luxurious music, German restaurants, and dinner parties, and the poverty of the Fakihani quarter, family responsibilities, and the constant threat of death—sets the life of the revolution in sharp relief. When upon his return he attempts to meld these two worlds, to share news from Louisa with Su'ad and Jinan, Su'ad responds, half joking, half serious, with a common Arab saying, "God make her happy, but keep her away from here!" (79). Su'ad has nightmares of losing her husband, not to another woman, but to death; and when Umar insists that Louisa means nothing to him, she says, "I know. It's something else I'm afraid of" (64). Against the backdrop of revolutionary struggle, Umar's affair with Louisa takes on minimal significance.

Within nationalist discourse, these often-idealized constructions of family, home, and community serve to ward off the threat of annihilation. The women characters in *A Balcony* embrace an ever-elusive dream of domestic tranquility and stability. They fail, however, to confront their position within the domestic sphere and within the Resistance, perhaps because solidarity among women and men is critical to the survival of the community. Jinan, an organizer for the Women's Union and a close friend of Su'ad and Umar since their days in Amman, recounts the final section of this story. In their afternoons on the balcony, Jinan and Su'ad exchange news with Salwa, Jinan's cousin recently arrived from the Gulf. Through the women's conversations, Badr conveys the varying political attitudes of diasporan Palestinians. Salwa, for example, discusses the complacency of Gulf Palestinians: "All people seemed to look forward to over there was a pay raise and their annual leave . . . and there are still Palestinians outside who complain about the decision to mobilize" (Badr 1993a, 66). Su'ad responds, "You wait. The ones who've settled down and *made a secure future* for themselves will be the first to skip back to Palestine *when it's liberated*" (67, my emphasis). In contrast, the members of the Resistance, like Jinan, Su'ad, and Umar, cannot build a secure future for themselves except through their commitment to Palestine's liberation. When Su'ad thinks of all the places she's lived since leaving Jordan, she says, "Heavens, it's a hard life, always packing up and moving on!" Su'ad's comment reminds Jinan of her mother, who spoke "as if peace and quiet and settling down were just a dream" (67). In exile and war, where the domestic sphere is constantly under attack, the confinements of domesticity are both obscured and disrupted by the struggle for survival.

On July 17, 1981, Israeli aircraft bombed the Fakihani quarter, destroying tall apartment blocks and killing 350 civilians (Gilmour 1983, 160). Within the story, the narrative of "normal life" is shockingly disrupted when Jinan, standing on the rooftop of Salwa's apartment, is jolted by a tearing quake as black smoke rises from the Fakihani quarter. Here the text breaks into poetry, as the characters' lives are fragmented by four consecutive raids. "I lose the faces I know," thinks Jinan. "Feeling crushed, desperate, I remember her." In the streets, the wounded weep and others search for family in the rubble, while Jinan, thinking she has witnessed "the end of the world," searches desperately for Su'ad and her children. Su'ad survives the raid; however, all her premonitions of disaster are fulfilled when Umar's body is found in the wreckage, his last expression "full of wisdom and irony" (Badr 1993a, 83). Ironically, only in death is Umar allowed to return to his homeland, Tunisia, and he seems to take his laughter with him. In the hospital, where Jinan goes to bid Umar farewell, she grows nauseous from the stench of death and steps outside to breathe. "Things won't always be like this," she thinks, "there's still some fresh air left in the world" (84). Even in this time of despair, Jinan maintains the will to survive and a bitter hope for the future of her people.

The constant disruption of Palestinian homes has been justified in Israeli ideology by the rhetoric of "defense of national borders" (Harlow 1992, 224). Despite the role of transnationalism in the Palestinian struggle, which has been played out across many borders, transnational theories are finally inadequate in the Palestinian context, where borders remain a persistent site of contestation. Indeed, an emphasis on transnationalism here produces contradictory effects. On the one hand, Said's formulation of transnationalism situates the Palestinian struggle for independence within the discourse of human rights, emphasizing human dignity and the right to a homeland above fixed notions of national identity. This discourse of transnationalism, I have argued, is potentially liberating for women, as it releases them from the burdens of a patriarchal nationalism even as it provides space to examine the interlocking oppressions of patriarchy, occupation, and exile. On the other hand, transnationalism ignores the implications of borders for the Palestinians, who continue to struggle without a "home" or nation. With the founding of the state of Israel in 1948, the borders of the new nation-state became impermeable to Palestinians. Furthermore, because the Palestinians are identified in geopolitical terms as an "ethno-nation" (Verdery 1994, 3) rather than as a nation-state, they have been denied the right to live within safe and secure borders. These tensions among various forms of transnationalism, and between transnationalism and nationalism, are evident in Badr's complex representations of home, homeland, and the borderlands that sever diasporan Palestinians from their native place.

The impermeability of borders and forced movement across borders figure as dominant tropes in the final story in Badr's collection, "The Canary and the Sea." This story, told in the voice of Abu Husain, documents the official history of the Resistance from the Exodus in 1948 through the

1982 Israeli invasion, and tells Abu Husain's family history through the language of historical fact and military struggle. The fence erected around his border village, Shuwaika, after 1948 provides a vivid representation of the impermeable borders established by the Israeli state. Palestinians are shot dead by Israeli soldiers for stretching a hand over the border fence; family members, separated during the Exodus, stand on opposite sides of the fence conversing but not embracing. Abu Husain can cross the border into Palestine only as a prisoner of war, and must view his home village only from a distance. After 1948, the borders of national identity between the Arabs also become less permeable. Palestinians are told by the Lebanese, "This is our country. You shouldn't be here at all" (Badr 1993a, 96). Abu Husain's proposal to a Lebanese girl is initially denied until the family learns that his grandmother is Lebanese. These borders of the ethno-nation and the nation-state drawn after the 1948 war mark the unnatural divisions of families from their land and from each other.

In this section, Abu Husain chronicles the hardships of growing up in the refugee camps in Lebanon, making explicit the power differential between the Lebanese and Israeli forces and the Palestinians: "For them the clashes sprang from a desire to dominate, for us it spelt the defense of our very existence" (Badr 1993a, 97). He points out the atrocities of the war, including the Israeli's use of bombs prohibited under international law, and their dropping of 200,000 bombs on Beirut in a single day. "The only things they didn't use against us," he says, "were nuclear weapons" (107). Taken as a prisoner of war, Abu Husain is transported blindfolded over the border—ironically in his homeland at last but unable to see it —and interrogated by Israeli agents. Abu Husain's experience is an apt metaphor for the limits of transnationalism for the Palestinians, whose movement (and vision) is so constricted by their oppressors. After weeks of inhumane treatment and torture, he is finally released in an exchange of prisoners. As he is driven back to Lebanon through his boyhood village, this time without the blindfold, Abu Husain surveys the landscape from which he feels strangely alienated: "There was the country that was beyond my reach, and there was the sea—the sea shimmering and gleaming behind the roofs of Shuwaika, the village which I was even now leaving behind me! It had nothing to say to us, as if it had no understanding of the secret of our tears" (125).

In this final of three stories, Badr chooses to end her narrative from the male perspective. However, Abu Husain's account of the struggle, while masculinist in its celebration of the male martyrs, presents a transgression of gender borders. Lying in the road with nine bullet wounds, Abu Husain has a vision of his newborn baby daughter, an image that subverts traditional gender roles wherein men exalt in the birth of sons. As a *fedai*, he embodies his people's history of displacement, indignities, and sacrifice to the struggle. His consciousness is rooted not in male machismo and violence, however, but in the preservation of life, as evidenced in his appreciation of his daughter, his canaries, and the shimmering beauty of the sea. This emphasis on the nation as home, resplendent with warmth and life, suggests a nationalism beyond ideologies of domination, and draws boundaries that are not exclusive, but inclusive.

Significantly, all of Badr's writings are punctuated by images of the sea, which functions as the mirror-image of the nation. The sea signifies both the intangible Palestinian nation, even as the shifting elements of the sea replace the rigid concept of the nation with a more fluid one. The epigraph of the final story is excerpted from a poem by Mahmoud Darwish, "In Praise of the Tall Shadow":

> The sea is the deep-seated land of our call
> The sea is our portrait.
> Who has no land
> Has no sea. (quoted in Badr 1993a, 89)

The sea as the beloved nation further signifies a nationalism in flux, a people set adrift from their country, the turbulent state of Palestinian landlessness. In her most recent novel, *Najoum Ariha* (Stars over Jericho), Badr writes, "Maybe I'll create a poetic sea to throw myself in, to forget the failure of others to find a sea in which to throw us and rest forever. To swim inside language searching for a homeland that accepts us" (Badr 1993b, 9, my translation). However, the poetic sea, the sea of language that forms

the national narrative, argues for the inadequacies of mere artistic representations to provide a secure homeland for the Palestinians. The sea ultimately exposes the need for a real land base, a nation-state rather than an
illusory mirror-image of a homeland.

Critical Nationalism in *The Eye of the Mirror*

In many ways an expanded version of "Land of Rock and Thyme," *The
Eye of the Mirror* (1991) recounts the bloody siege of Tel al-Zaatar (the Hill
of Thyme) with a sharpened critical eye for the limitations of nationalist ideology and its consequences for Palestinians expected to sacrifice their selfhood and responsibility to their families in duty to the nationalist struggle.
This historical retrospective, probably the most complex of Badr's narratives, also confronts the violence of the right-wing Lebanese militias and
oppressive gender roles within the family. Tel al-Zaatar, a huge refugee
camp sheltering 50,000 Palestinians and Shi'ites from the south and situated in the eastern (Christian) sector of Beirut, became the site of the bloodiest incident of the civil war, with 4,000 casualties; 12,000 Palestinians were
driven out, mostly into Muslim West Beirut (Faqir 1994, v). Tel al-Zaatar
symbolizes the Palestinian people's will to survive incredible brutality, and
this may be one reason Badr returns again to this haunting episode in Palestinian history. The narrator, a journalist like Badr herself, goes to the camp
during a brief cease-fire to "report on the steadfastness of the camp on the
anniversary of the emergence of the resistance" (Badr 1994, 125). Badr's
narrative, developed from a collection of oral histories, celebrates the rich
oral tradition in Arab culture (Faqir 1994, viii), and eschews political rhetoric and "the slogans we've become weary of " (Badr 1994, 2). It also exposes the tragic absurdities of the demand by the national leadership that
the residents of Tel al-Zaatar practice steadfastness against overwhelming
odds of deprivation, siege, and systematic annihilation.

Whereas earlier texts seemed to require a nationalist ideology with
idealized notions of home, Badr here exposes the violence and confinements of the patriarchal household and implicates women in the perpetu-
ation of oppressive practices. As Harlow points out, "Critical to the
contested construction of 'home' is the position a woman occupies in it, a

position to which she may be confined as much by the resistance as by the state" (1992, 211). Aisha, the story's main character (whose name means "life"), represents the Palestinian woman's struggle for survival against both the external forces of the war and the internal gender oppressions of her society. Born to a poor refugee family, Aisha works as a maid in a convent school where the nuns ostracize her from the daughters of influential Lebanese families and reprimand her for her small attempts to hold onto her Muslim faith. After twenty Palestinians are killed in a bus by Christian forces, an intractable line is drawn between Christians and Muslims, and Aisha's mother takes her daughter back to the camp, thereby destroying the prospects for Aisha's education. At home, Aisha is forced to contend with the domestic violence of her alcoholic father, whose abuse and addiction are symptomatic both of patriarchal practices and his own personal and military defeat as a Palestinian male. Aisha considers escaping from her family's scheme to arrange her marriage; her predicament is representative of many Arab women: "As she confronts her clear feminine destiny, the same eternal treatment meted out to millions of women like her awaits her. Even qualified women with careers and means of their own are no different to Aisha in our part of the world. They do not know how to enjoy the independence of taking their own decisions, however much society may appear to appreciate them" (Badr 1994, 90). The war, the barricades in the street, in fact, inhibit Aisha from taking action, revealing how her options for liberation as a woman are restricted by her oppression as a Palestinian. However, Badr's commentary also holds women responsible for their own liberation, their own decisions to either resist or submit to what is socially constructed as "feminine destiny."

By contrasting Aisha's condition with that of Hana, a middle-class woman who works as a wireless operator for the Resistance Movement, Badr exposes how class position often dictates women's freedom both within the struggle and within the social order. Because Hana's family enjoys financial stability, she receives more care and pampering than the other girls in the camp and is allowed to have a say in choosing her husband (Badr 1994, 77). When Aisha first meets Hana, she is struck by her expression of self-confidence, a mark both of her class privilege and of her participation in the Resistance. In fact, throughout the novel, we see how women's participation in the nationalist struggle allows them access to the public sphere, adds vitality to their lives, and imbues them with self-confidence. Khazneh, Aisha's sister-in-law, for example, would have liked to enroll in the armed resistance training for women had it not been for the paralysis of her leg from polio. Instead, she works in the hospital as an aide, a job which fills her with a confidence that matches or even outstrips that of able-bodied people. Aisha, in contrast, struggles against a pervasive sense of invisibility and lifelessness: "she is present on this earth, yet does not exist" (82). Aisha's discovery of a small mirror amidst the ruins of a bombing raid symbolizes her own self-discovery and reaffirms the role of the individual within the collective struggle. She is also strengthened by the prophetic lessons of her mother-in-law, Um Hassan: "My child, we shall all become strong women. Have they left us any other choice? They take everything from us. Marriage, children, homes, stories, old people . . . everything. So, all of the time, we defend ourselves as though we were not women, but standing in the trenches" (260). War and exile violently sever women from their traditional roles as wives, mothers, housekeepers, and the bearers of culture. Their new roles, however, can only be de-scribed by the older generation of women as masculine, "as though we were not women." Yet war both erases and reconfigures gender distinc-tions; the younger generation of women, such as Khazneh and Hana, rec-onciles their position in the organization with a new construction of what it means to be a woman.

This reconstruction of "feminine destiny" is implicitly tied to the de-construction of masculinist codes of nationalism. Aisha's debilitating in-fatuation with the *fedai* George, who is in fact engaged to Hana, signifies those Palestinians who idealize their fighters as "holy heroes" and "wallow in the romance of the revolution" (Badr 1994, 129), as well as the passive attitude taken by some women toward the nationalist movement. George, however, represents a new generation of Resistance fighters who voice their convictions "irrespective of slogans" (129). While the nationalist struggle is depicted as giving strength to women and men alike, *The Eye of the Mirror* also confronts problems of disorganization within the move-ment, criticizes the leadership for operating out of spontaneity with no long-term strategy, and questions the sacrifices the fighter makes to "professional duties at the expense of his humanity" (239). As George hides out alone in enemy territory, in the borderland between life and death, he contemplates his duty to Hana and his obligations to the nationalist struggle, "to the country, the family, the extended family; then the organization, the establishment, the party" (244). He concludes, "the collective dream was certainly not enough for life. He had to love her well, pay attention to her problems and help her more clearly than before" (255). Like Aisha, he suffers from the submersion of self within the collectivity, and yet his gender accords him seemingly more freedom of movement. Both characters represent the complex conflict between selfhood and collectivity: Aisha, trapped by the tyrannies of gender, class, and national oppression, is expected to sacrifice herself to traditional domesticity, yet finds herself through participation in the Resistance. George, in contrast, sacrifices himself entirely to the struggle at the expense of his selfhood and his relationship with Hana. Nationalism remains the life source for Palestinian resistance and existence, yet it is implacably intertwined with the search for individual and collective humanity in the face of systematic annihilation. In Badr's narratives, nationalism is in a constant state of redefinition, shifting with and reconfiguring gender roles and social structures, as well as individuals' relationship to the movement.

During the final siege, as the refugees flee the camp to face either another bitter journey or massacre, the older generation is haunted by the recurrent dream of return to their homeland. Um Jalal dreams that she returns to her family's home in Acre only to confront the new inhabitants who refuse to let her in. Her husband, Assayed, transformed by the war from his abusive ways, dreams that he reaches the border of Palestine but cannot enter through the barbed-wire fencing. He flies upward, but is transported back to Beirut; then, on the horse of Mohammed, he rides into an unfamiliar and hostile Palestine. While Um Hassan desires to become a bird rising above the suffering and injustice around them, her husband recounts a dream of their uncertain destination: "I am walking across the land of Palestine, guided by the morning star. I walk carrying the gun across my shoulder. Suddenly, a horseman appears on a blue mare, coming slowly towards me. A horseman as green as the spring is approaching. He asked, do you want anything? I said to him: I want your well being. He said, where are you going? I answered: I don't know" (Badr 1994, 223). This recurrent dream with the green promise of spring signifies a persistent hope for return even in the most desperate of situations, as Maronite forces massacre Palestinian boys and men, execute hospital workers, and cart off women and children in trucks like animals. In a similar affirmation of life, Aisha emerges from a trancelike withdrawal to claim with "an accustomed boldness" (264) her dignity and responsibility for the child within her womb, the promise of the future.

Conclusion

For the Palestinians living under occupation who have not yet been able to create their state, and for those of the diaspora, who continue to resist outside of their occupied lands, the continuous reconstruction of the national narrative has been critical to their survival. This national discourse produces a transnationalism rooted in the definition of the ethnonation—"Palestinians wherever they may be." Palestinian nationalism can therefore be measured by the narrative conceptualizations of a nation in the process of formation, with its unresolved conflicts and contradictions. Badr's narratives, written over twenty years of resistance, provide a processual understanding of the shifting relationships between exile, nationalism, and feminism within the Palestinian diaspora.

Today, with the resurgence of Palestinian resistance in response to the injustices of "peace" negotiations, the meaning of al-Awda, "return," has been transformed from the paradisiacal dream often painted in Badr's stories to an uncertainty. In the years since the publication of Badr's novels, the "official" Palestinian narrative on the Right of Return, namely that dictated by the Israeli state, has been rewritten, so that for exiles of 1948, al-Awda can no longer refer to "return to the same home, piece of land, or grove which a certain Palestinian owned before 1948" (Abu Zayyad 1994, 77). Some Palestinians, however, remain hopeful that al-Awda will mean a return to an independent Palestinian state, although Israeli officials continue to deny this possibility. Recently, the Palestinian leadership has come under "intense international pressure to formally disavow the validity and applicability of a binding resolution of international law, on the pretext that consigning millions of Palestinians to permanent exile will serve the cause of Middle East peace" (Rabbani 2001). In other words, to fulfill their most minimal nationalist aspirations, Palestinians are being pressured to sacrifice their Right of Return. As Badr has written, the promise of return has consistently been an empty one. However, her portrayal of Palestinian refugee experience asserts that nationalism cannot readily be transcended without a nation-state, and that any just, humane, and lasting resolution in the Middle East must allow the Palestinians of the diaspora to return to their homeland rather than consigning them to permanent exile.

7 Strategic Androgyny

Passing as Masculine in Barakat's
Stone of Laughter

MONA FAYAD _____

Khalil disappeared. He turned into a laughing male. While I've remained a woman who writes.

— *Hajar al-Dohk* (The laughing stone) (my translation)

Hoda Barakat. *Courtesy of Hoda Barakat*

Hoda Barakat is considered one of the most prominent contemporary Arab writers. She was born in Lebanon in 1952. Raised in Beirut, she graduated in 1974 with a degree in French Literature from the Lebanese University. She left a year later for Paris to work on a Ph.D., but returned to Lebanon after the civil war broke out, preferring to contribute to her country during the war. She worked as a journalist, teacher, and translator, as well as being an active member in a number of organizations. In 1985 she published her first book, al-Za'irat *(The visitors), a collection of short stories and articles. In 1988 she helped establish a women's magazine,* Shehrazade. *In 1989 she moved to Paris, where she completed her novel,* Hajar al-dohk *(1990), translated into English as* The Stone of Laughter *(1995). The novel received the* al-Naqid *Award for first novels and was acclaimed as one of the best novels depicting the Lebanese Civil War. It has been translated into numerous lan-*

guages. In 1993 Ahl al-hawa (People of love) was published. She has contin-
ued to write articles in Arabic and French, including an autobiographical
essay, "I Write Against My Hand," which appeared in Fadia Faqir and
Shirley Eber's In the House of Silence: Autobiographical Essays by Arab
Women Writers. *In the year 2000 Barakat won the prestigious Najib Mah-*
fouz Medal for Arabic Literature for her third novel, Harith al-miyaah *(The*
Tiller of Waters, English, 2001).

H oda Barakat's novel *Hajar al-Dohk* (The laughing stone) (1990)
won the prestigious prize of *al-Naqid* for best novel by a new writer.[1]
Described by Edward Kharrat, one of the judges, as "the best novel written about the Lebanese Civil War," *The laughing stone* deals with the
struggle of a gay man to resist involvement in the fighting and to define his
identity in alternative terms. In a complex, painful, and remarkably skillful
narrative, Barakat represents two figures who are marginal to the war: a
gay male, Khalil, and a narrator, whose voice is often interwoven with
Khalil's, but who emerges at the end as a woman. In effect, the narrator is
androgynous, until the circumstances, specifically those in which Khalil is
obliged to classify himself as masculine in order to take up his role as
fighter for his community, force her to forgo her androgyny and declare
herself as feminine.

Barakat presents the war situation as one where gender identity is
rigidly overdetermined, where participation in the community through
fighting is the basic touchstone of masculine identity, and where dedication to an ethnic group is measured by one's willingness to sacrifice oneself
in battle. As such, *The laughing stone* reveals the mechanisms through
which collectivity is established, and the ways in which identity itself becomes nothing more than a construct that serves the interest of various
systems of control that begin at the local level and extend outward to the
international. In a narrative that fluctuates between the first person and

1. Hoda Barakat 1990, *Hajar al-Dohk.* All quotations in this paper are my translation. Any reference to *The laughing stone,* therefore, indicates my version of the Arabic and
does not refer to the English translation (*The Stone of Laughter*).

third person indiscriminately, however, Khalil is able to create for himself a phantasmagoric space that enables him, if only briefly, to resist the hegemonic discourse that defines gender and that seeks to appropriate him as a male national subject. By establishing a character that has not yet accepted the mark of gender, the narrative shows the process through which masculinity and femininity come to be defined.

Barakat's use of androgyny as a strategy through which to approach gender construction implies what Ursula Le Guin has called in her essay on *Left Hand of Darkness* a "thought experiment" (1989, 151). In the case of a novel in which a character chooses to remain "neutral," both in terms of the civil war raging outside and in terms of how he is willing to participate in it, the very attempt to identify gender polarities raises a question about the nature of war itself.[2] Thought of in terms of passivity and activity, feminine and masculine polarities are articulated by the general social context as a *lack* of participation in the war (feminine) as opposed to *active* participation (masculine). In the novel overall, however, lack of participation, which is constituted as feminine, is written as a sign of resistance that is far from passive. In fact, the main character's frantic activity throughout the first section—domestic activities traditionally classified as "feminine"—is represented as far more difficult than the act of going out to fight (which none of the males agonizes over). In contrast, the "martyred" males of the text, whose pictures are posted in the street as examples of the heroic, are little more than representations meant to be emulated by the males who are still alive.

The novel, then, uses androgyny as a means of going beyond the binarism of masculine/feminine.[3] Reducing all such binaries to the level of

2. The association between masculinity, violence, and war in the context of the Lebanese Civil War has been studied extensively by Evelyne Accad in *Sexuality and War: Literary Masks of the Middle East*. Accad argues that war is an outgrowth of the masculine perception of sexuality as violence and dominance. In *War's Other Voices*, miriam cooke sees the civil war as an occasion that enabled women writers to inscribe female identity through the breakdown of civic society.

3. In a short article, "Thukura wa Inutha" (Masculine/Feminine), Barakat advocates that our other side, "masculinity" or "femininity," is the "absence that fills our lives." She

representations by extracting one character and placing him outside representation, the status of representation itself comes into question. As Ali Bensaoud points out, the primary aim of *The laughing stone* is to strip the war of many of the illusions surrounding it (1991). For although the war seems to imply a breakdown of social structures and control of identity, it in fact represents the opposite: the creation of the ideal citizen who is compelled to conform fully to the normative rules it establishes. The title, *The laughing stone,* is a take on the philosopher's stone, the medieval alchemical stone believed to have the ability to transform iron ore into gold. By using the stone as a metaphor for Khalil's gradual change from a marginalized figure to one who is fully integrated into his community, Barakat emphasizes the constructed nature of identity. Like the vision of gold dreamt up by the alchemists, the identity that is forged by the end of the novel is illusory. Furthermore, Khalil's entrance into a communally defined identity is presented as a violation, a transformation that, like that brought about by the philosopher's stone, arrives at a new product that bears little resemblance to the original. Nor is the end achieved actually desirable. By the final pages of the novel, Khalil has been transformed into "gold," the perfect "masculine" subject. But this transformation is only accomplished through a process in which he dehumanizes both himself and others.

The novel presents Khalil's transformation in two sections. In the first, the pre-hospital section, Khalil struggles to maintain his integrity as a subject, but faces as a result increasing social isolation and a self-loathing that threatens to destroy him. The beginning of the novel provides us with a more fluid, open conceptualization of identity, where Khalil has the opportunity to explore his options. The language in this section is more amorphous and poetic, relying on metonymic relations to establish meaning. Because the boundaries between masculinity and femininity have not yet been rigidly drawn, Khalil is associated with femininity in several different ways. He is represented as a mother-figure, a wife, and a sister, and

---

argues that one of the strongest and most primary human drives is to be "both sexes together, at the same moment" (Barakat 1993b, 18). It is possibly this drive, she asserts, that leads us to write.

he spends a great deal of his time cleaning, cooking, and waiting, all deliberately depicted as stereotypically "feminine" actions. Meanwhile, he keeps himself apart from the war, does not participate in any of the activities related to it, and is generally alienated from the young men his age. Because the subject's relation to war is always already gendered, it is only through Khalil's representation as feminine that his resistance to the war can be articulated.

The post-hospital section takes place after a severe illness, during which Khalil grows thinner and thinner and throws up blood. He is operated on for an ulcer and nurtured by a male doctor who pulls him back from a close encounter with death. After the operation, Khalil determines to survive, no matter what. Gradually, after an occasion in which he is almost killed in the street by a group of young men, he determines that survival depends on hate, not on love. He grows increasingly misogynistic, an attitude that culminates in his cold-blooded rape of his neighbor, a young mother who reminds him of himself. In the final pages of the novel, Khalil is "masculinized," but only at the price of destroying his "femininity." He violates his feminine side in order to participate fully in the fighting, and becomes actively involved in smuggling weapons into the country and storing them in his building.

Formulating Gender Identity

Much of the resistance of the text lies in its rejection of gender stereotyping. Gender is problematized, both by reinforcing constructed representations of gender and by recording Khalil's reluctance until the end to abandon one type of gender identity in favor of another. Lu'ai Abdul-Ilah asserts that the male/female polarity in the novel represents the conflict between the death drive (masculine) and eros, a drive for survival (feminine) (1991, 68–69). Within such a reading, Khalil's resistance to the logic of death represents a triumph of the feminine pole. However, I would argue that Barakat's critique of the war is more complex precisely because Khalil does not inhabit one gender or the other. He enters a gendered world reluctantly, finding in a pregendered self a refuge from having to make choices. Indeed, Khalil undergoes a second moment of rupture, not unlike the Lacanian mirror stage, this time when his voice breaks: "When his voice fell and its high wave broke like the glass of a lantern, he was too taken by surprise to know what it was he had now lost, forever. His voice became thick like a thick wound. His green leaves fell in an instant, reducing him to a large brown dry trunk which would carry him on the ebb of language to a screen with lights that blinked on and off" (Barakat 1990, 167).

As his body begins to be contoured by language, his entrance into masculinity is traumatic rather than triumphant. Khalil falls out of his prelapsarian world where he had "the all-encompassing happiness of being outside gender" (Barakat 1990, 168) into a language that defines him against his will. Prior to that, the "I" is undifferentiated in terms of gender. Rather than opening up a space for him, it forecloses his identity, setting up an obstacle between his former self and the language that has now come to define him. The broken glass of his voice wounds his body, marking it, inscribing it with the traces of loss, with an impossible plenitude that can never be his once he has entered the realm of gender. He has become a *sujet clive,* a split subject, but in a more complex sense of the word, for he is unable to rid himself of the semiotic that is constantly disrupting his ability to speak his new gender. As a result, he is both self and other to himself.

Khalil's resistance lies in that he refuses to forget. Unable to give himself up to a normative notion of identity, he clings to his memory, and by doing so hangs on to a self that is defined by language as feminine. He is aware that his new language excludes women, and that once he lets go of his voice he, too, will define his world in terms of exclusion: "He began to talk to himself in his new voice but he was unable to hear its complaints, and he was unable to catch up with himself, with his gender, through his voice. Every time he spoke, his complaints would be afraid, would draw back in disgust and go outside, out of the kingdom that he knew, where the women would die. After that he did not speak with a voice but with language, and he had to know whose language it was" (Barakat 1990, 168).

Khalil's first impulse, as he struggles to deny his loss, is to occupy the space of that "feminine" loss himself. Consequently, the text spends some time presenting Khalil as functioning within a code that would define him as so-called feminine.

Narrating the Androgyne

Initially, Khalil is presented as androgynous. The narrator, who is not identified but who weaves in and out, sometimes becoming the "I" of Khalil, at other times treating him as a third person, describes Khalil as lying outside masculinity, which consists of two types. In the first category of the "masculine" are the men who are younger than Khalil but similar physically, those "who had torn open the door of masculinity, had gone in through the wide entrance, the entrance of history, and were manufacturing, daily, the destiny of an important area on the world map" (Barakat 1990, 17): in other words, those with brute strength. The second category consists of those who were the brains behind the formation of that "important area," through leadership, journalism, political thought, and the general wielding of power. Either way, masculinity is defined through its relation to the area on the map. By giving us only two options, Barakat mimics a discourse that posits these kinds of masculinities as the only possibilities available. Anything outside these two cannot be defined, and ultimately cannot exist. Khalil's position itself, then, destabilizes the two options by providing another. According to the narrator, Khalil fits into neither category: "These two masculinities had closed the door on him and he had remained alone in a narrow corridor, in touch with two areas which were highly attractive. He dwelt in what resembled a stagnant femininity that had surrendered to a purely vegetable existence, and active masculinities that exploded the volcano of life" (17).

By placing him in the corridor between passivity and explosive activity, the narrator presents his condition as a suspension of identity rather than as a space in which identity can be formulated. His identity is always on the verge, but remains constantly outside one or the other category. It is the narrator, in fact, who can find the words to describe his situation, and to explain how and why Khalil cannot be simply defined through preconceived categories. S/he enables him to shift backwards and forwards between self and other by alternating the first person with the third.[4]

At the heart of the novel, therefore, is Khalil's struggle to find an intelligible mode of being that survives the contesting representations that seek to appropriate him. By refusing to become one or the other, Khalil resists gender as a vector of power. However, his resistance to being foreclosed as either male or female renders his very existence impossible. He is neither one nor the other; but to situate himself as an in-between, an *interdit*, as Irigaray expresses it (1985), cannot help him, for setting himself up "between" language does not finally lead to the breakdown of the two binary oppositions that continue to define his boundaries.

The narrator places this fluctuation between two extremes within his body itself—a fluctuation that is described as inhabiting his sleeping body independently of his consciousness. The focus on the body throughout the course of the novel is an attempt to move Khalil out of the realm of textuality into that of the irreducible materiality of the body, to use the body to ground his identity away from the totalizing narrative that reigns in the war-torn streets outside his room. Hence the novel relies on space and a systematic enumeration of Khalil's physical activities to provide an alternative to a constructed notion of identity that is externally and socially defined.

Gendering the Body

Thus begins Khalil's long journey into the body. His only access to an alternative identity lies through a body that, by resisting heterosexual desire, sets up desires of its own that define Khalil against others. Because Khalil is "different," his body represents, in the words of Judith Butler, a "failure to materialize," and therefore provides "the necessary 'outside,' if not necessary support, for the bodies which, in materializing the norm, qualify as bodies that matter" (1993, 16).

---

4. I should emphasize here that the narrative shifts abruptly and unpredictably from the first person to the third, sometimes within the same sentence. Until the last two pages of the novel, there is no difference, in fact, between Khalil and the narrator, whose presence is puzzling but not ultimately intrusive.

Consequently, because Khalil's body is outside the normative discourse, because it is not a body that matters, it escapes its function as a site where identity can be located. Since Khalil at different times redefines his body, it is constantly escaping its materiality, shaping itself through language rather than as an anchor of the absolute. This amorphous tendency of Khalil's body extends itself to other bodies, too. Even corpses have no stability. Bodies litter the text, fragmented into pieces that cannot be put together, that defy any unitary presence, that are undergoing repeated transformation.

Why this concern with fragmented bodies? To answer this, we must return to Judith Butler and the notion of regulatory norms. The need to assert the "bodies that matter" inevitably produces a domain of abject bodies through its exclusion of what does not matter, by definition "a field of deformation which . . . fortifies the regulatory norms" (Butler 1993, 16). Much of the energy of the characters in the novel, who are usually seen as a collective unit in a series of parties and gatherings Khalil attends, is spent on affirming their survival, whole, despite the debilitating war that is happening outside. A whole realm of meaning is consequently generated through the contrast between the abjected fragments that have been claimed by death and the laughter of those who have not.

A perfect example of this contrast is the story somebody tells at a party Khalil attends, and which the listeners perceive as wildly funny: "During a battle he wanted to save one of his wounded men so he carried him by the legs for several kilometers at night. But when he was about to unload the man from his shoulders, he discovered that he was only carrying his lower part" (Barakat 1990, 150). The audience laughs, because the deformed body only reinforces the fact that the man who carried him has survived and is alive to tell the story. At the same time, however, the fragmented body intrudes, creating an unease that is also part of the reason for laughter. The abjected body, like that of Khalil, challenges the symbolic hegemony by reminding it of its limitations.

Nationalism, "Masculinity," and Death

The projection of the body as fragmented, moreover, brings together the associations of laughter with war by drawing attention to the Arabic expression *yanfajiru duhkan* (to explode with laughter). Barakat deliberately uses the language of violence to express the kind of laughter that predominates in the novel. The laughter, because it is "explosive," does not express joy. Rather, it is a result of the war itself and is consequently connected with the ability to distance oneself, to reject empathy, and to use explosives to destroy the other. In the novel, it becomes an antidote to the pain of nationalism, which demands the sacrifice of the individual at the expense of collective identity. Such a sacrifice, as represented in the novel, equates nationalism with death. Note, in the following quotation, the way the gender roles are clearly established: "The only emotion appropriate to nationalist feeling is deep sorrow. Tragedy. Death. Nationalist feeling means death. Death. You walk with it side by side, converse with it, iron its clothes, feed it from your plate. Love it. Death" (Barakat 1990, 130).

The association of nationalism with death is double. Nationalism is the death of subjectivity, but it also implies sacrifice. Khalil links both nationalism and history with death, interpreting the history upon which national identity is constructed as a catalogue of death: "Nationalist feeling hurts if it is distanced from death, and history is made only through death" (Barakat 1990, 131). Surprisingly, as Khalil turns more and more to nationalist feeling, he finds himself, contrary to traditional narratives, rejecting his mother more and more, and becoming increasingly misogynistic. He recalls an episode in his childhood, when his history teacher tells the class about the great sacrifices of the past, and especially about the Phoenicians who set themselves on fire in their temples rather than accept defeat by the enemy. When Khalil returns home, he tries to find out what his mother would do if the occasion called for a sacrifice:

> "If I were your only son . . . would you agree to send me with the soldiers to die defending my country? . . ." "Against whom?" asked the mother, throwing out the dishwashing water onto the earth in front of the house. "Against the enemy who wants to take away our independence," he an-

swered, "whoever that enemy is." "No," she replied, laughing, arranging the gleaming kitchen utensils on the large rocks in the sun. "I would tie you by your ankle to the foot of a bed." "But that way the enemy would tear down our walls and burn our temples and libraries and mutilate our corpses, and they would kill me anyway." "No," said the mother, "They'd kill the men, but I would tell their leader that you were a little girl, one of my daughters, and when he saw you he'd believe it and go away." "You mean I'd stay alive and my homeland would die in disgrace?" "I don't give a damn about a homeland or a thousand homelands. Come here." She hugged him. He ran away. She laughed loudly. (132)

I have quoted the passage extensively because it articulates a number of the novel's basic preoccupations. The first is the presence of the mother herself, who is both naïve and down-to-earth in her responses. Then there is her laughter, which goes against the association established in the novel of nationalism with sorrow. The mother, concerned more with the survival of her child than with the "honor" of the nation, refuses to take nationalism seriously. To make matters worse, she is willing to sacrifice Khalil's masculinity rather than allow him to participate in the nationalist struggle. The passage as a whole displaces several nationalist themes. Although the mother is associated with nature, with water, earth, and rock all metonymically related to her, she resists becoming a symbol of the nation. Moreover, she is not interested in reinforcing his masculinity, nor in transforming him into the ideal male citizen, if it is at the expense of his life. She also insists on identifying the enemy, refusing to dehumanize it, demanding specificity, while Khalil tries to project a vague other that is faceless and ahistorical.

Because his mother does not fit history's description of the ideal nationalist woman, he begins to be ashamed of her. He sees her unpatriotic statements as a betrayal. Barakat reinforces, however, the impossibility of such an ideal. Khalil's model is the stuff of legend, the women of Carthage, who "melted down their gold and jewels and the kitchen utensils to make weapons, and cut their long shining hair to braid ropes for the national fleet that was defending the country's honor" (Barakat 1990, 133). Practically speaking, however, it is impossible for his mother to do so, and the young Khalil acknowledges this: "Well, she didn't have any jewelry. Her hair wasn't very thick . . . and wouldn't amount to a clothesline. And she laughs a lot." Despite the reality check that Khalil is faced with, he continues to resent his mother: "Khalil started to dislike his mother a little, to dislike laughter a lot, and to do well in history" (133).

As Khalil grows older, however, he is faced with another form of nationalist pedagogy, manifested in his high school teacher Mr. Muqbil. Muqbil suppresses laughter on any level: "He was serious to the extent that violent drama would explode in the classroom at the mere hint of a laugh or smile" (Barakat 1990, 133). Mr. Muqbil's version of history, apparently illogically, is focused on language, and specifically on an obsessive insistence on pronouncing the letter "q" from the back of the throat. His concern with the correct use of language, however, reflects another aspect of nationalism; the use of language as a marker of identity. Yet, despite the fact that Khalil clearly identifies himself in terms of Arabic rather than French, language remains a barrier to his identity rather than a means of constructing it.

The adult Khalil, consequently, rejects both versions of history: that based on a legendary Phoenician past and that based on an Arab linguistic present. His own version of the past is simple, and far closer to his mother's than he could have imagined as a child. It brings together a protective instinct with positive laughter, emphasizing that a need for preservation rather than for destruction lies at the basis of nationalism: "Khalil began to laugh along with nationalist feeling. For Yusef had returned, and he had not died" (Barakat 1990, 135). His laughter is an alternative laughter, one that differs from that of those around him. Rather than being "explosive" and detached, it is based on identification *with* others, rather than on objectifying them. His laughter is hence closely connected with his vision of national identity, which is based not on a process of othering, but rather on a sense of communion and common understanding.

Because of the fluctuations of Khalil's visions of history, the text overall dismisses history as an authoritative basis for building identity. In fact, the novel is remarkable in removing the Lebanese Civil War from any historical context. A war is being fought in the streets, explosions are heard, the damage is visible, but the participants are faceless, the enemies undefined, just like the enemy that the child Khalil tries to present to his mother. As such, the historical becomes devoid of meaning, irrelevant to a situation where destruction is the aim of both sides, where there is no attempt to provide a constructive notion of national identity, and where the concept of loyalty is ruthless in its need for sacrifice and death. The novel overall consequently resists any attempt to provide a justification for the war based on a historical narrative.

Rather, in the absence of any other foundation upon which to build identity, the novel explores the possibility of death itself as an absolute, bringing together the abstraction of death with the concreteness of a dead corpse. As he tries to comprehend his loss of his first love, Naji, Khalil reflects on what Naji's corpse represents. The body itself, however, can provide no certainties; if anything, things grow more confused, since any attempt to establish the connection between the body and its previous owner is rendered problematic: "Eyes examine it again, and women touch it. Not because it is difficult to part from it, but because the body so little resembles its owner when he was alive that it leaves a fissure through which doubt moves back and forth" (Barakat 1990, 67). This doubt is further reinforced by the way corpses are given a new gender, since the common practice is to use feminine terms to describe a corpse, even if it is that of a male.[5] As such, the dead body confuses the issue of gender for Khalil even further, since he has gradually grown to associate dead men's bodies with the ultimate ideal of masculinity: "How could he explain the flaring of his desire when he saw in the newspapers the bodies of the dead men whose torsos were always exposed. . . . It was because their still, naked bodies proved to him beyond a shadow of a doubt that they were men, and that it was the sharp flame of their virility that had led to their death" (170).

In the case of Naji, however, the rigid finality of that masculine ideal dissolves, partly because the body has been feminized through language, but mostly because Naji's masculinity has been cast into doubt by the dubious nature of his death. Rather than representing an ideal masculine commitment to his group, Naji has been playing the double agent, and his

---

5. The Arabic word for a dead body, *al-jutha,* is feminine, and is distinct from the general words used for a body, *al-jism* or *al-jasad,* which are masculine.

death is a result of being discovered by his "own" people: "Khalil did not possess the body of Naji, and he no longer possessed, after Nayif's visit, what had been there before the body. A large stick had stirred the warm cauldron of his memories and transformed it into a decomposing mess with bubbles that resembled those that surfaced in witches' stews" (Barakat 1990, 68).

The death of his friends emphasizes Khalil's own lack of defining boundaries. Unable to fully mourn either Naji or Yusef, the second man he loves, he is envious of the women who can enact their rites and thereby claim the dead. But he also envies the men who can transform the dead into martyrs for an imaginary cause. Khalil, however, can do neither: "They left him with a lack of crying, with the absence of the gift of burial, as a constant reminder that he was neither a man to create illusions, nor was he a woman to believe in them" (Barakat 1990, 157).

Khalil encounters his body on the operating table in its extreme form during a moment that is outside enunciation because it is the moment between life and death, portrayed, like his gender position, as a narrow passageway connecting the two. He struggles between resisting his rebirth and accepting it at the hands of Dr. Waddah, who becomes a surrogate male mother. Neither alive nor dead, in a moment between the two, on the operating table, his language is reduced to the barest minimum, his physical condition eluding words:

> you do it.
> i hear. i can't. say that i am. i can't hear. hear. hear. here. i
> i
> "Breath!"
> you don't. please.
>   . . .
> i don't see my body. i don't know. i can reach
> i'm beyond it. i hear. do with it. you
> (Barakat 1990, 194)

He is cut up, stitched up, and "cured." Having reached the limit between dissipation and self-preservation, he chooses the latter. After the operation, he slowly turns into a male, motivated by the gentle maternal prompting of Dr. Waddah to become a "hero."[6]

Passing as "Masculine"

In the end, however, despite his choice, Khalil's body is sacrificed, in the sense that Jean-Luc Nancy uses the word: "Sacrifice designates a body's passage to a limit where it becomes the body of a community, the spirit of a communion of which it is the effectiveness, the material symbol, the absolute relationship to itself of sense pervading blood, of blood making sense" (1994, 22). In this he follows in the footsteps of Naji, Yusef, and the other males whose bodies have become "bits and pieces" of paper, the remains of superimposed funeral photographs stuck on the neighborhood walls.

Barakat makes it clear to us, moreover, that Khalil's entrance into the community does not imply a new integrated self that is grounded in certainty. When the Boss, who is interested in him physically, takes him underground to a plushly furnished hiding place, talks about how isolated they are, and offers Khalil cocaine, Khalil rejects him angrily: "Do you want to rape me here?" Later, while they are on a yacht on the sea, Khalil dismisses the Boss's claim that he loves him: "You are talking to me like Yusef Bek Wahbi. . . . As if I'm the prostitute you want to bring out of the mud into a pure clean life. . . . As if I'm The Lady of the Camelias and you are the good hearted person, from a good family, who fell in love with me and wanted to bring me to the light" (Barakat 1990, 235). Khalil still only represents himself in terms of other texts, of discourses that he sees as generating who he is. He also still represents himself as "feminine." It is only when he has become completely engrossed in the world of weapons smugglers, drug addicts, and ruthless godfather figures that Khalil allows his

---

6. *Ya batal*, literally "hero," is a word used playfully by adults, usually males, to address small boys. The doctor treats Khalil like a child, particularly just before the operation as he undergoes anesthesia, when he actually reverts to childhood: "Start counting. Let's see if you're good at math. The voice of a small child said . . . they love me a lot. I'm a happy child" (Barakat 1990, 193).

identity to become completely contoured by the boundaries of that world. As Khalil is transformed by the masculine script, developing into a "hero," he moves from a marginal position to one of dominance in which he assumes power over and marginalizes others. Thus, he rapes the woman upstairs, a person he had consistently protected in the previous part of the novel. Then he violates her basic rights as a tenant by breaking the rental agreement he has set up with her and threatening to throw her out on the street if she protests.

Finally, Barakat transforms Khalil's alternative homosexuality into what Fedwa Malti-Douglas has identified as male homosocial desire—one that, while marked by the homoerotic, is normalized within the discourse of masculinity and set within the limits of male bonding (1991, 15). His relationship with the Boss, consequently, despite the fact that it goes against the heterosexual norm, emphasizes his integration into the male homosocial realm rather than situating him as an outsider. It is not his sexual preference that is of concern; it is his relation with "femininity."

In the final three pages of the novel, Khalil's resistance to the discourse of gender, which is very clearly tied in with his status as a national subject, disappears completely. He is swallowed by the discourse, incorporated, losing his identity completely and becoming no more than a representation in a script that has already been written. His transformation is replete with irony. He has lost his chance for forming an alternative notion of identity. But, more importantly, the moment he is written as a male subject he loses his autonomy, just as he submits to the authority of the "Boss" as his only means of survival. It is the Boss's name, printed on a card, not his own, that saves him from being beaten to death. At the same time, having become part of the Boss's entourage, he is implicated in a global arms smuggling operation that in fact violates and effaces national boundaries, and places Lebanon in a neocolonial context in which its fate is decided by powers beyond its control.

It is particularly noteworthy that, once Khalil has succumbed to this discourse, he loses his identification with the female narrator, the "woman who writes." In a twist that comes as a surprise in the last two pages of the novel, the narrator declares her own gender identity clearly. The "I" of the narrator, which had never been clearly differentiated from that of Khalil, separates from him/her, turning Khalil finally and conclusively into a "he." By so doing, the narrator disclaims her relation to him. The two become separate characters, and since Khalil has given up, it is the narrator that will continue the resistance. The final paragraph of the novel, despite Khalil's apparent authority, shifts control of the text completely to her:

> I approached the rear window. . . . Khalil had a moustache and dark sunglasses. Where are you going? I asked, but he didn't hear me. It's me, I said, but he didn't turn. The car moved. Through the rear window Khalil looked broad-shouldered in his brown leather jacket.
>
> The car went off. . . . How you have changed since I described you in the first pages. You know more than me now. Alchemy. The laughing stone.
>
> Khalil disappeared. He turned into a laughing male. While I've remained a woman who writes.
>
> Khalil, my dear hero. (Barakat 1990, 264)

From the scrawny androgynous figure she describes him as being initially, he has transformed into a broad-shouldered masculine figure, his leather jacket and dark glasses forming an impossible barrier between them. However, since it is she who has written him, she can also frame his story by reminding us of the original Khalil she created. She retains his memory, even if he has entirely forgotten it, and she reminds us that throughout the novel, except for the last pages, he has been able to avoid being appropriated. At the end, she *excribes* the new Khalil, making him disappear after he refuses to hear her calling his name. It is particularly noteworthy that she does not identify him as a *man,* but as a *male,* emphasizing the new gender role that he has assumed at the expense of leaving her behind, and thereby ending his story. Her separation from him marks *his* entrance into the community, while she has chosen to stay outside it, and through that separation to be able to continue to write.

In this carefully crafted novel, Barakat creates an alternative space, one that can be termed androgynous, that challenges an equally phantasmagoric space, that of the masculine national subject. And if Khalil does appear at the end to have lost the ability to resist, our awareness of him as a construct prevents us from accepting the transformation. The laughing stone's magic depends on a belief in the power of the stone, just as did that of the medieval alchemists dreaming of gold. And belief is simply what we, as readers, are taught not to have.

Part Three

Embodied Voices and Histories

8 The Fourth Language

Subaltern Expression in Djebar's Fantasia

NADA ELIA

> The blood in my writing? Not yet, but the voice?
> —Assia Djebar, *Vaste est la prison* (my translation)

> The women's shrill ululation improvises for the fighting men a threnody of war in some alien idiom: our chroniclers are haunted by the distant sound of half-human cries, cacophony of keening, ear-splitting hieroglyphs of a wild, collective voice.
> —Assia Djebar, *Fantasia: An Algerian Cavalcade*

Assia Djebar. *Courtesy of Assia Djebar*

Assia Djebar (née Fatima-Zohra Imalhayene) is an award-winning poet, novelist, and film-maker. Born in 1936 in Cherchell, she was the first Algerian woman admitted to the prestigious École Normale Supérieure de Sèvres. Between 1958 and 1962, she worked for a Front National de Libération newspaper in Tunis. In 1996, she received the Neustadt Inter-

A version of this chapter was originally published in *Trances, Dances, and Vociferations: Agency and Resistance in Africana Women's Narratives,* by Nada Elia, pages 11–34 (Garland, 2001). Reprinted by permission of Routledge, Inc.

183

national Prize for Literature. Her novels and short stories have been trans-
lated into sixteen languages. Her works available in English include the nov-
els A Sister to Scheherazade *(1993; French edition 1987),* Fantasia: An
Algerian Cavalcade *(1993; French edition 1985), and* So Vast the Prison
(1999; French edition 1995), and the collection of short stories Women of Algiers in Their Apartment *(1992; French edition 1980). Djebar currently*
lives in self-exile in the United States, where she is Distinguished Professor
and Director of the Center for French and Francophone Studies at Louisiana
State University.

A ssia Djebar's reputation as a feminist postcolonial novelist and film
director is by now firmly established. Numerous articles have examined the rich aspects of her oeuvre, and *World Literature Today* devoted its
autumn 1996 issue to her as she was awarded that year's Neustadt International Prize in Literature, second only to the Nobel. As I write this,
Djebar's accomplishments have also earned her the African Literature Association's 1997 Fonlon-Nichols prize, as well as the recognition of international organizations in Austria, Germany, Italy, and Belgium. My own
essay does not seek to further explicate Djebar's texts, nor does it attempt
a synopsis of what has already been written about her. Rather, I intend to
explore her treatment, in *Fantasia: An Algerian Cavalcade* (1993), of the
body as "wild collective voice," a venue of expression, and counterdis-
course among the subaltern: Algeria's women under French colonization.
The reference to the body as medium of expression immediately brings to
mind French feminism's *écriture féminine,* with its critique of hegemonic
discourse. Indeed, Djebar herself refers to French variously as the enemy's
language, the oppressor's language, and the stepmother tongue. She does
so, however, because to her French is first and foremost the language of
the colonizer. In this, she differs from the advocates of *écriture féminine,*
for whom all dominant discourse is oppressive because it is phallocentric—
regardless of ethnic or national origin. This difference becomes greater
when one realizes that the prime proponents of *écriture féminine,* Julia
Kristeva, Hélène Cixous, Luce Irigaray, and Monique Wittig, all have
some personal awareness of French as a foreign language and hence

should be aware of its oppressive nature not merely as the discourse of the patriarchal order, but also that of the outside transgressor/conqueror.[1] Djebar's focus on Algeria's women procures an additional dimension to *écriture féminine*, for the women whose voices she examines, being illiterate, do not write. With no access to literature, these women nevertheless undermine the discourse that oppresses/suppresses them, by preventing it from re-presenting them with finality. Free from the structures of the written form, they articulate their feelings viscerally, and their own bodies become an alternative medium for expression, a "fourth language" (see Djebar 1993, 180) that no official discourse can record, for it falls outside of French as well as the two patriarchal discourses native to Algeria, Arabic and Berber. Thus, their subversive power is greatest because of their alterity: they can best dismantle the master's house because they are not using the master's tools.

When Djebar herself set out to write her autobiography, that of a young Arab girl, she was confronted with the realization that she could only do it in French, the master's tool, the language of her former oppressor. "Autobiography practiced in the enemy's language has the texture of fiction," she confesses. "The language of the Others, in which I was enveloped from childhood, the gift my father lovingly bestowed on me, that language has adhered to me ever since like the tunic of Nessus," she continues, with a reference to the mythological, half-human, half-horse monster with poisoned blood (1993, 127). Yet she could not renounce French, which helped her escape her own country's stifling fundamentalism, a neotraditionalism that dictates that women should be domestic creatures, their very lives threatened by their refusal to wear the *hijab* as they step out, into "male territory." But Djebar is also an Algerian nationalist who, during the War of Liberation, had worked for the revolutionary paper *El-Mujahid* (Zimra 1992, 190). A historian by training, she additionally knows too well the atrocities the French committed against her people, atrocities that partly explain (though they certainly do not justify) the dismal circumstances in postrevolutionary Algeria.

Djebar's predicament is by no means unique. One of the many facets of

---

1. For an excellent synopsis of "écriture féminine," see Jones 1985.

the postcolonial condition is a problematic relationship to bilingualism, a familiarity with the colonizer's language that at times exceeds that with one's "native" tongue. Many radical postcolonial thinkers have stopped producing in the language of their conqueror. In the Francophone Maghreb, one thinks of Rachid Boujedra, who, shortly after winning the French world's most coveted and prestigious literary prize, the Prix Goncourt, stopped all writing in French in order to revitalize Arabic literature. Other writers, such as Morocco's Tahar Ben Jelloun, take a different approach to the fact that they write, think, and otherwise express themselves in French. "[W]e're trying to make the most of this situation," writes Jelloun, "not to keep complaining about it, to keep making it into a big issue, and every time say 'oh la la, we write in French because we've been colonized.' It's true, but you have to go beyond that, try to be a little more calm about it, and say OK, we write in French because it happened that way but let's try to get the most out of it for everyone" (1990, 30).

Between these two poles is yet another approach to bilingualism, a conscious problematizing of the use of the former oppressor's language, a realization that greater familiarity with the dominant discourse always/already implies some degree of alienation from one's culture, but is not necessarily accompanied by an acceptance of the hegemonic discourse. Indeed, the use of that language becomes itself a subversive practice, as it strips it of its exclusive membership rules, decentering and deterritorializing it.

Djebar locates herself in that middle ground, as she feels indebted to French for her own personal liberation, while remaining aware of that language's subjugation of the greater community she identifies with, Algeria and, more specifically, Algerian women. An insider without, she oscillates between quasi-gratitude to French, which allowed her to escape the harem, and nostalgic attachment to conversational Arabic, which bonds her with the Algerian women she interviewed, whose oral histories she inscribes in *Fantasia*.

The median position she occupies is, in part, her way to resolve her failure to write in Arabic. In 1969, following the publication of a collection of verse, *Poèmes pour l'Algérie heureuse,* as well as a play, *Rouge L'aube,* Djebar stopped writing to devote herself to learning Arabic, which she determined to use for her future publications. Her attempt at erasing colonial education proved futile, however, since in her case the hegemonic French discourse seemed to have permanently displaced Arabic, relegating it to the status of spoken, conversational language, a status that Djebar, as a writer, perceives as precarious. "My oral tradition has gradually been overlaid, and is in danger of vanishing," she comments in *Fantasia* (1993, 156). Still unreconciled to writing in French, Djebar resorted to the visual arts, and in 1978 directed *La nouba des femmes du Mont Chenoua,* which was awarded the Prix de la Critique Internationale at the 1979 Venice Film Festival. Mildred Mortimer correctly points out that, "For Djebar the gaze is crucial because the prohibition against women seeing and being seen is at the heart of Maghrebian patriarchy, an ideological system in which the master's eye alone exists; women challenge the patriarchal system by appropriating the gaze for themselves" (1996, 859). *La nouba,* which features some of the interviews and oral histories later recorded in *Fantasia* under the subheading "Voices," foregrounds women's role in the oral transmission of Algerian history, and is an "investigation of . . . the world of space and time as perceived by women, the world of body and thought as experienced by Algerian women" (Bensmaia 1996, 877).

Djebar's reappropriation of the gaze is empowering not only in its challenge to Maghrebian patriarchy, as Mortimer states in her analysis, but also because it effects a conscious reversal of the Orientalist gaze North African women were subjected to by French artists. In an interview, she explained that it was her experience with filming, that is, with controlling the gaze, that allowed her to return to writing in French. Her second film, *La Zerda et les chants de l'oubli,* is a documentary covering the period 1912–42 in North Africa, from the perspectives of Maghrebians generally and women in particular. In 1980, her stories of two decades were collected and published, in French, as *Femmes d'Alger dans leur appartement.* The title of that work, as well as the cover illustration, are taken from the 1834 oil painting by Eugène Delacroix, depicting three voluptuous women in exotic setting, dressed in luxurious silks, and being waited on by a turbaned servant. The profession of these women—providing men with sexual gratification—is affirmed by their sleepy looks, supine positions, bare faces, bare feet, and the door that stands suggestively ajar in the background.[2] Djebar felt it necessary to redress this image, part of the permanent collection at the Musée du Louvre. And, in a moment that crystallizes her agency, her power of subversion from within, she writes to counter the visual impact of the Orientalist painter.

As an individual artist, then, Djebar writes in French. As a member of the community of North African women, she foregrounds other means of communication, the vocal and the physical. She writes: "The fourth language [after French, Arabic, and Lybico-Berber], for all females, young or old, cloistered or half-emancipated, remains that of the body: the body which . . . in trances, dances or vociferations, in fits of hope or despair, rebels, and unable to read or write, seeks some unknown shore as destination for its message of love" (1993, 180). The venue left these disenfranchised women is the preverbal, physical expression, movements and sounds, "dances and vociferations," functioning outside the reach of any Symbolic discourse, and which, by virtue of this, can communicate the unsayable. And, just as an energetic body's movement will not be stilled by the *hijab*, Djebar's use of French to revive these "trances and vociferations" disarms that language, reducing it to the role of medium, rather than agent, or oppressor.

Uncritical speakers of the dominant discourse adhere to a rigid language that does not allow for great liberties in interpretation and that does not accommodate great variations in meaning. As they have never had to negotiate a space for their own representation in the dominant discourse, such speakers uphold, and seek to impose on various others, the Law of the Father, which stipulates a one-on-one equivalence between a sign and its signified. The Law of the Father is Jacques Lacan's theory that language is the medium through which we enter society and are capable of functioning therein, and that language is represented, and enforced, by the authoritarian figure of the father in the family.[3] In contrast to the rigidity and orderliness of phallocentric discourse, female expression is viewed

2. For a study of the depiction of North African women as exotic-erotic, see Alloula 1986.

3. See "The Agency of the Letter in the Unconscious or Reason Since Freud" in Lacan 1977. Lacan's theory is aptly discussed in Lemaire 1977.

as poetically fluid, replete with ambiguities and uncertainties. Thus French feminists, despite their internecine differences, have denounced Western discourse's systematic repression of women's experience, as it placed (white, upper-class) man as its defining center. This claim to centrality is expressed in religion, philosophy, politics, and language—it is no surprise that Euroman's first impulse, indeed irresistible urge, upon recognizing a child as his own is to bestow his name, the Name of the Father, upon that child. Children who bear their mother's name are stigmatized as outside the Law, literally "illegitimate."

Yet in a striking illustration of their own repression of alterity, French feminists, in their discussion of Symbolic discourse as agent of alienation, have not mentioned the role that colonialism plays for all non-Westerners. A prime example is Hélène Cixous, who grew up as a French Jewish (white) girl in Algeria, and who discusses "blackness" and Africa in strictly symbolic terms, co-opting these to represent European women's experiences. Cixous writes: "As soon as [women] begin to speak, at the same time as they're taught their name, they can be taught that their territory is black: because you are Africa, you are black. Your continent is dark. Dark is dangerous. . . . We the precocious, we the repressed of culture . . . we are black and we are beautiful" (1981, 247–48). Implicated in a Symbolic discourse of colonialism that includes them because they are white, these French feminists fail to adequately address the flip-side of Euro-phallogocentrism, its effacing of the non-Western experience, both male and female. Similarly, Julia Kristeva erases the reality of Algeria's oppression as she levels differences between foreignness within and foreigners per se. This leveling is most obvious in her recent work *Strangers to Ourselves*, although it constitutes a natural progression of her writings since her own exile as a (welcome) East European political and intellectual dissident in France. Thus, in *Strangers to Ourselves*, where she discusses Albert Camus' stranger, Mersault, Kristeva writes, "Mersault is just as, if not more, distant from his conationals as he is from the Arabs. At what does he shoot during the imporous hallucination that overcomes him? At shadows, whether French or Maghrebian, it matters little" (1991, 26). As Winifred Woodhull points out in *Transfigurations of the Maghreb*, her excellent study of the (ab)uses of feminine tropes in Maghrebian literatures,

"By virtue of focussing on foreignness within and systematically dissociating it from social inequalities, Kristeva ends by ignoring the foreigners whose foreignness, unlike her own, sparks hostility and violence in France" (1993, 92). What strikes me as even more offensive is the fact that no one, in looking at Camus' so-called masterpiece, has ever indicated that during France's lengthy occupation of Algeria not a single French person was ever tried for shooting an Arab.

Growing up Arab in occupied Algeria, Djebar could not ignore colonialism. It was her father, a schoolteacher, who introduced her to French, the "oppressor's language," but also, as she refers to it, the "father tongue." Djebar opens *Fantasia* with a warning, an awareness of the potential danger involved in the acquisition of French:

> A little Arab girl going to school for the first time, one autumn morning, walking hand in hand with her father. A tall erect figure in a fez and a European suit, carrying a bag of school books. He is a teacher at the French primary school. A little Arab girl in a village in the Algerian Sahel. . . . From the very first day that a little girl leaves her home to learn the ABC, the neighbours adopt that knowing look of those who in ten or fifteen years' time will be able to say "I told you so!" while commiserating with the foolhardy father, the irresponsible brother. (1993, 3)

For the colonized, French is invested with a mythical dimension: learning it seems tantamount to initiating a metamorphosis that does not provide for turning back. And clearly, the danger is gendered: the male relatives, the "foolhardy father" and "irresponsible brother," have allowed a woman to taste of that forbidden fruit, to lose her innocence. These men, however, seem to be themselves immune to the "danger" that threatens the young girls. Like sexual experience, which traditional discourse views as shameful behavior in single girls and women, while celebrating it as entry into adulthood for men, learning French carries different values depending on whether the student is male or female. Yet at the very foundation of this "fear," specifically as the danger threatens women, is an awareness of the fact that French may well provide the entryway into enfranchisement.

Later, we see that French does indeed open up unprecedented possibilities for women. Particularly, it allowed for an evolution of the relationship between Djebar's parents, who became almost accomplices in love as Djebar's mother learnt French.

> After she had been married for a few years, my mother gradually learnt a little French . . .
>
> I don't know exactly when my mother began to say *"My husband* has come, my husband has gone out. . . . I'll ask *my husband,* etc. . .* ." Nevertheless, I can sense how much it cost her modesty to refer to my father in this way.
>
> It was as if a flood-gate had opened within her, perhaps in her relationship with her husband. Years later, during the summers we spent in her native town, when chatting in Arabic with her sisters or cousins, my mother would refer to him quite naturally by his name, even with a touch of superiority. . . .
>
> Years went by. As my mother's ability to speak French improved, while I was still a child of no more than twelve, I came to realize an irrefutable fact: namely that, in the face of all these womenfolk, my parents formed a couple. (Djebar 1993, 35–36)

Nevertheless, even as it brought the parents closer, French alienated Djebar's mother from "the womenfolk," with whom she could only chat in Arabic, and among whom her modesty always suffered. For by accessing French, Djebar's mother had moved away from full membership in the community of disempowered women and aligned herself, if only through her claim to be part of a couple, with a speaker and teacher of that alien and alienating language. Her use of the expression "my husband," like her referral to him by his first name, suggests an intimacy that is absent from common references among other women to their spouses, references such as the impersonal "him," or even "the enemy." Moreover, the implicit counterpart of "my husband," namely "my wife," identifies her in the position of individual partner, not merely one of the "womenfolk," a member of the harem with no particular claim to selfhood.

French, with its emancipatory associations, must have been equally alienating to the young Djebar. A 1939 photograph of her father's village school shows her as the only girl among forty-five boys. How can Djebar record the thoughts of people whose looks she recalls, but whose statements she only hypothesizes as future utterances? How then can she, writing in French, inscribe the experiences of the female neighbors who never stepped inside her father's school gates, never learned to read and write?

The mere fact of Djebar's being female cannot alone qualify her for the role of spokesperson for "the womenfolk." One must avoid the trap of essentializing women as biologically determined, even as one asserts that we express ourselves in a multitude of alternative ways. I maintain that our alternative modes of expression are a result of our socially constructed roles, which have historically relegated us to the margins of the social text, the official, hegemonic discourse. Yes, women can take liberties with language, and we have historically done so whenever we have sought to see ourselves represented in language. In various aspects of life, past and present, from the secular to the sacred, women have had to interpret, manipulate, and modify language, have had to transgress its rigidity, in order to secure ourselves a forum of expression, of representation.

Women have resorted to interpretation whenever statements were made that supposedly applied to all. Indeed, if language is to make sense to us at all, there must be more in it than Lacan's "word-to-word connection." The hegemonic, dominant discourse keeps us limber, increases our flexibility through the intense linguistic maneuvers we undertake to make it relate to our experiences as women. It is all the more so when that dominant discourse is twice removed from us, as foreign and colonizing.

Almost two decades before *Fantasia,* as she attempted to gain fluency in Arabic, Djebar had already confronted the traumatic realization that she had been schooled in the language of her alienation. A generation earlier, her mother, too, had suffered communally as she gained individually from her knowledge of French. Upon receiving a letter from her schoolteacher husband, for example, she was at once flattered and embarrassed; the French written word leaving her at a loss for words in spoken Arabic:

"He wrote his wife's name and the postman must have read it? Shame!
. . ."

"He could at least have addressed the card to his son, for the princi-ple of the thing, even if his son is only seven or eight!"

My mother did not reply. She was probably pleased, flattered even, but she said nothing. Perhaps she was suddenly ill at ease, or blushing from embarrassment; yes, her husband had written to her, in person! . . .

The murmured exchanges of these segregated women struck a faint chord with me, as a little girl with observing eyes. (Djebar 1993, 37–38)

The experiences of Djebar and her mother, a full generation apart, are similar in that both women can no longer express themselves fully in Ara-bic, as a direct consequence of their schooling in French, a schooling moreover conducted by a man. Yet what is most significant is that Djebar can still relate to that moment of embarrassment that her mother must have felt, although the immediate circumstances are themselves different. The mother had received a postcard written by a man, probably mention-ing what he has done while away from home, or relating some other su-perficial news about himself. The reception of such a postcard, naming her as the addressee, makes her so uncomfortable as to silence her socially, even as it pleases her personally. Djebar, on the other hand, is a woman seeking to record intimate feelings and experiences—an autobiography is essentially different from a postcard. She is the sender, not the recipient. Yet she too is frustrated by her familiarity with French. And it is this feel-ing of frustration that bridges the gap between her and her mother, and between her and the broader community of women whose unity was dis-rupted by imposition of the foreign language. Thus Djebar's writing, like that of many feminists, is a validation of sensual and intuitive knowledge, of a history passed down orally and through the body, for it is not to be found in the trivia reported by her father on his postcards, much less in the textbooks she read in French school.

In the above passage, Djebar recalls both the postcard and the segre-gated women's "murmured exchanges" surrounding it. Elsewhere, she continues to foreground women's voices, recovering them and reintro-ducing them into the historical narrative that had omitted to record them. Some of the interviews and oral narratives she had collected for *La nouba* are included in part 3 of *Fantasia,* "Voices from the Past," in several chapters each entitled "Voice." The resulting polyphony, while clearly not exhaustive, suggests the heterogeneity of the subaltern experiences, as it produces an echo effect with its myriad variations, its infinite repetitions.

Fantasia's many "voices" recount the experiences of women as individual agents, as well as members of the subjugated community. Thus one "voice" speaks up, only to fall silent again when her older brother seeks to shelter her from the brutality of death: "My elder brother Abdelkader came up behind me and suddenly said angrily to the others, 'Why did you show her the body? Can't you see she's only a child?' 'I saw him fall!' I said, turning round suddenly. 'Right in front of me!' And my voice gave way" (Djebar 1993, 121). Another "voice" gives the alarm as she hears French spoken and is quickly surrounded by death:

I could hear French spoken, not far away. I asked in surprise, "Who's speaking French?"

The old woman said, "One of our men, probably!"

"No," I replied. "You know perfectly well we're forbidden to speak French now."

I turned around to look and spied French soldiers. I gave the alarm, shouting, "Soldiers! Soldiers!"

I'd barely started running when the firing began. A child (some of the married women had children) had just got up and came tottering out first: a bullet hit him in the middle of the forehead and he fell down on the ground in front of me. (132)

In another episode, yet another "voice," having informed the freedom fighters about the impending arrival of French soldiers, must suffer for it: "When I got back from meeting with the Brothers, I found out in the village that the French were going to make a raid into the mountains. I had passed on the information. . . . And that's how I found myself facing the French officer! . . . This time they questioned me with electricity until . . . until I thought I'd die" (160–61).

Indeed, the voices resonate in the mountains, in the caves, coming from everywhere, inundating *Fantasia.* The pain of the victims becomes a primal scream, a powerful shudder, repeated ad infinitum. In this respect, it becomes irrelevant that the individual woman who uttered it has fallen, for the echo-like structure magnifies the voice, multiplying its call. The "wild collective voice" is heard by everyone, including those in charge of silencing it. Eugène Fromentin, a chronicler of the conquest of North Africa, records that breach of silence: "A heart-rending cry arose—I can still hear it as I write to you—then the air was rent with screams, then pandemonium broke loose" (quoted in Djebar 1993, xxii).

Djebar comments in *Fantasia* that none of the thirty-seven accounts of the 1830 siege of Algiers was written by a woman. The multitude of voices she herself cites in that novel helps remedy that silence. As Dorothy Blair points out in the introduction to the English translation: "The hero of the Algerian resistance to the French conquest was the legendary Sultan Abd al-Qadir, but the episodes which stand out here are those featuring the sufferings of women" (Djebar 1993, n.p.). *Fantasia* also functions as gazing back, as it opens with a scene of women looking out to the sea, watching the French armada approaching their shores. Here too, by foregrounding the women's physical presence in open space, she counters the masculinist blindness to women's presence at historical moments, and debunks the Orientalist myths that Arab women are always passive, always "absent": "I can imagine Hussein's wife neglecting her dawn prayer to climb up too to the terrace. How many other women, who normally only retreated to their terraces at the end of the day, must also have gathered there to catch a glimpse of the dazzling French fleet" (Djebar 1993, 8).

Despite its focus on women's experiences, *Fantasia* is not all oral and feminine history. It features episodes drawn from obscure archives, from letters by petty officers to their families in France, or from the private journals of the early colonizers, all punctuated by Djebar's own voice, in the autobiographical chapters, or by the voices of the numerous women she interviewed, the *porteuses de feu*, women who took part in the War of Liberation. While some sections show women as agents, others depict them as victims of utterly barbaric conquests: many had their hands and feet cut off by the French for their jewelry, thousands died in the fumigation of rebel tribes in the caves in which they had taken refuge. Significantly, none of the passages depicting women as victims is narrated by these women themselves. Rather, it is the male French gaze that sees them as such, symbolically stripping them of the agency they enact in the episodes featuring their own "voices." Djebar, bilingual and bicultural, fuses past French reports with contemporary Arabic narratives. By so doing, she belies the assertion that official (male/victor) reports are definitive, while oral (female/vanquished) narratives constitute at best a distant memory, to be ultimately obliterated by the "self-evident truth" of history books. Moreover, Djebar's subversive use of written/printed French to record those oral narratives renders that very language "feminine"—equivocal, ambivalent, ever evading closure.[4]

"Biffure," the last chapter in part 1, is a prime illustration of this *"écriture féminine,"* an exposition of intuitive knowledge and feelings, emphasizing the physical, her own body—not official documents—as the agent of continuation, and expression, of her kind. Djebar narrates her impressions upon entering the dark cave where a tribe had been obliterated. Visiting the site where her ancestors were killed ("fumigated") during the French conquest of Algeria, she experiences their agony gutturally: *"To read this writing, I must lean over backwards, plunge my face into the shadows, examine the vaulted roof of rock or chalk, lend an ear to the whispers that rise from time out of mind, study this geology stained red with blood. What magma of sounds lies rotting here? What stench of putrefaction seeps out? I grope about, my sense of smell aroused, my ears alert, in this rising tide of ancient pain. Alone, stripped bare, unveiled, I face the images of darkness. . . . And my body reverberates with sounds from the endless landslide of generations of my lineage"* (Djebar 1993, 46).

The undermining of the dominant discourse, French, is here rendered through Djebar's reading its reflection on the wall, a reflection read from right to left, as in Arabic: *"The flickering flames of successive fires form letters of French words, curiously elongated or expanded, against cave walls, tattooing vanished faces with a lurid mottling. . . . And for a fleeting moment I glimpse the mirror-image of the foreign inscription, reflected in Arabic letters, writ from right to left in the mirror of suffering"* (Djebar 1993, 46).

---

4. For an excellent discussion of Djebar's use of French for the purposes of "écriture féminine," see Ghaussy 1994.

The "Arabic" text that she senses in the dark tells a different story than that superscripted in French. It tells of a suffering that could not be articulated in French, nor even in the Arabic language, itself Symbolic, patriarchal as the culture it bespeaks, and which also seeks to relegate women to a position of passive recipient rather than active agent. Instead, it is with her body bent backwards, her bare face plunged in the shadows, that Djebar interprets the dark signs of the suffering, leaning over the memory of the victims, groping about, her ears alert, her sense of smell aroused. Her own literacy is of no avail—it is impossible to read in pitch darkness. But all her other senses are receptive to the cave's myriad messages. The counter-discourse she channels is multiple, as was the oppression. It "reads" in Arabic rather than French, it produces a mirror-image, that is, a negative/negating image, and it is transmitted through the body, site of feminine alterity.

The next "episode" of *Fantasia,* chapter 1 of part 2, is "official history," what Ranajit Guha, writing on "The Prose of Counter-Insurgency" in colonial India, has described as "primary discourse," explaining that "it is almost without exception official in character. . . . It was official also in so far as it was meant primarily for administrative use—for the information of government, for action on its part and for the determination of its policy" (1988, 7). Djebar, schooled in French and seeking to express the voices of the various participants in the Algerian revolution, does not fail to include the texts inscribed "from left to right," texts that the French officers wrote for their compatriots, explaining military strategy and logistics. These official texts, however, will never again read with the same aura of authority and/or objectivity, because of their juxtaposition with those that articulate and inscribe the screams of the victims. Her citing of the chroniclers is subversive in another way, for she reveals them to be affected by the sight of the massacred tribes, vulnerable to feelings of remorse, guilt, outrage at their own barbarism. They foster ambiguous feelings about the orders conveyed by the dominant discourse, undermining the very validity of that discourse, its claim to authority. Thus Pélissier, who was responsible for the fumigation of numerous tribes in the caves that Djebar visited, is shown as transformed by his contact with his own victims' corpses: "Smoke them out mercilessly, like foxes!" ordered

Bugeaud, and Pélissier obeyed: "That is what Bugeaud had written; Pélissier had obeyed, but when the scandal breaks in Paris, he does not divulge the order. He is a true officer; a model of *esprit du corps,* with a sense of duty; he respects the law of silence" (Djebar 1993, 70).

"The law of silence" could not, however, forever obscure the sinister sights Pélissier witnessed. Once again, bodies, even in their deaths, prove stronger than words, defeat attempts at official reporting, are turned over to the person most worthy of narrating their suffering: not the French male aggressor, but the Algerian female kin of the fumigated tribe:

> After Pélissier emerges from this promiscuous contact with the fumigated victims clad in their ashy rags, he makes his report which he intended to compose in official terms. But he is unable to do so; he has become for all time the sinister, the moving surveyor of these subterranean *medinas,* the quasi-fraternal embalmer of this tribe which would never bend the knee . . . Pélissier, speaking on behalf of this long drawn-out agony, on behalf of fifteen hundred corpses buried beneath El-Kantara, with their flocks unceasingly bleating at death, hands me his report and I accept this palimpsest on which I now inscribe the charred passion of my ancestors. (Djebar 1993, 79)

The scandalous official written reports were censored in Paris, but the bodies' eloquence still recounts Algeria's subterranean/subaltern stories, long after literal death. The cave is at once communal tomb, interring the massacred tribe, and life-giving womb, (re)birthing Djebar into her native community.

Another chronicler of the French massacres, Bosquet, is challenged by the sight of a woman's corpse: "Bosquet muses over the youth killed defending his sister . . . he recalls the anonymous woman whose foot had been hacked off, '*cut off for the sake of the khalkhal'* [ankle bracelet]. . . . Suddenly as he inserts these words, they prevent the ink of the whole letter from drying: because of the obscenity of the torn flesh that he could not suppress in his description" (Djebar 1993, 56). Flesh prevents the ink from drying, from formulating the definitive report of the conquest. Flesh allows Djebar to experience her culture's pain, as she assumes a cramped position inside the darkness of the womb-like cave. It also allows her to reverse the French script and frees her from the intellectual shackles the French language would have imposed on her. The wild, collective voice rings on, for "Writing does not silence the voice, but awakens it, above all to resurrect so many vanquished sisters" (204).

9 Voice, Representation, and Resistance
Etel Adnan's Sitt Marie Rose

LISA SUHAIR MAJAJ _____

The imagination's object is not simply to alter the external world, or to alter the human being in his or her full array of capacities and needs, but also and more specifically, to alter the power of alteration itself, to act on and continually revise the nature of creating.

—Elaine Scarry, *The Body in Pain*

Etel Adnan. *Photograph © Simone Fattal*

Etel Adnan, a poet, writer, and visual artist, was born in Beirut, Lebanon, in 1925 to a Muslim Syrian father and a Greek Christian mother. She studied philosophy at the Sorbonne in Paris, at the University of California at Berkeley, and at Harvard University, and taught philosophy of art at the Dominican College of San Rafael, California, for many years. She has also lectured widely at academic insti-
tutions throughout the United States and has exhibited her artwork through-out the United States, Europe, and the Middle East. Adnan's publications include Moonshots *(1966);* Five Senses for One Death *(1971);* Jebu Suivie de l'Express Beyrouth-Enfer *(1973);* Sitt Marie Rose *(1978);* l'Apocalypse Arabe *(1980);* From A to Z *(1982a);* Pablo Neruda Is a Banana Tree

200

(1982b); The Indian Never Had a Horse *(1985);* Journey to Mount Tamalpais *(1986);* The Spring Flowers Own & The Manifestations of the Voyage *(1990);* Of Cities and Women (Letters to Fawwaz) *(1993a);* Paris, When It's Naked *(1993b); and* There: In the Light and the Darkness of the Self and of the Other *(1997). Originally written in French,* Sitt Marie Rose *won the France-Pays Arabe Award in 1978 and has since been translated into English (1982), Arabic, Italian, Dutch, German, and Urdu. Adnan currently divides her time between the United States, France, and Lebanon.*

*S*itt Marie Rose, Lebanese/Arab-American writer Etel Adnan's novel about the 1975 Lebanese war, is well-known for its critique of Lebanon's social and political conditions during the war and for its strong feminist analysis.[1] The novel, which occupies a significant position in the emerging canon of Arab feminist literature, offers particular insight into the intersection of gendered, political, sectarian, class-based, and colonial hierarchies of power in Lebanon. As critic Thomas Foster notes, *Sitt Marie Rose* posits "the writing of the gendered body as crucial for understanding recent Lebanese history," charting the pivotal role of "women's ideological repression within the political struggles of national formation, religious affiliation, and ethnic identities" (Foster 1995, 60, 67). As both the first novel to be published on the Lebanon war and a landmark Arab feminist text, *Sitt Marie Rose* demonstrates the necessity of situating Arab feminism within its political contexts.

In conjunction with this sociopolitical critique, however, *Sitt Marie Rose* also functions on a self-reflexive textual level, using its own narrative form and thematic content to raise questions about the efficacy of artistic representation in challenging structures of oppression and about the role

1. First published in French by Des Femmes (Paris, 1978), *Sitt Marie Rose* was translated into English by Georgina Kleege and published by Post-Apollo Press in 1982. All references herein are to the 1982 English translation and are reprinted with permission. I am grateful to Deborah Najor, Julie Olin-Ammentorp, Therese Saliba, Ranu Samantrai, and Paula Sunderman for commenting on versions of this chapter.

of the artist in resisting injustice and violence. On its most fundamental level, the novel affirms the possibility of challenging oppressive power and suggests that artistic representation may play a significant role in such resistance. It thus functions as a "resistance" text (see Harlow 1987), a text that seeks to expose, challenge, and transform structures of oppression. At the same time, however, *Sitt Marie Rose* also makes clear that representation is inscribed within, and may become complicit with, structures of oppressive power. This tension between resistance and complicity is encapsulated most clearly in the novel's portrayal of articulation: the act of voicing, and hence representing, oneself or others. While the novel insists on the necessity of speaking out against oppression even within contexts of powerlessness, it also demonstrates the complexities inherent in trying to give voice to and depict subaltern experience.

Articulation, *Sitt Marie Rose* makes clear, functions as a fundamental vehicle of agency, understood as the ability to affirm the self and to take action in the world. Central to the novel's exploration of resistance and its complexities are themes of communication and failed communication, voicelessness and speech. The silencing of the powerless is dramatized in *Sitt Marie Rose* in several ways: metaphorically, through the political voicelessness of women, laborers, and other subalterns; literally, through the physical voicelessness of the "deaf-mute" children (who function in the novel as representative subalterns); and pragmatically, through the interrogation, torture, and execution of the protagonist, Marie Rose. But although it champions resistance, the novel suggests that such silencing cannot simply be challenged by speaking out on behalf of the voiceless, because articulation is caught up in the problematics of representation: in particular, the tension between speaking for the "other" and empowering the "other" to speak for herself.

These tensions are particularly acute in resistance literature, in which the need to speak out on behalf of the oppressed is complicated by the hierarchies of power implicit in such representation. Resistance literature, in Barbara Harlow's definition, is a "category of literature that emerged significantly as part of the organized national liberation struggles and resistance movements in Africa, Latin America, and the Middle East" (1987, xvii). "The term 'resistance,' " Harlow notes, "was first applied in a description of Palestinian literature in 1966 by the Palestinian writer and critic Ghassan Kanafani in his study *Literature of Resistance in Occupied Palestine: 1948–1966*" (2). Given the difficult contexts within which such writing arises, resistance literature "insists on the historical reality and consequences of works of literature and their specific place in the events of the world which they transcribe" (111). Frequently testimonial in nature, resistance texts use literary forms to expose specific social and political conditions, to suggest alternatives to these conditions, and to elicit responsive action from their readers. They provide counter-narratives through which subaltern voices may be heard or represented, and put forward alternative political perspectives. As a result of this focus on communicating suppressed narratives and empowering subaltern voices, through which the literary act of testifying to oppression, or "writing human rights," is crucially linked to political intervention, or "righting political wrongs" (Harlow 1992, 244, 256), articulation plays a central role in resistance texts. However, this link between "writing" and "righting" situations of oppression is complicated by the difficulties of narration and by the complexities inherent in the multilayered act of representation. Among these complexities is the unequal relationship between, on the one hand, writers/artists, who possess access to modes and forums of production, and on the other hand, subaltern subjects of representation, who are rescued from silence through another's narration or artistic mediation. While Adnan's novel affirms the need to speak out against oppression, it also provides a self-reflexive critique of the representational modes through which such articulation may be achieved.

On the narrative level, *Sitt Marie Rose* offers a fictionalized account of the outbreak of the Lebanese war in 1975 and of the abduction and murder by Christian Lebanese militiamen of an actual person, Marie Rose Boulos, a Christian Syrian-Lebanese woman active in organizing social services among Palestinian refugees in Beirut (Harlow 1987, 110). Divided into two sections, "Time I: A Million Birds" and "Time II: Marie Rose," the novel explores the possibilities of resisting oppressive power within the context of intersecting "circles of oppression" and "circles of repression" (Adnan 1982c, 104), featuring female protagonists who seek to challenge, whether on their own behalf or on behalf of others, the boundaries that confine them. "Time I: A Million Birds," written from the perspective of an unnamed first-person female narrator, depicts Lebanon at the outbreak of the 1975 war, situating both the war's violence and Lebanon's social and political hierarchies within the context of its colonial legacy. This section portrays the narrator's failed attempt to collaborate with her friend Mounir, one of a group of wealthy Christian Lebanese men with a penchant for hunting, on a film that she hopes will give voice to the problems of Syrian migrant laborers in Beirut. The section thereby introduces both the problem of representing subaltern subjects and the question of the relationship between artistic representation and political/social resistance. "Time II" depicts the capture and execution of Marie Rose, a childhood friend of Mounir, as narrated through the voices of seven characters: Marie Rose herself, her captors (Mounir, his friends Fouad and Tony, and the priest Bouna Lias), the collective voice of the "deaf-mute" children whom Marie Rose teaches, and the narrator from "Time I," who functions in "Time II" as an omniscient observer. As if in answer to the questions raised in "Time I" about how subalterns may be represented, "Time II" presents the transgressive figure of Marie Rose, who, as a teacher of "deaf-mute" children, empowers silenced subalterns to find their own voices and modes of communication. In contrast to the insular group definitions that her captors seek to uphold through violence, Marie Rose challenges the rigid binaries of gender, nationality, sect, and class, grounding her resistance to oppression in an engagement with difference. Yet although "Time II" posits Marie Rose as a heroic figure, this section also makes clear the difficulty of achieving individual resistance within situations of unequal power. Read in conjunction, the novel's two sections suggest a framework of interpretation through which art as a mode of political activism is affirmed even while its limitations are acknowledged.

As the narration of a "true" story, *Sitt Marie Rose* provides the occasion for a discussion of the Lebanese war that moves beyond the binarisms of religion to a more complex analysis of the various factors contributing to the violence. This discussion is situated within a critique of the problems facing the Arab world—problems portrayed as stemming from an inability to articulate (speak about, give voice to, make connections between) the oppressive and repressive forces that situate individuals.

"Voice" thus emerges as a central concern of the novel, both metaphorically and thematically. Indeed, the narrator asserts in "Time II" that the "illness" troubling the Arab world, depicted here as a patient, is the inability to speak: the illness is "not the blood clogging his [the patient's] throat but the words, the words, the swamp of words that have been waiting there for so long" (Adnan 1982c, 100). The novel's attention to issues of voice is similarly evident through its portrayal of characters who are literally or symbolically voiceless—the "deaf-mute" children, Syrian migrant laborers, women—and through narrative strategies such as the direct interior monologues of "Time II." However, this focus on voice is situated within a narrative framework that not only raises questions about the possibility of achieving subaltern articulation, but also opens its own narrative project to scrutiny.

Representation may be understood both as artistic/linguistic depiction and as the process by which an individual is spoken for (represented) in a political context. At stake in the representational process is the relationship between articulation/expression and agency: between the ability to speak, whether for oneself or others, and to take action in the world. This relationship is the subject of Elaine Scarry's meditative study *The Body in Pain: The Making and Unmaking of the World*. Scarry examines the ways in which language serves as "a consistent affirmation of the human being's capacity to move out beyond the boundaries of his or her own body into the external, shareable world" (1985, 5), and the extent to which situations of violence destroy this capacity for self-extension. While linguistic expression both results in and reflects an expansion of the self into the world, violence and pain lead to the "contraction of the universe down to the immediate vicinity of the body . . . bringing about an immediate reversion to a state anterior to language, to the sounds and cries a human being makes before language is learned" (4). In other words, violence enacts a schism between body and voice, reducing the individual to aversive embodiment while simultaneously stripping the subject of his or her voice.

One particularly concrete example of such a schism occurs in situations of torture and interrogation, such as that undergone by Marie Rose in Adnan's novel. In such contexts, the voice of the dominated victim is not only silenced but is, in fact, taken over by the interrogator. The domination of the prisoner "both in physical acts and verbal acts" means that "the prisoner's ground become[s] increasingly physical and the torturer's increasingly verbal, that the prisoner become[s] a colossal body with no voice and the torturer a colossal voice (a voice composed of two voices) with no body, that eventually the prisoner experience[s] himself exclusively in terms of sentience and the torturer exclusively in terms of self-extension" (Scarry 1985, 57). This bifurcation of body and voice is taken to its furthest extension in the act of execution, in which the prisoner is permanently silenced, leaving the power of articulation and representation in the hands of the executioner.

But the schism between body and voice is not limited to situations of overt violence. Rather, it is characteristic of situations of oppressive power relations more generally. Indeed, Scarry asserts, a political situation "is almost by definition one in which the two locations of selfhood (body and voice) are in a skewed relation to one another or have wholly split apart and have begun to work, or be worked, against one another." As a result, "power is in its fraudulent as in its legitimate forms always based on distance from the body" (Scarry 1985, 37, 46). This schism between body and voice may be seen in a variety of situations defined by unequal power. For instance, in patriarchal gender relations, women are reduced to emotionality and the body while men are viewed as rational agents of culture and intellect. In class relations the working class is associated with physicality while the upper class is defined in terms of intellectual activity. In race relations, people of color are stereotyped in bodily, often sexualized terms, while white people are rarified as the "standard bearers of civilization." In all of these situations, articulation is associated with the dominant group, silent embodiment with the subordinate group.

Such schisms of power are evident throughout *Sitt Marie Rose*. In "Time I," for instance, Syrian laborers, women, and Lebanese civilians are silenced and reduced to aversive embodiment by poverty, patriarchal oppression, and the violence of war. Meanwhile, in "Time II" the correlation between silencing and embodiment is exemplified through the powerless "deaf-mute" children and through Marie Rose herself, whose heroic attempt to speak out on behalf of the voiceless is foreclosed by her brutal execution. Although both the children and Marie Rose "speak" within the context of the novel, and indeed achieve their agency primarily through articulation, their speech is only possible within the discursive parameters of the text, and is represented through pragmatically "impossible" interior monologues. The novel thus provides structural as well as thematic acknowledgement of the difficulties inherent in achieving articulation in contexts of oppressive power.

Such difficulties, Adnan makes clear, circumscribe the possibilities of agency. Agency involves both self-affirmation and action in the world; it requires the capacity for protecting the embodied self from physical domination, and the capacity for self-representation (the verbal extension of the self into the world, and the corresponding assertion/extension of the self as subject within a political realm). These two capacities are aptly combined in the metaphor of "voice"—a term which, like agency, involves both a physical dimension (the vocal nature of speech) and a representational dimension (the metaphorical role of voice in representing the self). The centrality of voice to agency is particularly clear in the political realm, where, Scarry argues, power depends on the capacity for articulation, and more specifically on "the power of self-description" (1985, 279), and where the failure to achieve articulation leads to a failure of agency. Indeed, Scarry asserts, "the relative ease or difficulty with which any given phenomenon can be *verbally represented* also influences the ease or difficulty with which that phenomenon comes to be *politically represented*" (12).

Given this linkage between articulation and political power, "voice" takes on great significance in projects of subaltern resistance, often becoming a metaphor for agency itself. Indeed, implicit in many resistance texts is the suggestion that the subaltern is able to transcend her location through the fact of articulation alone—that the act of speech is in and of itself a revolutionary act. As Sidonie Smith and Julia Watson comment, "For the colonial [or marginalized] subject, the process of coming to writing is . . . a charting of the conditions that have historically placed her identity under erasure" (1992, xx). Articulation thus becomes "a process and a product of decolonization" (xxi). Similarly, "giving voice to the voiceless"—through testimonials meant to convey the sufferings of the common people with no access to literature—is often a central goal of resistance texts. However, what is often inadequately acknowledged in such projects is the problematic role of power—for no matter how liberatory the intention, to speak on behalf of others is implicitly to participate in the same power structures that make it possible for some people to speak while others are spoken for. Gayatri Spivak's essay "Can the Subaltern Speak?" provides one of the best-known discussions of the problematic underlying subaltern articulation and representation of the subaltern. In this essay Spivak calls for a critique of the "transparent" role that intellectuals (and by extension, all who seek to represent subaltern subjects) play in the constitution of subaltern subjectivity. In their discussions of "the nonrepresented" subaltern subject, Spivak argues, intellectuals are "complicit in the persistent constitution of Other as the Self's shadow" (1994, 74–75). However, intellectuals nonetheless play a necessary role in facilitating the voice of subaltern subjects who otherwise would disappear "between . . . subject-constitution and object-formation." Even if "there is no space from which the sexed subaltern subject can speak," Spivak points out, intellectuals have "a circumscribed task" to fulfill—that of speaking to the subaltern subject at the same time as they critique their "institutional privileges of power" (102–4, 75).

This complex relationship between power, agency, and articulation informs Adnan's literary project of testimony and empowerment. Implicit in the act of representation is not only a power differential between representer and represented, but also a tension between the represented subject's inner voice/reality and the image/expression of this reality—between what Rey Chow calls "the politics of the image," a politics that is "conducted on surfaces," and a corresponding politics of authenticity—of "depths, hidden truths, and inner voices" (1993, 29). While articulation is presumed to emanate directly from the speaking subject, and hence is granted authenticity and immediacy, representation (whether visual, textual, or political) of necessity functions at a remove from this immediacy. Attempts to give voice to subaltern subjectivity frequently falter over this tension between self-expression and representation. In *Sitt Marie Rose* these dynamics of power and privilege are brought to the foreground through the role of the narrator and her relationship to various "others" in the text. The narrator appears to share a number of characteristics with both Marie Rose and Adnan herself, including gender, class, nationality, and postcolonial background. Moreover, all three women "speak" not only for themselves but also for others positioned as silenced subalterns: Syrian laborers, "deaf-mute" children, women victimized by the intersecting forces of patriarchy and militaristic violence, civilians caught in the war's violence. The narrative functions to rescue Marie Rose's voice from the silence of death, thereby challenging her captors' consolidation of power and articulation. At the same time, it empowers not just Marie Rose's voice, but also the voices of both the narrator and Adnan herself. And while these narrative voices insist on the necessity of testimony as a mode of resistance, the complex positions of intertwined power and powerlessness from which they emerge both facilitate and complicate the possibilities of articulation as a mode of resistance.

These subject positions are grounded in the postcolonial contradictions that inform Adnan's writing, artwork, and personal life. Born in Lebanon to a Syrian Muslim father and a Greek Christian mother, Adnan spoke Greek and Turkish as a child, and is fluent in French (her first language of composition), English (the language of her most recent texts), and Arabic (the "language," she has stated, of her paintings).[2] She currently resides at different times of the year in the United States, France, and Lebanon. As a child in Lebanon, Adnan was subjected to the French educational system imposed on Lebanon under the colonial mandate, "a system of education totally conforming to . . . schools in France, an education which had nothing to do with the history and the geography of the children involved" (Adnan 1990a, 7). As a result, Adnan has said, she grew up "thinking that the world was French. And that everything that

2. A visual artist as well as a writer, Adnan creates paintings, drawings, calligraphy, and tapestry designs, in addition to publishing poetry, fiction, and nonfiction prose. In an interview with Hilary Kilpatrick, Adnan said, "In 1960 I began to paint, and I heard myself say out loud, 'I paint in Arabic!' At that moment my soul was at peace, as if I'd been given the answer to an important problem" (Kilpatrick 1985, 119). Adnan's work often crosses over between visual and textual artistic mediums, as if to probe the limitations of representational forms and to interrogate the relationship between form and meaning. This is perhaps most evident in *The Arab Apocalypse,* in which graphic symbols are used to convey meaning at the boundaries where language breaks down.

mattered, that was 'in books,' or had authority (the nuns), did not concern our environment" (7). The implications of this legacy of alienation are evident in Adnan's own distance from the Arabic language, which she was forbidden to speak in school. Indeed, *Sitt Marie Rose* was written not in Arabic, but in French, and the novel was first published in France. This use of the language of the colonizer to portray the experiences of the colonized situates Adnan's authorial voice in complex relation to the Arab readers—themselves often French-speaking—to whom, and for whom, she attempts to speak.

Such complexity of identification and location leads to a stance paralleling what Rosi Braidotti has called "nomadic" subjectivity—a "kind of critical consciousness that resists settling into socially coded modes of thought and behavior" and that functions as "a form of political resistance to hegemonic and exclusionary views of subjectivity" (1994, 5, 23). In childhood, Adnan writes, she "got used to standing between situations, to being a bit marginal and still a native, to getting acquainted with notions of truth which were relative" (1990a, 11). This childhood experience of moving between cultural and religious backgrounds, like her adult experience of traveling between Lebanon, France, and the United States, undergirds a stance of identification that is fluid and adaptive. And indeed, Adnan suggests, despite its difficulties, a marginal stance has its uses, among which is the ability to interrogate structures of power. (As she observes in *Paris, When It's Naked*, "People from the Third World are better at seeing through [mainstream media manipulation of information]; for them it's a matter of survival. Citizens from dominant countries fool themselves by thinking that they don't need to know: that's the beginning of the beginning of their downfall" [Adnan 1993b, 60].) However, as Elspeth Probyn has cautioned, "the recognition that the subaltern works across her positioning does not immediately entail a form of free agency" (quoted in Kaplan 1994, 149). A marginal stance may yield insights but not the power to act upon them. Moreover, marginalized subjects also run the risk of becoming implicated in the structures of power that situate and constrain them. Indeed, in *Paris, When It's Naked* Adnan openly acknowledges the ways in which she is simultaneously marginalized from, resistant to, and yet drawn by French culture: "Paris is beautiful. Claude can say it innocently. It's harder for me to say so, it's also more poignant. It tears me apart. Paris is the heart of a lingering colonial power, and that knowledge goes to bed with me every night" (1993b, 7).

Such tensions are central to *Sitt Marie Rose*, in which the contradictions of postcolonial identity are critiqued by female protagonists who are themselves caught in these contradictions. Although both the narrator and Marie Rose attempt to speak out against repression and oppression, whether their own or that of others, they are not able to disrupt the hierarchies of power that situate them as at once privileged and subordinate. Critically aware of the ways in which colonialism has constituted the modern Lebanese subject, they are nonetheless implicated in the hierarchies of value and power that situate them as upper-class, Christian, educated women, and that view them as "Western" and "modern." This location and identification empowers their articulation even while it circumscribes their attempts at resistance.

The problem of speaking from a marginalized position is first addressed in "Time I: A Million Birds." This section evokes situations of victimization and silencing, drawing implicit parallels between the birds shot down by hunters wielding machine guns, civilians slaughtered in the war, women subordinated by patriarchal structures, and exploited, objectified migrant laborers. Although the narrator of "Time I" offers sardonic insights into Lebanese gender relations and postcolonial subject positions, and stunned testimony to the ravages of war, she is unable to take significant action against the prevailing ideologies and perversions of power. Notwithstanding the narrator's efforts to challenge both her own silencing as a woman and the exploitation of the Syrian laborers Mounir plans to film, "Time I" traces the breakdown of both agency and articulation. This breakdown is made clear in the narrator's failure to assert her own voice in the film project, in the difficulties she faces in attempting to narrate the war's violence, and in her own retreat to inaction in the face of the violence.

"Time I" is structured around two films: the hunting film that opens the section and the film that Mounir proposes to make with the narrator. These films serve as a lens through which the dichotomies of power underlying Lebanon's social and political contexts are brought into focus.

The most obvious dichotomy operative here is that of gender, reflected in the masculinization of power. Mounir's hunting film opens with images of hunters "aim[ing] their rifles toward the sky like missile launchers," showing "their teeth, their vigor, their pleasure" (Adnan 1982c, 2). As the birds fall, "All their faces glow. Except Fouad's. . . . He suffers from never having killed enough. . . . Fouad hunts as though obsessed. He prefers killing to kissing" (2). As these interwoven phallic and militaristic resonances suggest, underlying the hunters' hypermasculinity is reliance upon force and a strategic maintenance of gendered oppositions, with their concomitant power differentials. Thus, to the women who watch his film Mounir comments disparagingly, "You didn't see anything, really. . . . I can't tell you what the desert is. You have to see it. Only you women, you'll never see it" (4). Positioning himself as a privileged possessor of knowledge by virtue of his masculinity, Mounir seeks to keep power— whether gendered or representational—firmly within his locus of control.

The film Mounir proposes to make with the narrator similarly functions as a means of asserting his gendered, sectarian, and class authority. Mounir intends this film to stand as a monument to his commercial success, his artistic vision, and his patronizing view of the Syrians, whom he views as pastoral but primitive. His perspective on the film as an aesthetic and commercial project with no responsibility to external facts or to their political implications subsumes the voices of those he seeks to represent under his own. Similarly, although Mounir invites the narrator to write the screenplay, he co-opts her voice and agency, making it clear that he will control the final product and its message. "It will be my film," he tells her. "I just want to make it with you" (Adnan 1982c, 4). To her suggestion that the film explore the actual lives of Syrian laborers, he retorts, "No, no. You don't understand. You'll write the script. I'll make the film" (7).

Mounir's exclusion of the female narrator from the domain of agency, and his appropriation of her voice as a function of his own, is paralleled by the general silencing of women throughout this section. Of the women in "Time I," only the narrator actually speaks, and she voices her ironic critique not directly to Mounir, but indirectly, to the reader. Meanwhile, the narrator makes no verbal protest to Mounir's positioning of her as a helpmate rather than as an active partner on his film project. Despite her feminist perspective, her subversive commentary, and her admission of the role she herself plays in her silencing, she too is circumscribed by her female status. In response to Mounir's claim that the women will never be able to really see the desert, she admits, "It's true. We 'women' were happy with this little bit of imperfect, colored cinema, which gave, for twenty minutes, a kind of additional prestige to these men we see every day. In this restrictive circle, the magic these males exert is once again reinforced. Everybody plays at this game" (Adnan 1982c, 4).

Such silencing and self-silencing are not simply a function of gender, however. Rather, they indicate the broader difficulty of achieving articulation within contexts of hierarchical power. The images that open the book, like the gendered metaphors that inform the text as a whole (Beirut as a raped woman, Marie Rose as a bird shot down by hunters, Lebanon as a woman drawn and quartered), emphasize the gendered aspects of oppression. However, the novel also moves beyond a simple linkage between male sexual aggression and violence to a broader critique of binary power structures, exemplified through religion, sect, class, nationality, and colonial relations. Within this critique, hierarchies of gender are inflected by the postcolonial context that situates Arabs more generally. Thus, for instance, the conflation of masculinity and violence evident in Mounir's hunting film reflects not only anxiety about gendered roles, but also a fundamental anxiety about Lebanese identity in the context of internalized colonial structures. As the narrator notes, "Before, it was the Europeans with faces like the ones we saw on the screen, who went hunting in Syria and Iraq, and elsewhere. Now it's the Christian, modernized Lebanese who go wherever they like with their touristo-military gear. They bring their cameras to film their exploits, their puttees, their shoes, their shorts, their buttons and zippers, their open shirts and their black hair showing" (Adnan 1982c, 3).

As this passage suggests, the hunters' construction of masculine identity through dominance over bodies (female and animal) and tools (cars, guns, and cameras) is embedded within the lingering structures of colonial relations that situate the Lebanese Christians at the site of conflicting locations of power and oppression, at once dominated (by the French colonial legacy) and dominant (in relations with Muslim Lebanese, Syrian laborers, and Palestinians). Although Mounir insists that he "loves" Syria, his education in French colonial schools is predicated on a denial of his Arab identity. Like other Christian Lebanese, Mounir and his friends were "taught by Jesuits who oriented them toward Paris and the quarrels of the French kings" (Adnan 1982c, 47). As a result of this early education, they longed to be "European" and "dream[ed] of a Christianity with helmets and boots, riding its horses into the clash of arms, spearing Moslem footsoldiers like so many St. Georges with so many dragons" (47). The dilemma posed by this orientation is summed up in a childhood anecdote recalled by Marie Rose. Seeing Mounir dressed up like a Crusader to march in a procession, she tells him, "You come from here. . . . You don't come from France or England. You could never be a Crusader." In response, Mounir asks sadly, "Then what am I going to become?" (48). Mounir's identification with Crusader imagery and with Europe, Christianity, and the West—an identification representative of the Lebanese Maronites more generally—provides the underpinnings of Mounir's political identity. From this perspective, Lebanese identity is predicated upon the establishment of clear boundaries between Christian and Muslim, East and West, Lebanese and Palestinian, "civilized" and "primitive"—and upon the implicit relocation of the Christian Lebanese to the "Western" side of the divide. The war simply accentuates this desire for decisive boundaries; as Mounir asserts, "It will be clean and definitive. There will be a victor and a vanquished, and we'll be able to talk, to reconstruct the country from a new base" (33).

As Kaja Silverman has noted, "It is by now a theoretical truism that hegemonic colonialism works by inspiring in the colonized subject the desire to assume the identity of his or her colonizers" (1989, 3). In Adnan's depiction, this desire is evidenced through the hunters' attempt to internalize not just the colonizer's identity but also the colonizer's modes of expression and representation: in particular, filmmaking and photography. Their cameras act as emblems of representational power, enabling them to refute the identity of "native" and to claim instead the identity of tourist, militarist, photographer, voyeur. However, this gesture only serves to highlight their inscription within colonial relationships of power. By filming themselves, the hunters associate themselves with modern (read:

Western) modes of representation, yet simultaneously acknowledge their status as mute objects of this representation. Although they replace the "European . . . faces" that once dominated the screen, their representational power is only possible in relationship to other Arabs; as even Mounir admits, "a young Syrian in Beirut, it's like us in Paris" (Adnan 1982c, 3, 6). Their attempts to identify as both European *and* Arab can only be enacted at the expense of those who more unambiguously occupy a subordinate role. Thus, for instance, in discussing the film that he wishes to make with the narrator, Mounir views the Syrians as "naturally" pastoral, primitive, and silent, while the Christian Lebanese are just as "naturally" assumed to be modern, European, articulate, and possessed of representational, social, and political power. As he tells the narrator, "I want to make [the film] from the point of view of the hunters. They're proud of their superiority. . . . I want to show how happy [the villagers] are in those Syrian villages, what wisdom they had there, how integrated they are with Nature" (6, 8). Furthermore, in a comment that makes clear the violence underlying these hierarchies, Mounir conflates European identity with modern weaponry: "You see, before it was foreigners, now it's we who represent all that's modern. . . . The power of our guns was unimaginable to them" (5).

Mounir's film project participates in what Johannes Fabian describes, in *Time and the Other*, as a "discourse which construes the Other in terms of distance, spatial and temporal" (Fabian 1983, xi). Within this discursive framework, the distance between Western and non-Western subjects is measured temporally as well as geographically and culturally, with the "other" situated outside of the space of modernity that defines the observer. For Mounir, the Syrian villages with "everything made of earth, everything golden in the sun" and "the people . . . very simple, very hospitable, not at all ruined" represent both a pastoral innocence and an indicator of how far he and other Lebanese Christians have traveled toward "modern," "Western" identity. It is only with the arrival of the Lebanese, Mounir suggests, that the Syrians can escape their state of "pastoral innocence" and enter the "modern" world—the world of change. Describing his planned film, he states, "I go back more than once to this Syrian village. Each time they recognize us, and each time they have changed"

(Adnan 1982c, 6). Construing Arab culture as Muslim, Muslims as backwards, and both Muslims and Arabs as outside the space of modernity occupied by the Christian Lebanese, Mounir sets up a framework of postcolonial identity that is dependent upon colonial as well as patriarchal models of identity formation. In particular, he draws on what Barbara Harlow terms "cultural paradigms of the colonized as either prelapsarian innocents or unschooled ignorants, the most 'deserving' among whom still await tutoring by their more politically advanced, 'developed' colonizers" (1992, 37). Much as the women watching Mounir's hunting film provide a backdrop against which the hunters construct their sense of masculinity, the Syrian villages provide a backdrop against which Mounir can articulate his own "modernity" and "Europeanness" while also laying claim to the cultural "authenticity" that the Syrian villages offer. As Thomas Foster observes, "Mounir's film resolves his contradictory desire both to participate in the European narrative of modernity and to narrate Lebanon's 'return' to a precolonial condition of autonomous national identity that never actually existed since the boundaries of Lebanon were artificially imposed by the French" (1995, 61).

But as the narrator realizes, the predication of subjecthood upon intersecting oppositions between Syrian and Lebanese, female and male, East and West, primitive and civilized depends upon the silencing and subordination of those with less power. Whether as representatives of backwardness or symbols of pastoral innocence, the Syrians do not function as agents in their own right; rather, they emerge as mute emblems of Mounir's projected desires. This silencing bothers the narrator, whose sense of affinity with the voiceless is informed by her own experience with the ways in which patriarchal social structures silence women. In contrast to Mounir, who plans to portray silent images of beautiful desert skies and happy peasants, the narrator wants to give voice to the concerns of the marginalized and to represent the individual lives and suffering behind these images. "This film should say something," she argues. "These people have problems, their own lives. There's something very important to be said" (Adnan 1982c, 7). While Mounir believes it is possible to make a "nonpolitical" film, the narrator's insistence on the importance of speaking for the subaltern and the silenced makes claims for the moral and political role of art. Moreover, in contrast to Mounir, who is unwilling to let the material reality of the Syrians' lives jostle his preconceived ideas, the narrator seeks to ground her representation of the Syrians in actual facts. "Find me two or three construction sites," she says, "where I can go to familiarize myself with the life of Syrian workers in Lebanon" (6–7).

Despite her politically engaged stance, however, the narrator's role in the film project raises questions not only about the political efficacy of artistic representation, but also about her own subject position within a world structured by power relations, in which no location is entirely innocent. Despite her insights into gendered and postcolonial identities and relationships, her own position within the society of wealthy Lebanese complicates her attempt to speak on behalf of others, and ultimately undercuts her ability to levy an effective social and political critique. This position becomes particularly clear when she attempts to interview the Syrians for the film. The seasonal laborers she seeks out at construction sites are, in her description, "small, supple, muscular, shy, furtive, and above all, silent" (Adnan 1982c, 10). They are spoken to by the contractor at the site, who "arrives in superb and enormous cars," as if they are "beasts of burden who go on two legs only because the narrowness of the stairways makes it impossible to go on four" (10). Within the context of this disparity of wealth and poverty, power and vulnerability, the narrator's own identity as an educated, well-off Christian Lebanese involved in the arts, and her relationship to the poor, uneducated migrant workers she hopes to represent, stand as an unaddressed problem. Arriving at the construction site, the narrator expects to find them willing to speak openly to her about their situation, and is frustrated by their reticence:

> I try to get them talking. They refuse. According to them everything is always all right. At noon they sit on the ground, even in the dirt, as they did in their villages. A little cement mixes with their food. At night they sleep on the story where they are working. . . . When it rains it's the same. They remain riveted to their places in the wind and the wet and wait for it to end. . . . If a stone needs to be raised ten stories, it goes on foot. That's all.
>
> I talk to them about their village. They say it's back there. Very far.

Beirut is very nice. . . . Do they like the Lebanese? Of course, they say.
They're our brothers. They're just more advanced. They have big cars
and beautiful houses.

When I tell Mounir that there is nothing to be had here but the circles under the eyes, the bent backs, the sorrow, the infernal noise of the
cement mixers, the sun that beats, and the rain that gnaws, and that it
could all be said very briefly with a few big images and nothing more,
he's disappointed. His film, decidedly, turns around nothing. (Adnan
1982c, 10–11)

Notwithstanding the narrator's ironic awareness of the constraints on the
Syrians' self-representation—clearly everything is *not* "always all right"—
the ambiguity of her concluding comment, that the film turns around
"nothing," is telling. On some level the narrator appears frustrated with
the laborers for failing to cooperate in the representation of their suffering. But like the "deaf-mute" children of "Time II," the Syrians are voiceless not because they have nothing to say, but because they do not have
access to dominant languages and modes of representation. Moreover, as
economically vulnerable workers they are, unsurprisingly, reluctant to
voice complaints to a strange woman at their work site. But these issues are
not addressed by the narrator, despite her earlier recognition of both the
ways in which power silences and the ways in which the powerless may participate in their own silencing. Failing to acknowledge in the laborers'
withheld articulation the complex relationship between political, social,
economic, and representational power, and frustrated at their apparent inability to provide the material she needs for the film, she appears to accept
their silence at face value.

Underlying this response are the narrator's implicit views on political
engagement, representation, and agency—views that in some ways repli-
cate rather than challenge existing power relationships. For instance, despite her wish that the film should serve the role of empowering the
voiceless, the narrator's expectation that the Syrians will cooperate with
her plans is based on the implicit view that their agency will be made possible through her own articulation—in other words, that she will give
voice to them. This privileging of her own voice over theirs is made appar-

ent at the level of narrative, as the narrator distills the laborers' voices into her own discourse rather than reporting their actual dialogue. Implicitly portraying them as silent victims, rather than as subjects whose lack of self-articulation is due to the material workings of power, she concludes that "there is nothing to be had here" but the "big images" of mute bodily suffering: "the circles under the eyes, the bent backs . . . the sun that beats, and the rain that gnaws" (Adnan 1982c, 11). But by thrusting the laborers into the role of timeless, suffering peasants instead of agents in the modern world, such depiction replicates in striking ways the schism between body and voice described by Scarry as characteristic of situations of unequal power. Although the narrator wants to represent the laborers' plight, her attempt founders not only on her inability to create conditions under which their articulation might become possible, but also on her failure to analyze the implications of her own position of privilege and power. As a result her stance, however principled, bears an uncomfortable resemblance to that of Mounir, for whom the Syrians are nothing more than a projection of his own assumptions.

These complexities of voice and representation take on greater resonance because they are played out against the backdrop of the war's outbreak, a context that brings to crisis the problem of agency and articulation more generally. While the war reinscribes power along lines of gender, situating men at the center of violent interactions and pushing women back into traditional female realms, it also forces the narrator to confront not only her own helplessness but also her own desire for power and her capacity for violence. "I understood this need for violence one day in front of an electric wire torn from its socket," she admits. "In the two holes there remained two little bits of brilliant copper wire which seemed to call out to me. And I wanted to touch them, to reunite them in my hand, to make that current pass through my body, and see what it was like to burn. I resisted only with an extraordinary effort" (Adnan 1982c, 13). Although she struggles to find a way of opposing the war's brutality, the only recourse she can imagine is a different form of violence. "I tell myself that it would be better to let loose a million birds in the sky over Lebanon," she says, "so that these hunters could practice on them, and this carnage could be avoided" (17).

The narrator's inscription into, and inability to intervene in, structures of violence is similarly reflected in the tensions underlying her narration of the war. "On the thirteenth of April 1975 Hatred erupts," she begins. The capitalization of "Hatred" evokes the enormity of the war's events through near-mythologization, as does the narrator's charged, poetic discourse—for instance, her portrayal of the city as "an electromagnetic field into which everyone wants to plug himself" (Adnan 1982c, 11, 13). But this poetic discourse eventually falters, replaced by abrupt, declarative sentences conveying the shocked contraction being brought about by the war: "They fight in the moonlight. At night sounds are more distinct. . . . The artillery booms" (15). As if searching for a language commensurate to the violence, the narrator turns to journalistic accounts of the war. But the remote, disembodied language of journalism reflects a disconcerting disconnection between articulation and bodily reality. When the narrator picks up the paper, all she finds is a "rapid list of names and facts" (22) that fail either to do justice to the human potential of the victims or to grapple with the meaning of their deaths. Instead, each murdered individual is ticked off—sometimes named, sometimes anonymous—as one more "incident." In the face of this schism between war's reality and the language used to describe it, the connections between actor and action become obscured: even "bullets seem to leave by themselves" (15). Although the narrator wants to take action against this violence—if only by using the film project to portray the fate of Syrian workers rounded up and shot—in such a context she can do or say little. Even her withdrawal from the film project to protest Mounir's refusal to address the politicized wartime realities of the Syrian laborers in Beirut proves irrelevant. Mounir reassures her patronizingly, "Don't worry about it. Tony, Fouad, Pierre and I will discuss it. . . . You come to the house for dinner tonight" (24). Thus reminded of her "place" as a woman, she is simultaneously recuperated into the comfort of her class status, her voice and agency subsumed both by her marginalization and her privilege. It is perhaps no surprise that when the narrator reemerges in "Time II," she does so as simply an observer, her narration but one of many voices, with no power to interfere in the inexorable movement toward Marie Rose's death.

While "Time I" depicts a schism between articulation and the gendered, subjected body, "Time II," which stands in synchronic relationship to the diachronic narrative of "Time I," seeks to breach this schism, levying a social and political critique that brings to the foreground issues of communication and their relationship to agency. As if in response to the narrative and representational crises of "Time I," "Time II" posits a new mode of narration, depicting the action entirely through the unattributed voices of individual characters. This strategy forces readers to discard their stance of uninvolved spectatorship and to enter into the time and space of the narrative, participating in the construction of meaning through careful listening. The multiple subjectivities of this section not only stand in contrast to the monolithic discourse and faceless violence of "Time I," but also bring to the foreground the dialogical contexts within which agency and articulation become possible. At the same time, however, the narrative framework also contains and isolates individual voices, suggesting at a structural level the ways in which articulation is appropriated within structures of power.

At the center of "Time II" is the transgressive figure of Marie Rose, a woman who unsettles social, gendered, religious, and political boundaries of identity. Like the actual Marie Rose Boulous upon whom the novel is based, Adnan's Marie Rose is a divorced Christian Lebanese woman living in Muslim West Beirut and active in educational reform, labor strikes, women's liberation, and the Palestinian cause. Her challenge to insular group power and to the boundaries, both actual and metaphorical, that maintain group identities results in her being considered a "traitor": after the war breaks out she is kidnapped by Christian militiamen and murdered. As one of her captors in the novel puts it, "I don't understand. She's a Christian and she went over to the Moslem camp. She's Lebanese and she went over to the Palestinian camp. Where's the problem? We must do away with her like with every other enemy" (Adnan 1982c, 36). In contrast to her captors' belief in maintaining closed circles of identification through physical violence, Marie Rose argues for a transgressive and liberating "love of the Stranger" that takes as its central element a willingness to listen to and engage with others across exclusionary boundaries of identification (Adnan 1982, 94–95). Yanked out of "the world of ordinary speech" (32) by her kidnappers—a world defined by a "language of coercion and violence, a discourse of power which suppresses the voices of its victims" (Harlow 1987, 112)—Marie Rose posits an alternative mode of articulation and communication, one that takes as its goal the act of listening to and empowering the voice of the subaltern. While her captors' agency is predicated on physical coercion, Marie Rose's agency is predicated on the concept of dialogue: of listening and speaking to, rather than speaking for, others.

This mode of agency is exemplified in "Time II" through Marie Rose's impassioned debate with her captors, in particular with Mounir, whose prior relationship with her complicates the binary opposition of friend versus enemy that structures the other men's world views. (As he admits, "I know her, and knowing is an extraordinarily strong bond" [Adnan 1982c, 34–35].) The power dynamics structuring their interaction is clear: Marie Rose is caught in her captors' net like a "fish torn from the sea . . . thrashing with the same impotence" (32). Similarly, the fatal outcome of the encounter is evident early in "Time II": as the narrator states, "I doubt Marie Rose will leave this confrontation alive" (40). Yet Marie Rose nonetheless dares to speak out, challenging her captors' political and social ideologies, their assumptions about the role of women in the political order and about group loyalty, and their violent power. When Mounir warns her, "Marie-Rose, it's you who's being judged here, not us," she replies, "And who would prevent me from saying what I think since this is perhaps my last opportunity. . . . There are knots to untie, abscesses to drain" (56–57).

Marie Rose's ability to speak out in the face of such overwhelming power is striking, particularly in light of the problems suggested in "Time I" about the limited possibilities of articulation in contexts of oppression and violence. What "Time II" suggests is that Marie Rose's articulation, moral efficacy, and agency are grounded in her attempt to listen to, rather than simply speak for, others, and to empower others to find their own voices. Because of this stance of caring and receptivity, Marie Rose's voice is heard across sectarian lines, as news of her capture ripples through the city, touching people in all sectors of the city regardless of political or religious affiliation. " 'Allah bring her back,' some said, while others said

'Blessed Virgin, we'll light a hundred candles for you if you just send her back to us safe and sound' " (Adnan 1982c, 72). In engaging with others across group lines, Marie Rose also destabilizes the boundaries of her own privilege as well as the structure of traditional group affiliations—the "concentric circles" that contain the individual within widening spheres of power. She crosses the green line dividing the war-torn city to teach the societally outcast "deaf-mute" children; she supports the Palestinian cause despite the risk such support entails; and she refuses an offer to save her own life at the expense of that of her Palestinian lover.

However, her heroism is not unique; rather, it is part of a growing movement of resistance. As Marie Rose notes, "half of the country, made up of as many Christians as Moslems . . . are fighting for and with the Palestinians. I'm not the only one to do it" (Adnan 1982c, 57). Moreover, her stance is the result of a progression of events and changing structural conditions. As even Mounir recognizes, a "series of roads, of stages, of turning-points" made possible Marie Rose's resistance: rebellion against an unhappy marriage, a growing public life, participation in "conferences, protests, social action, planning committees, causes of all kinds" (35, 49). By stressing this progression, the novel points toward the growing role of Lebanese women in challenging Lebanon's political and social structures. As Barbara Harlow comments, *"Sitt Marie Rose* charts a trajectory by way of which women's access to the public arena of political activism can transform the structures of sectarianism that have killed [them]" (1992, 54). Moreover, the suggestion that Marie Rose is not unique in her resistance is reflected on a structural level by the narrative framework of "Time II," for although this section focuses on the events leading up to Marie Rose's death, it does not unconditionally privilege Marie Rose's voice. Rather, "Time II" refracts the narration through different voices, suggesting— even as it makes clear Marie Rose's structural overdetermination—that resistance is not a singular event, and that its story cannot be told through one voice alone.

The emphasis in "Time II" on direct speech and active listening is reflected metaphorically through Adnan's authorial decision to depict Marie Rose not as a teacher of retarded children, as was the real Marie Rose Boulos, but as a teacher of speech- and hearing-impaired children. In her role as a teacher of communication skills, Marie Rose does not speak for the children, but empowers them to speak for themselves. Hence, she offers an alternative to the problem confronted by the narrator in "Time I" of representing subaltern subjects: acknowledging the children's exclusion from dominant forms of discourse, she also gives them the tools of self-articulation with which to redress this marginalization. Her call for a wholesale reform of modes of relationship and communication contrasts sharply not only with the moral "deafness" of her captors, but also with the narrator's uninvolved but authoritative stance. At the same time, the children's discursively realized "voice" not only asserts the possibility of subaltern articulation, but also holds the possibility of disrupting the monolithic discourse upon which the narrative of communal identity is predicated. The militiamen view the children as societal outcasts who are there to learn their place within the normative boundaries of the group, and to discover, as Fouad states, "what it costs to be a traitor" (Adnan 1982c, 92). But the children are not simply mute witnesses to the events. Rather, they provide their own commentary and their own perspective. Instead of accepting Marie Rose's execution as a demonstration of the fact that, as Fouad puts it, "might makes right" (92), the children testify to the incomprehensible horror of her murder. "They've forgotten all about us, but we see everything," they cry. "Devils have come up from underground and they've fallen on her. . . . No human being would ever do what they're doing" (82). Refuting the militiamen's attempt to define violence as "normal," the right of those with power, they testify to the atrocity of Marie Rose's murder, making clear that such acts remain outside of the boundaries of "human" behavior.

But this testimony is circumscribed by the forces, discursive, social, and political, that call both the children's voice and their agency into question. As they themselves acknowledge, "Perhaps one day speech and sound will be restored to us, we'll be able to hear and speak and say what happened. But it's not certain. Some sicknesses are incurable" (Adnan 1982c, 82). The tenuous nature of their resistance is accentuated by their marginalization within the Lebanese social structure. Fulfilling a role similar to that of the Syrian villagers of "Time I," the children are situated in "Time II" as subaltern representatives of "the People," whose inclusion within the boundaries of the group is predicated upon their acquiescence to the status quo. As they observe, commenting on an Egyptian movie Marie Rose has taken them to see, "We have been told that to be The People is to be like in the film, lots and lots of smiling folks. When we grow up, we'll be The People too. And it's not only because we're poor. We're not all poor. It's not enough just to be poor to be The People. You have to be docile and innocent. You have to be a part of things like clouds are a part of the sky" (45). This pastoral inscription glosses over not only the violence underlying the homeostasis of the national body, but also the children's own internalization of the forces that render them "docile and innocent." For like the women watching the film in "Time I," the children are to some extent complicit with the larger structures that situate them, longing not to transform so much as to participate in the structures of power. They comment, "She [Marie Rose] doesn't like the war. Neither do we, because we can't take part in it" (30). Their inability to speak or hear functions within the text not only as a sign of their subaltern status, but also as a metaphor for the perils of silence in a world of violent power relations, where silence too often becomes complicity. As the children themselves observe, "There's no noise in this world. That's why the war doesn't stop. Nobody wants to stop it. . . . From the Gulf to the Atlantic, on our geography maps, the Arabs are all silent" (43).

The tensions underlying the relationship between voice, agency, and resistance are brought more clearly into focus in "Time II" through the relationship between the narrator and Marie Rose. As various commentators have noted, the narrator and Marie Rose share many similarities.[3] Both challenge the intersection of gendered, class-based, sectarian, nationalistic, and religious hierarchies of power while also implicitly presenting a challenge to stereotypes of Arab women. (For instance, the revelation early in "Time I" that the narrator has been to Taos, New Mex-

---

3. Thomas Foster argues that "the position shared by the narrator and Sitt Marie Rose provides a basis for . . . a critique of both Western representations of 'the Arabs' and of the Lebanese nationalism's representations of its own 'others.' " (1995, 64). Similarly, Madeline Cassidy notes that "Marie-Rose and the film writer occupy a similar space, unbounded by delineations of gender, ethnicity and class" (1995, 284).

ico, unsettles conventional assumptions about Arab women's lives.) Both seek to give voice to the sufferings of subaltern "others." And in their attempt to articulate an agency that will transform not only their own situation but that of others, both move uneasily between positions of privilege and marginalization. However, there are significant differences between the two. In contrast to Marie Rose, who stands in "Time II" as an exemplar of agency, courage, and activism, the narrator in "Time II" does not seek to intervene, but functions strictly as an observer. Describing the men who kidnap Marie Rose, she depicts herself as "hover[ing] above this city, this country, and the continent to which they belong. I never lose sight of them. I have devoted myself to observing them up close" (Adnan 1982c, 39). In a sense, this stance positions her as director of the film she wanted to make in "Time I," the film in which she would finally "say something . . . important." Her omniscient commentary at the close of each subsection of "Time II" not only analyzes the political context in which Marie Rose's story is played out, but also hints at the unfolding plot. Observing, from a safe distance, a drama unfolding toward a foregone conclusion, the narrator predicts the outcome of Marie Rose's captivity in much the same way she predicted the denouement of Mounir's film. Describing Marie Rose as a challenge to the natural (or rather, naturalized) order of things, she concludes, "When the impossible mutation takes place, when, for example, someone like Marie-Rose leaves the normal order of things, the political body releases its antibodies in a blind, automatic process. The cell that contains the desire for liberty is killed, digested, reabsorbed" (76).

The precisely choreographed narrative structure of "Time II" echoes the homeostasis of the political and social body within which Marie Rose is but an errant cell to be contained and killed. Situating each character within a patterned narrative form, "Time II" privileges individual voices while at the same time making clear their structural overdetermination. The role of the narrator as both an omniscient narrator and a separate character whose voice is juxtaposed to, and at times intersects with, that of Marie Rose accentuates this tension between individual agency and structural inscription. Moreover, the narrator's position as the concluding speaker in each of the three subsections of "Time II" serves as a reminder of the mediating role of the artist/intellectual, bringing the narrator's role under scrutiny and disrupting the illusion of narrative transparency assumed by the film project of "Time I."

This mediating role, and its corresponding implications for Adnan's own relationship to the text, is most evident in the final chapter of the novel. This chapter, an interior monologue by the narrator, opens with an aesthetic statement that emphasizes the narrative's status as a literary artifact and that points toward the authorial need to wrest resolution and meaning from tragedy. "I want to talk about the light on this day," the narrator begins. "An execution always lasts a long time. I want to say forever and forever that the sea is beautiful. . . . It's only in it, in its immemorial blue, that the blood of all is finally mixed" (Adnan 1982c, 98). Trying to encompass the horror of Marie Rose's execution, the narrator searches for understanding. But her search founders on the tension between visionary transcendence and brutal fact. "To discover a truth is to discover a fundamental limit," she says, "a kind of inner wall to the mind, so I fall again to the ground of passing time, and discover that it's Marie Rose who's right" (99–100). Notwithstanding her sense of Marie Rose's "rightness" (which perhaps refers to Marie Rose's engagement, commitment, and grounding in the local), the narrator understands that Marie Rose is situated within a context of structural oppression, beneath the weight of which even the most visionary modes of activism falter. Indeed, she suggests, Marie Rose's death is the outcome of "universal Power" oppressing the Arab world more generally: "Marie-Rose is not alone in her death. Second by second the inhabitants of this city that were her comrades fall. . . . Airplanes have become the flies of the Arab world, conceived in a frenzy of power, and the plague they carry is the vehicle of its new curse" (104).

Power, to return to Elaine Scarry's argument, depends on the capacity for articulation and specifically on the power of achieving self-description. While *Sitt Marie Rose* affirms both the possibility and the necessity of articulation in the face of oppression, and grants moral primacy to Marie Rose and her impassioned articulation, it also makes clear that narration, like other forms of representation, is too often co-opted by the structures of power. "It must be said," the narrator states, "so that this civilization . . . hears what its masses want to tell it"—the untold stories of oppression and repression, the words "that have been waiting there for so long" (Adnan 1982c, 100). But the act of narration is caught up in the hierarchical relationship between those possessing the power of representation and those who are represented. In a clear reflection of this structural hierarchy, it is not Marie Rose's words or vision with which the text concludes, but the narrator's surreal description of the "deaf-mute" children dancing to the reverberations of bombs in the wake of Marie Rose's execution.

This final image brings to a crescendo the ambivalence surrounding the possibilities of subaltern articulation and resistance in *Sitt Marie Rose*. "Whether you like it or not," the narrator asserts, echoing the recognition put forward in both "Time I" and "Time II" of the seductive nature of violence, "an execution is always a celebration. It is the dance of Signs and their stabilization in Death. It is the swift flight of silence without pardon. It is the explosion of absolute darkness among us. What can one do in this black Feast but dance? The deaf-mutes rise, and moved by the rhythm of falling bombs their bodies receive from the trembling earth, they begin to dance" (Adnan 1982c, 104–5). The stabilization of the "dance of Signs" refers, of course, to Marie Rose's literal silencing in death, as well as to the discursive containment of her voice through the narrative structure of "Time II." But the image also raises questions about the aestheticization of violence inherent in the use of artistic forms to narrate violent events. The "embodied articulation" of the children's dance in some ways functions to extend Marie Rose's singular voice beyond the limits of narrative frame, and thus to heal the schism between voice and body enacted in her death. But the novel's narrative structure also emphasizes the literary, discursive status of her voice, implicitly situating both narrative and narrator at a remove from the political context that makes the novel, as a resistance text, both possible and necessary. Although providing a powerful closure to Marie Rose's story, the final image of the children dancing propels the reader into an aesthetic realm where poetic transcendence provides perhaps the only possible response to unthinkable horror. As the narrator queries, "What can one do in this black Feast but dance?" (105).

This question, and the self-reflexivity of its narrative gesture, returns the reader to the questions raised in "Time I" regarding the efficacy of artistic representation in representing oppression and in giving voice to the voiceless. Like the children's dance, the novel offers an aesthetic response to a violent event. While "Time II," as we have seen, challenges the failure of "Time I" to make possible subaltern articulation by putting forward the voice of both Marie Rose and the "deaf-mute" children, these voices are discursively constructed and contained. Thus, the narrative attempt in "Time II" to empower subaltern voices and to resist violence and oppression is ultimately recuperated within the confines of poetic discourse. Moreover, while it is true, as Elaine Scarry argues, that any artifact of human creativity, whether a coat, a chair, or a poem, holds the potential to challenge the isolation of pain and thus to function as a vehicle of resistance, it may also be true that the complexities inherent in the act of representation work to undermine the efficacy of this resistance, rendering resistance literature on some level a poetic "dance" in the face of death.

This anxiety about the political efficacy of resistance literature is particularly significant in the case of *Sitt Marie Rose* because of the postcolonial tensions informing the text. As a novel written in French and published in France by an author who is situated, like her narrator, at a remove from the events she depicts, *Sitt Marie Rose* confronts the problem of reaching a Christian Lebanese audience resistant to acknowledging their own social, religious, economic, political, and military power, and their role in the war's violence. The novel's efficacy as a resistance text depends upon whether or not it will be heard and responded to by those implicated in the social and political power structures it critiques. Similarly, the efficacy of Marie Rose's resistance within the novel rests on whether or not her speech will be heard by her captors, and, more generally, by the Christian Lebanese whom they represent.

It is this anxiety about the text's wider political efficacy that seems to underlie the ambivalence with which the "deaf-mute" children's final *danse macabre* is presented. Located on the ground of history, where no action is innocent and not all illnesses are curable, the children's dance is situated, like the novel itself, within a literary and poetic space circumscribed by a violent political context. The surreal dimensions of this dance accentuate its literary and discursive status. And indeed, unlike human rights reporting, which "entails both documentation and intervention" (Harlow 1992, 244), literary texts such as *Sitt Marie Rose* do not necessarily function as vehicles of explicit political intervention. Yet both the children's dance and the novel itself also gesture toward what Scarry calls the "sharability of sentience" (1985, 326)—the possibility of speaking beyond the structures of power that silence and isolate individuals. Although *Sitt Marie Rose* makes clear the problematics of representation, the novel stands as testimony to the crucial significance of speaking out against oppression, and to the possibility of healing the schism between body and voice. As Barbara Harlow asserts, "The silence imposed by the torturer is challenged by the demand for political resistance, raising again and again the urgent and critical relation between writing human rights and righting political wrongs" (1992, 256). This relation is never uncomplicated. But out of that complication rises the fierce power of *Sitt Marie Rose*.

10 Hanan al-Shaykh's *Hikayat Zahra*
A Counter-Narrative and a Counter-History

SABAH GHANDOUR

And Earth?
I found her wounded
—is she in agony?—
        Has chaos
returned?
        —Etel Adnan,
            Manifestations of the Voyage

Hanan al-Shaykh. *Photograph*
© *Michael Ward, courtesy of*
Hanan al-Shaykh

Hanan al-Shaykh (b. 1945) is one of the leading contemporary women writers in the Arab world. Some of her novels have been translated into English, French, Dutch, German, Danish, Italian, Korean, Spanish, and Polish. Although she was born and raised in Beirut, where she received her high school education, her family was originally from southern Lebanon. At the age of sixteen, al-Shaykh published essays on freedom,

An earlier version of this chapter was presented at the Middle East Literature Seminar, University of Pennsylvania, April 3–5, 1992. I would like to thank Michael Beard for his valuable comments.

231

boredom, and infidelity. After leaving Lebanon for Cairo to pursue her college education, she wrote her first novel, Intihar rajul mayyit *(Suicide of a dead man), at the age of nineteen; this novel was later published in Beirut in 1970. Al-Shaykh's other novels include* Faras al-shaytan *(Praying mantis, 1975);* Hikayat Zahra *(1980; translated as* The Story of Zahra, *1986);* Misk al-ghazal *(1988; translated as* Women of Sand and Myrrh, *1992);* Bareed Bayrut *(1992; translated as* Beirut Blues, *1995); and* Inna a Londan ya azizi *(2001a; translated as* Only in London, *2001b). Her collections of short stories include* Wardat al-sahraa *(Desert rose, 1982);* Aknus al-shams 'an al-sutouh *(1994; translated as* I Sweep the Sun off Rooftops, *1998).*

This chapter proposes a reading of Hanan al-Shaykh's *Hikayat Zahra* (*The Story of Zahra*) that traces its motion against the grain of established history, the discursive history of the state.[1] On one hand, what we read in history books and chronicles or archives is a history speaking for the state; indeed, most of the literature produced in Lebanon before the civil war speaks for the "authorized" history of the dominant discursive practices. On the other, we find that as a personal history, *Hikayat Zahra* derives its significance from its historical moment, the Lebanese Civil War. In *Zahra*, we lack the historical truth traditionally implied by the narrator's seemingly neutral voice. Rather, we find another kind of "truth" being produced—a truth related to personal, political, or socioeconomic history. *Hikayat Zahra* is itself a personal discourse inscribed within a totalizing discourse of patriarchal history and yet questioning its completeness.

The discourse of the novel in general has developed from a well-structured and delineated narrative—a clear beginning, middle, and end—to a fragmentary but more sophisticated one (see Ghandour 1993,

---

1. *Hikayat Zahra* (Beirut: Dar al-Adab, 1989) was first published in Arabic in 1980. The English text, *The Story of Zahra,* was published in 1986 by Quartet Books, translated by Peter Ford with the cooperation of the author. Another edition appeared in 1987 from Pan Books (Pavanne edition). The references included in the body of the text are to the Dar al-Adab and Pavanne editions, respectively and are reprinted with permission.

xiv-xv). In Lebanon, this change in discursive practice can be linked to the disintegration of the social structure of the state. With the collapse of civil society and the emergence of various political and power entities, and hence the disappearance of a singular truth, writers have come to experience not only a frustration with the political structure and its mechanism operating in the state, but also a disbelief and doubt in everything that goes on around them, even a disbelief in their own identity and subjectivity. Writers are left with bits and pieces from which to draw, and around which to build their fictional worlds in their search to comprehend their continuously changing reality.

Hikayat Zahra tells of the pain and suffering of a Southern Lebanese girl who lives with her family in Beirut. The novel is divided into two major sections. The first part comprises Zahra's personal history: her upbringing, her fear and reluctance, her intimidation, and her sense of self. This part is divided into five chapters all of which are narrated through first-person narrative voice. Three out of the five chapters are narrated by Zahra, the third and fourth by Hashem (her uncle) and Majed (her husband), respectively. Each of Hashem's and Majed's discourses constitutes a history by itself, whether personal/political or personal/socioeconomic. The second section of the novel is narrated solely by Zahra.

Narrative, as it will be employed in this study, relates mainly to how a story is being told, not merely the succession of events presented for us, but more fundamentally the structuring of these events in a novelistic format. In other words, we have narrative as a story (the chronological ordering of events) and narrative as discourse (the presentation of the events). By analyzing the narrative structure of *Zahra*, we will be able to map out the multiple voices in the narrative, to see how they function at the level of both story and discourse.

Discourse, however, embodies the whole spectrum of language as it is understood and analyzed in its sociohistorical context. Even when discourse is analyzed at a very basic level, as a dialogue between two people who are engaged in an exchange of ideas, it still evokes a complex spectrum of social formations related to a particular time in a particular place (see Bakhtin 1981). Since discourse evokes such a vast range of power structures and relations, history will inevitably be among them. We usually know about history through the various discourses that are available to us: books, documents, and archives. History is traditionally understood as the presentation of events in chronological order, with an emphasis on the interpretation of cause and effect. History is also characterized as a coherent and a continuous narrative.

In *Hikayat Zahra,* by telling her own (hi)story Zahra is, in fact, disrupting the coherent continuous narrative of the patriarchal story of the state. In other words, Zahra's story subverts the dominant discursive narrative of the patriarchal story, the prevalent discourse in Lebanon. Hence my analogical reading of *Hikayat Zahra.* While we are reading a personal (hi)story of Zahra, the story of her being used and abused, we are reading Zahra's story, at the same time, as a metaphor of Lebanon, a country that has been used and abused by its own people. In a sense, Zahra's body, which is private and personal, cannot be separated from its function as public and communal. What my reading offers is an analysis of the intricate connectedness between the sociopolitical and the personal; how one story can be read as two stories simultaneously. For Zahra's personal history is told on two levels: one at the level of the narrative, and another at the level of history.

Memory plays a major role in *Hikayat Zahra,* as it is closely related to the presentation of history and narrative alike. The three narrative voices in this novel tell their (hi)stories by invoking memory. Each of them, Zahra, Hashem, and Majed, invokes her/his memory under the pressure of some kind of challenge and/or oppression. To put this another way, memory, by being invoked, presents itself as having its own history and hence its own narrative. Hence, by personal history, I mean what comprises one's actions and behavior at a certain moment in time. This moment needs to be seen as the culmination of the societal and psychological makeup of the individual. Coupled with this for Zahra is a gender issue. The violation of her body is invoked time and again in the novel; and the memory of such violation is presented in a disjunctive narrative. Each time the invocation of her bodily violation takes place, her body is being violated once again.

Hikayat Zahra: A Counter-Narrative

At the level of the narrative, *Hikayat Zahra* presents a counter-narrative to the patriarchal story of Lebanon. The novel generates a tension between the narrative's and the characters' voices. Zahra, by telling a story about herself is, on one hand, repeating the patriarchal story of women as an object of contestation, while on the other hand, undercutting or parodying the patriarchal story of Lebanon, the story of male authority and dominance. Zahra is, in fact, transgressing an official code of history by telling her own story, which is itself a story of transgression. To put it differently, *Hikayat Zahra* shows that "it is no longer possible to maintain that there are two spheres of social reality: the private, domestic sphere of the family, sexuality, and affectivity, and the public sphere of work and productivity" (de Lauretis 1987, 8). Rather, these two spheres present closely "interconnected sets of social relations" (8). Zahra, by transgressing a patriarchal code, shows in fact that this code is inextricably intertwined with the personal code. The personal is political, as "woman's place . . . is not a separate sphere or domain of existence but a position within social existence generally" (Kelly, quoted in de Lauretis 1987, 9). Zahra is not only positioned within "social existence," but is constituted by the very fact of being a woman circulating in a symbolic economy. Zahra's body acts as the gendered space where "the two orders, the sexual and the economic, operate together" (de Lauretis 1987, 8).

In order to appreciate how the counter-narrative in *Hikayat Zahra* works, we have to differentiate between narrative as story and narrative as discourse, by taking into consideration the difference between Zahra, the narrative voice in the novel, and Zahra who is a character in her own story. Such an approach is important because it enables us to appreciate, later, how the structure of the novel itself functions as counter-history. This approach will also enable us to decipher when Zahra's voice is acting as the narrative voice in her story, and when it represents a character. This difference in the two voices—as a narrative voice, on one hand, and as a character, on the other—will help us find out where each of these voices stands alone and where and when they merge and become one. In other words, we have to differentiate between what Genette calls extradiegetic and homodiegetic voices, that is, between free indirect speech where "the narrator takes on the speech of the character, or . . . the character speaks through the voice of the narrator, and the two instances are then *merged*," and immediate speech where "the narrator is obliterated and the character *substitutes* for her" (Genette 1980, 174). This difference in narrative level will elucidate for us how the narrative voice of Zahra, separated in time and space from the character's voice, is able to look back, comprehend, and analyze how Zahra the character was constituted among other discourses.

Zahra, as a character in her own story, orients the events of the narrative. These events are simply the basic succession or the arrangement of incidents within the text. They comprise Zahra's personal history: Zahra as a child witnessing her mother's extramarital affair; Zahra's affair with Malek (her brother's friend), and the consequences of this affair (the loss of her virginity) that prompt her to go to Africa to run away from an arranged marriage in Beirut; her other ordeals in Africa with her uncle Hashem and with her husband, Majed; and, finally, Zahra's return to Lebanon and her subsequent affair with the sniper that leads to her pregnancy and death.

But these events are not always narrated by Zahra, the character in her own story. For the narrative voice that we get throughout the novel is a voice detached in time yet extremely intimate in knowing, remembering, and retelling the events. This *extradiegetic* voice is the one that parodies the patriarchal story of Zahra, the story that constitutes Zahra through and by other discourses. It is the voice that tells us, "Yet what I attempted to understand was, at best, blurred" (al-Shaykh 1989, 7/1987, 1); or "was it because I had grown a little and could understand certain things better?" (10/4); or "I am at an age when I can fully distinguish between village and city life" (10/4).

It is worth pointing out here the difference between the Arabic source text and the translated English text. Where the Arabic says: "I am at an age" (10), the English translation reads: *"Here is another memory.* I am at an age" (4). This accretion gives the reader of the English text a clue or a hint on how to read a certain incident in the novel. In other words, the English text is making explicit what the Arabic text is hiding, while in reality, the power of the Arabic text lies in the confusion between the narrative voice and the character's voice. This confusion is especially fruitful in Arabic because of diglossia.

Diglossia is a major characteristic of Arabic. Strictly defined, it is variety within "the same language . . . used by some speakers under different conditions" (Ferguson 1959, 325): for instance, the difference between *al-fusha,* whose contemporary form is generally known as Modern Standard Arabic, and *'ammiyyah,* the language of everyday spoken communication. Throughout the short history of the Arabic novel, there has been a debate between the traditionalists, who call for preserving the purity of Arabic language, the *fusha,* and for the need "to be eloquent, to use Arabic correctly" (Allen 1982, 34) by adhering completely to the formal aspect of the language; and the modernists, who call for introducing the *'ammiyyah* into literary texts (Allen 1982, 34–35; Semah 1974, 13). Contemporary novelists utilize the colloquial in their narratives not only to mark the high and low status of speakers, but mainly to render as truthfully and authentically as possible a certain dialogue, or to convey the inner thoughts and feelings of characters.

In *Hikayat Zahra,* the distinction between the narrative voice and the character's voice is successfully problematized for us as we read. For example, in the wedding scene, when Zahra decides to try again to salvage her relationship with Majed (note that they're already married), she finds herself to be the only woman sitting down watching her guests having a good time, and she starts to entertain the idea of dancing herself: "I started to ask myself to get up and dance. To get rid of all the shyness. Right at this moment in order to become one of them (the women). *This is the evening of my decision to get married, and that's why this dancing and singing is taking place*" (al-Shaykh 1989, 136; my translation, my emphasis). The narrative voice is recounting what happens to Zahra the character. Zahra's body, which she experiences as being separated from herself, from her being as a woman, needs an invitation to get up and dance. This extradiegetic voice becomes homodiegetic with Zahra's voice, which is adamant about becoming like other women: "All at once, I found [*wajadtu*] myself in the center" (136/98). Zahra is quite aware of being a decentered subject, of being marginalized. However, her endeavor to be included with the others, in the dance, is not reported in a language implying an activity. It is instead reported that she "found" herself in the center; *"wajadtu"* is an emotive verb indicating that her activity is actually an involuntary act. Zahra, who wants to be integrated with the crowd at her house, is in fact longing to blend her body with the music so that there won't be any distinction between "the dancer and the dance," to borrow Yeats's expression. Zahra, who all along has felt separated from her body as she has watched it being violated, is anxious to make it part and parcel of herself as a woman.

In *Technologies of Gender,* Teresa de Lauretis critiques Levi-Strauss's reading of a Cuna myth where women are helped by a shaman's incantation to facilitate childbirth. The shaman reintegrates the pain of the woman by providing "the sick woman with a *language,* by means of which unexpressed, and otherwise inexpressible, psychic states can be immediately expressed" (Levi-Strauss; quoted in de Lauretis 1987, 44). De Lauretis explains that "the incantation aims at detaching the woman's identification or perception of self from her body. It seeks to sever her identification with a body that she must come to perceive precisely as a space, the territory in which the battle is waged" (2).

Substituting the incantation in Levi-Strauss's myth with the music Zahra hears while dancing in *Hikayat Zahra,* we get a comparable but inverse situation in which Zahra's body acts as a space that has to be integrated with her self, her being. The music that Zahra hears while dancing keeps shifting and changing, from the rhythm of an African drum to the Arab lute. This music, which plays a role like that of the incantation for the Cuna woman, has a similar influence on Zahra, for the shift in tune is not only indicative of Zahra's rejection of her condition in Africa, embodied in her marriage and her yearning for Lebanon; but more importantly, of her endeavor to possess and have control over her own body, which she perceives as a territory or a space "in which the battle is waged." In other words, she wants to be in harmony with her body: "Ah! from now on, I have no control over my body; I have to stop; I have to stand still. But I'm dizzy. Who is holding me? Who is saying that's enough Zahra?" (al-Shaykh 1989, 137/1987, 98). Zahra the character, iterating her inability to "control her body," blends in this scene with Zahra's narrative voice. These voices that converge at one point become diglossic immediately after that: "I turned on them screaming, 'You are all pathetic animals! What are you laughing about? You were all dancing yourselves. Leave my house! Get out!' " (137/99). It is important to note here that the distinction between the vernacular and the written, or between the spoken and Modern Standard Arabic, gets blurred, or merged together, in this quote; this merging is clearer to the reader of the Arabic text, in which this distinction becomes useful in mapping out the extradiegetic and homodiegetic voices. This tension in the narrative between Zahra's voice as a subject constituted by her body, and the narrative voice as the consciousness of Zahra able to analyze incidents that happened to Zahra, generates the counter-narrative that undercuts the patriarchal story of Zahra the subject. It is Zahra's personal history that is generated between other discourses and defined by social constraints.

These discourses make of Zahra what others wanted her to be, for Zahra, in fact, is afraid of changing others' perception of her. "[M]y image of myself might be overturned . . . the image of which I had run off hundreds of copies for distribution to all who had known me since childhood. Here is Zahra, the mature girl who says little; Zahra the princess, as my grandfather dubbed me; Zahra the stay-at-home, who blushes for any or for no reason; Zahra the hard-working student—quite the reverse of her brother, Ahmad; Zahra, in whose mouth butter would not melt, who has never smiled at any man, not even at her brother's friends" (1989, 42/1987, 32). What is at stake here is Zahra's subjectivity in relation to society. For Zahra is a "subject constituted in gender . . . though not by sexual difference alone, but rather across languages and cultural representations . . . a subject . . . not unified but rather multiple, and not so much divided as contradicted" (de Lauretis 1987, 2). The discourses by which Zahra's immediate and extended family construct her, along with the social discourses such as that represented by the narrator's comment "Zahra . . . has never smiled at any man, not even her brother's friend," are basically discourses that constrain and contradict her as an evolving human being. These discourses construct her, instead, as a speechless entity, a woman "who cannot object to anything" (1989, 42; my translation). For example, in her relationship with Malek, Zahra is only capable of watching what is happening to her; she keeps meeting Malek, who stretches her on a dirty bed, violating her body as if it belonged to someone else, without her uttering a single word or objection.

Moreover, Zahra is not only constructed as a woman who does not "object to anything," but she is also made into an object or an entity that is constantly "spoken for." In the scene where her husband, Majed, tells her uncle, Hashem, about her fits and her not being a virgin on her wedding night, her uncle dismisses the subject as not worthy of discussion in the twentieth century. However, Hashem begins to interrogate Zahra about the man who deflowered her, about his job, and about why she did not marry him. But, most importantly, Hashem provides his own interpretations and answers, saying: "Perhaps he was a Christian and you were afraid of your father. Perhaps there is another reason. . . . What is the real story, Zahra?. . . . Who is this man? We'll help you to return to him. We want you to be happy" (al-Shaykh 1989, 132/1987, 95). During the ordeal of her interrogation, Zahra remains silent, thinking, "how far off the track he was. . . . How could I express in simple terms and say that this was something which really had nothing to do with me—that, from beginning to end, I had been a mere spectator. . . . I cannot tell because I simply do not know" (132–33/95–96). Zahra, in fact, is relegated to being a "woman [who] is unspeakable." That is to say, her "reality is unspeakable," for she is "sublimated into ineffability . . . out of the agenda . . . either lost by or lost out of history" (Radhakrishnan 1989, 196–97). It is not that Zahra is shown to be a woman who cannot "speak," but more importantly she is shown as one whom no concept or accepted definition of a "woman" will fit. Zahra's story is presented as "unspeakable" by the very patriarchal structure that she is trying to undermine and subvert.

Moreover, Zahra dies at the end when she has dared to speak. During her relationship with the sniper, Zahra kept being both the "unspeakable" and a woman who cannot speak her mind. In order to divert the sniper from killing passersby at the beginning of their affair, Zahra flaunts her body by getting "undressed and wrapp[ing] a towel about [her] waist" (al-Shaykh 1989, 186/1987, 135). But her plan falters when she begins a stormy sexual affair with the sniper. When she finally dares to ask him, "if he is a sniper" (243/179), he kills her. During her last breaths she questions, "He kills me with the bullets that lay at his elbow as he made love to me. . . . Does he kill me because I'm pregnant? or is it because I asked him whether he was a sniper?" (247/183). Scenes of Zahra's body being violated and separated from her keep recurring in the novel, especially when her husband, Majed, approaches her in bed: "the things that I feel whenever Majed comes close to me! Cold winds, cold, crowding me close with thousands of snails closer. . . . I cannot keep away these things. I can't resist. . . . My resistance is to end this crawling. I have to extinguish this crawling with knives, to destroy it with fire. *I want to live for myself. I want my body to be mine alone. I wanted the place on which I stood and the air surrounding me to be mine and no one else's*" (1989, 111–12/1986, 78). [The following is not translated in the English version]: "*And if my husband agrees to leave my body alone, then I don't want him even to breathe within the boundaries of this space. My space.*" (1989, 111–12, my translation, my emphasis). Although the context vividly portrays the violation of her body, it is equally important to note the language in which Zahra the character describes this violation where her body and her physical space become interchangeable, where she becomes quite aware of what solely belongs to her. In fact, it is the first time that Zahra spells her oppression out literally and articulates how she feels about her body. Previously, it has been the narrative voice telling us how Zahra was constituted and violated by the others. Zahra's body evokes images of a specific economy of exchange. It becomes an image of Lebanon, whose different inhabitants fight over the land's—the body's—true genealogy. It is a genealogy that could be traced and explained patrilineally, going back to origins. Zahra, throughout her life, has been repeatedly violated by men who are supposedly close to her, who are considered to be "family." Zahra's body, in this sense, becomes invaluable particularly to her uncle, Hashem, and her husband, Majed, in constructing their own histories.

Hikayat Zahra: A Counter-History

The counter-history of *Hikayat Zahra* is embodied in the structure of the novel itself. As mentioned earlier, the novel is divided into two major sections where the first part is narrated by Zahra, Hashem, and Majed with the third and fourth chapters recounted by the major male characters, while the second part is narrated by Zahra alone. Taking into consideration what I've stated before with respect to narrative history—that is how the question of history is a question of narrative—it is fruitful to look at the third and fourth chapters within the structure of the first part of the novel. Zahra's voice in this section engulfs the male voices of these two chapters. It is important to note that, unlike the English translation, the Arabic text has no chapter titles, only numerical divisions, which provide the reader of the source text with a continuity and a flow and with a challenge missing in the English translation. We have to discover who the narrator is from a reading of the text itself. This narrative technique enables us to read these two chapters as part and parcel of Zahra's consciousness of herself, of Zahra's personal narrative. This reading becomes especially clear when we take into consideration the dialogue between Zahra and her uncle that ends chapter 2. This dialogue presents her uncle trying to convince her to tell Majed, the intended husband, about her fits, to which Zahra replies: "Whatever happened to me was your fault" (43/33). Zahra's answer is extremely important; it shows us for the first time Zahra confronting her uncle. But the importance of this dialogue lies on a structural level of the narrative. It opens up the space for Hashem's and Majed's stories to be included in the narrative, yet to be contained within Zahra's narrative.

At the level of represented history, Hashem's story presents an oppositional version of the formal history of Lebanon. His personal history is inseparable from that of the public history. The initiating moment for remembering his (hi)story occurs when he writes a telegraph to Zahra's parents. This moment accompanies Zahra's decision to marry Majed, but it is also saturated with emotions and intensity for Hashem, as he reviews his past history and remembers the reasons for being an exile, for taking Africa as a second home.

Hashem's political history is comprised of his membership in the Syrian Socialist Nationalist Party (SSNP),[2] and the moment of disruption in

---

2. The term "Partie Populaire Syrienne" (PPS) used in the English translation of *Zahra* is an inaccurate and outdated translation of the name of the party. The term PPS was introduced by the French mandatory authorities.

his political affiliation is the failure of the coup d'état in 1961.[3] Hashem's participation in the coup attempt prompted him to flee his country in search of a safer haven. However, Hashem's memory of a past Lebanon is indivisible from his present moment of Zahra's decision to marry Majed, for Zahra has symbolized for Hashem the missing homeland. Lebanon, which he could not change, control, or take possession of when he was in Lebanon has arrived now in Africa in the figure of Zahra: "Through her I hoped to absorb all my life, both here and in Lebanon. . . . I felt that Zahra was my key to making contact with my past and my present as well as my future" (al-Shaykh 1989, 82–83/1987, 57–58). At the level of narrative as history, Zahra, then, symbolizes for Hashem his dream of Lebanon, for he generates a nonrealistic image of her, an image of his lost Lebanon that he cannot retrieve. Hashem's understanding of what Zahra represents to him exemplifies a masculinist nationalist discourse that generally equates land and women.

As for Majed, his story presents a history of demystification of Lebanon. Majed's discourse constitutes Zahra as an object to be possessed. Majed's obsession in appropriating Zahra's body is an extension of his dream to be inscribed into the socioeconomic formal history of Lebanon. Majed, as a member of the working class, has always felt the gap isolating and separating him from other Lebanese in his country and even in his emigrant land, Africa. So, his objective in marrying Zahra is to climb the social ladder, for Zahra "comes from an illustrious middle class family"; he wants to become a "real human being" by having a wife and a family. In marrying Zahra, Majed has become "the owner of a woman's body that [he] could make love to whenever [he] wished" (al-Shaykh 1989, 98/1987, 69). Zahra, then, functions as a symbol of an economic exchange.

As she does for Hashem, Zahra also symbolizes Lebanon with respect to Majed. The Lebanon that Majed was excluded from while in Lebanon

3. The coup d'état was initiated by the Syrian Socialist Nationalist Party (SSNP) with the help of some military officers. The coup aimed at toppling the regime of President Shehab and initiating a secular state instead. The SSNP, founded in 1932, had frequently called for abolishing feudalism and sectarianism, and for unity of the fertile crescent states.

is brought to him now to Africa. Zahra is the "priceless" bride just because he doesn't have to pay a dowry as he would if he were in Lebanon. Despite all her silences, her noncommunicative and nonresponsive attitude, and sometimes her aggressiveness, Majed goes along with the marriage: "Her changing moods had never stopped me or made me alter my mind about us marrying. It was normal for a woman to be moody at the outset. I felt sure that, as she grew used to me, so things would change" (al-Shaykh 1989, 99/1987, 70). Majed has never attempted to know the essence of Zahra; to really understand her silences and her shifting moods. Instead, he keeps constituting her according to his own likings and imagination. In fact, he feels "sure" that things will change because that is what he believes should normally happen in such marriages. Even when Zahra is on the verge of a nervous breakdown, and her uncle wants to take her to the hospital for treatment, Majed keeps constituting her as a woman who is a "liar, frightened of her own shame and making a pretense out of her remorse and regret" (105/75).

Moreover, Majed can speak of Zahra only in monetary terms: "Certainly there was no reason for me to intervene with her uncle paying all the expenses" (al-Shaykh 1989, 105/1987, 75). For Zahra has never existed to him as a person with her own rights and thoughts. On the contrary, she exists only as a woman—a symbol of the speechless land—that can provide him with physical and/or psychological satisfaction, similar to that he used to get when visiting a whorehouse in downtown Beirut. In addition, his marrying Zahra is more profitable than his dealings in downtown Beirut, for he does not have to pay her as he used to pay the prostitutes. That is why he cannot stand having a woman in his house without sleeping with her, as he did after his argument with Zahra about the lack of her virginity.

At the level of narrative as history, Zahra's body, then, circulates in a symbolic economy of exchange, to be appropriated by men who see her as a symbolic substitute for the country they miss. The contestation, in fact, is between the two symbolic economies of Hashem and Majed, on one hand, and another symbolic economy represented by Zahra's voice and the narrative voice.

At the level of represented history, Majed's story demystifies the official history of Lebanon that says that it is for all the Lebanese, or that its story is about common origin and common heritage. Majed's story, in fact, tells us that Lebanon is characterized by social classes, misery, and poverty. His story clarifies what Ahmad, Zahra's brother, means when he claims later that he is "fighting against exploitation . . . to draw attention to the demands of the repressed Shi'ite minority . . . to destroy imperialism along with . . . [the] tattered regime" (al-Shaykh 1989, 167/1987, 121). In brief, Majed's narrative shows the incongruence between a historical account of Lebanon and its reality.

Reading these two histories (Hashem's and Majed's) as an intrinsic part of Zahra's narrative enables us to see how the question of history is in fact a question of narrative. Narrative in this equation relates to the issue of whose history prevails and becomes dominant in the whole novel. To put it differently, Zahra's discourse in such a reading not only contains the male discourses, but also relegates their discourses to the status of marginality, to the level of footnotes that help in understanding Zahra's story, the history of Lebanon. In fact, these two male voices are excluded from physical presence in Lebanon. It is as if they were sent to Africa to remain there, and this is why the second part of the novel is narrated only by Zahra and the narrative voice.

Narrative, History, and Memory

There is a close relationship between narrative, history, and memory in *Hikayat Zahra*. We find that Hashem's quest for his memory is, as Pierre Nora notes, "the quest for one's history" (1989, 13). In fact, Hashem believes that his past in Lebanon could be retrieved, that he could preserve his past by giving it form and meaning exemplified by Zahra. Hashem's memories of Lebanon, which he carries "with him as [he] carries [his] arm or [his] body" (al-Shaykh 1989, 73/1987, 52), are present with him all the time as he says, "the homeland is present and past together" (al-Shaykh 1989, 73/1987, 52).

Hashem's memory of his nation, however, a nation he believed to be fragmented, is confronted by the reality of a nation with "an army . . . capable of arresting, plotting and knowing everything about our party members, capable of tracking us all down" (al-Shaykh 1989, 49/1987, 66). As Pierre Nora observes, "The passage from memory to history has required every social group to redefine its identity through the revitalization of its own history" (Nora 1989, 15). Hashem's "own history" is his commitment to his political group. By reliving, while in Africa, every moment of the coup in Lebanon, Hashem sees himself only within the collectivity of his party. But his exile, in Africa, has given him a more acute sense of his past, of what Nora calls a "before" and an "after," for "a chasm had to intervene between the present and the past" (Nora 1989, 16). Hashem cannot retrieve his image as "the hero" in his homeland even though he still heads the party and its meetings in Africa. In his endeavor "to make the history [he is] reconstructing equal to the history [he has] lived," Hashem is in fact seeking an "ephemeral spectacle of an unrecoverable identity" (Nora 1989, 17–18), since that identity, along with his dream of an identity rooted in collectivity, has been forever lost with his departure from Lebanon.

In Africa, Hashem experiences routine instead of the "continuity" and the "details" of things: "When I used to tell them that these things are the nation, they used to laugh. Don't laugh, you people, I can't get used to anything but my nation. Even its fruits taste different. [You say] I think like a girl? That's your opinion. I want to understand if sincere emotions belong only to girls? It's obvious that we won't be able to communicate" (al-Shaykh 1989, 73–74; my translation). Hashem is consciously articulating a definition of personal history, against the distinction made by Nora that "memory attaches itself to sites, whereas history attaches itself to events" (Nora 1989, 22). Hashem's memories of small details, of basil pots, of sex and wrestling magazines under his pillow, of the kitchen tiles, cannot be separated from the events he describes. Running away from the police after the failure of the coup, he "found [him]self in a forest such as [he] had never known existed in Lebanon. . . . It seemed as though Lebanon, the struggle and its failure had never touched this place" (al-Shaykh 1989, 65/1987, 48). The site of "huge trees [with] the flutterings of roosting birds" is Hashem's memory of Lebanon. It is this site, a place that embodies Lebanon's historical and political signification, that Hashem carries with him into exile.

While Hashem's memories might seem "heroic," Zahra's memories function differently. Her memories serve as a subversion, a counter-memory of what is considered to be "improper." The relationship between the narrated self and the narrator, between the childhood self and the adult self telling the story of Zahra, is presented to us through memory. Zahra's subjectivity is constituted out of different discourses. These discourses, however, are presented to us through the narrative voice, which is able to comprehend, to analyze, and especially to retrieve them out of Zahra's memory. Hence memory is, in a sense, "historically situated," and the relationship between history and memory depends on the time and place in which a certain incident or event takes place. As Natalie Zemon Davis and Randolph Starn have noted in their introduction to a special issue of *Representations* on "Memory and Counter-Memory," "memory has a history, or . . . histories" (1989, 2).

Zahra, in her endeavor to live her present moment, to organize her past in order to make sense of what happened to her, has to suppress her memories—of fear, pain, and sufferings—of her earlier stages in life. For we cannot "separate contents from functions," as Davis and Starn observe, because "the identity-defining functions of memory are real enough" (1989, 4). What defines Zahra's subjectivity is her fear, while witnessing her mother's extramarital affair, that they might be caught; her pain while watching her father beating her mother; her suffering while continuing to meet Malek and knowing quite well that she abhors him.

These memories of emotional disturbances keep intruding on Zahra, even during her most intimate moments. For example, when she experiences sexual orgasm for the first time in her life with the sniper, she says, "My cries became like lava and hot sand pouring from a volcano whose suffocating dust was burying my past life" (al-Shaykh 1989, 179/1987, 130). Her "past life" of fear, pain, and suffering, which needed to be dismantled, is in itself a historical process by which Zahra was constituted. Zahra, the silent, the "unspeakable woman," has to come to terms with her own body and sexuality. As she puts it, "withdrawing back into my shell had been exhausting because it drained me of all control over my body" (181/131).

These memories of Zahra recounted through the narrative voice function, in themselves, as counter-memories that are buried in the unconscious, for they are usually considered "unethical," like Zahra's personal history, because they pertain to sexuality and are not customarily discussed in the open. In a patriarchal society, women are not allowed to discuss their sexuality for they, as individuals, are relegated to second-class citizens who are usually "spoken" for. The novel, quite explicitly, brings images of sexual repression to the forefront, hence allowing these issues to serve as counter-narrative and counter-history. These counter-memories, in fact, expose the hypocritical attitude of the Lebanese patriarchal society with respect to sexuality.

Narrative, history, and memory are thus inextricably intertwined in *Hikayat Zahra*. While memory and history go hand in hand, it is the narrative that gives them their ultimate form for survival. For the story of Zahra, besides being a counter-narrative that parodies the historical patriarchal story of Lebanon, is a narrative that, although it cannot keep Zahra physically alive, allows her to live discursively. Although Zahra dies, we are still reading her (hi)story and pondering about it. In other words, the narrative of silencing becomes a reversal of it, something that even survives the silenced one's death.

Conclusion

In retrospect, the opening scene of the novel in which Zahra's mother silences her by placing her hand over her mouth, suppressing Zahra's voice and her ability to express herself, becomes extremely helpful in interpreting Zahra's behavior throughout the narrative. Zahra, who has been reduced to a speechless woman, to a body, represents in fact the speechless Lebanon, the land that cannot voice its own sufferings. This "silencing" theme, which takes on different forms throughout the novel, presents in the last scene an entirely different register. When Zahra the character is killed, it is in fact the narrative voice that keeps speaking to us: "He kills me. He kills me with the bullets that lay at his elbow as he made love to me. . . . He's killed me. That's why he kept me there till darkness fell" (al-Shaykh 1989, 247/1987, 183). It is this narrative voice narrating the story of Zahra, the story of Lebanon that keeps pouring out Zahra's sufferings and her misfortune even after her death. This narrative voice does not die; it cannot be silenced. It represents the consciousness of Zahra and by extension the narrative voice of Lebanon. For *Hikayat Zahra* bears within it Lebanon's specific political history. It is this extradiegetic voice that has the last say on the history of Lebanon. It is a voice that counters or parodies the official history, and most importantly it contains the socioeconomic and political history of Lebanon, the diversified voices of Lebanon. It is the voice that challenges Lebanon's social formation.

Works Cited

Index

Works Cited

Abdo, Nahla. 1991. "Women of the Intifada: Gender, Class and National Liberation." *Race & Class* 32, no. 4: 19–34.

Abdu, Ibrahim, and Durriyya Shafik. 1945. *Tatawwur al-nahda al-nisa'iyya fi Misr min 'ahd Muhammad 'Ali ila Farouq* (The development of the women's movement in Egypt from the times of Muhammad 'Ali to those of Faruq). Jamamiz: Maktabat al-Aadaab.

Abdul-Ilah, Lu'ai. 1991. Review of "Mi'mar riwa'i mudhish" (An astonishing fictional work). *al-Naqid* Feb.: 68–69.

Abdullah, Yahya Taher. 1975. *al-Tawq wa'l-iswirah*. Cairo: Matabi' Al-Hay'a al-Misriyya al-'Amma li al-Kitab.

———. 1983. *The Mountain of Green Tea and Other Stories*. Translated by Denys Johnson-Davies. Cairo: American Univ. in Cairo Press.

Abu Zayyad, Ziad. 1994. "The Palestinian Right of Return: A Realistic Approach." *Palestine-Israel Journal*, no. 2 (spring): 74–78.

Accad, Evelyne. 1978. *Veil of Shame: The Role of Women in the Contemporary Fiction of North Africa and the Arab World*. Quebec: Naaman.

———. 1982. "Entretien avec Andrée Chedid." *Présence Francophone* 24: 157–74.

———. 1987. "Freedom and the Social Context: Arab Women's Special Contribution to Literature." *Feminist Issues* 7, no. 2: 33–48.

———. 1990. *Sexuality and War: Literary Masks of the Middle East*. New York: New York Univ. Press.

Adnan, Etel. 1966. *Moonshots*. Beirut: Les Editions du Reveil.

———. 1971. *Five Senses for One Death*. New York: The Smith.

———. 1973. *Jebu Suivie de L'Express Beyrouth-Enfer*. Paris: P. J. Oswald.

———. 1978. *Sitt Marie Rose*. Paris: Des Femmes.

———. 1980. *L'Apocalyse Arabe*. Paris: Editions Papyrus.

————. 1982a. *From A to Z*. Sausalito, Calif.: Post-Apollo Press.

————. 1982b. *Pablo Neruda Is a Banana Tree*. Lisbon: De Almeida.

————. 1982c. *Sitt Marie Rose*. Translated by Georgina Kleege. Sausalito, Calif.: Post-Apollo Press.

————. 1985. *The Indian Never Had a Horse & Other Poems*. Sausalito, Calif.: Post-Apollo Press.

————. 1986. *Journey to Mount Tamalpais*. Sausalito, Calif.: Post-Apollo Press.

————. 1989. *The Arab Apocalypse*. Sausalito, Calif.: Post-Apollo Press.

————. 1990a. "Growing Up to Be a Woman Writer in Lebanon." In *Opening the Gates: A Century of Arab Feminist Writing*, edited by Margot Badran and miriam cooke, 5–20. Bloomington: Indiana Univ. Press.

————. 1990b. *The Spring Flowers Own & The Manifestation of the Voyage*. Sausalito, Calif.: Post-Apollo Press.

————. 1993a. *Of Cities and Women (Letters to Fawwaz)*. Sausalito, Calif.: Post-Apollo Press.

————. 1993b. *Paris, When It's Naked*. Sausalito, Calif.: Post-Apollo Press.

————. 1997. *There: In the Light and Darkness of the Self and of the Other*. Sausalito, Calif.: Post-Apollo Press.

Adonis. 1974. *Al-Thabit wa al-mutahawwil: bahth fi al-ittiba' wa-al-ibda' 'ind al-'arab* (The Permanent and the changeable: A study of imitation and originality in Arab culture). Beirut: Dar al-'Awdah.

Ahmad, Aijaz. 1992. *In Theory: Classes, Nations, and Literatures*. London: Verso.

Ahmed, Leila. 1981. Review of *The Hidden Face of Eve*, by Nawal El Saadawi. *Signs: Journal of Women in Culture and Society* 6, no. 4: 749–51.

Al-Ali, Nadje Sadig. 1994. *Gender Writing/Writing Gender: The Representation of Women in a Selection of Modern Egyptian Literature*. Cairo: American Univ. in Cairo Press.

Alcoff, Linda. 1994. "The Problem of Speaking for Others." In *Feminist Nightmares: Women at Odds. Feminism and the Problem of Sisterhood*, edited by Susan Ostrov Weisser and Jennifer Fleischner, 285–309. New York: New York Univ. Press.

Allen, M. D. 1995. Review of *The Innocence of the Devil*, by Nawal El Saadawi. In *World Literature Today* 69, no. 3: 637–38.

Allen, Roger. 1982. *The Arabic Novel: An Historical and Critical Introduction*. Syracuse, N.Y.: Syracuse Univ. Press.

————. 1995. *The Arabic Novel: An Historical and Critical Introduction*. 2d ed. Syracuse, N.Y.: Syracuse Univ. Press.

Alloula, Malek. 1981. *Le Harem colonial: images d'un sous-érotisme*. Genève and Paris: Editions Slatkine.

———. 1986. *The Colonial Harem*. Minneapolis: Univ. of Minnesota Press.

Alternative Information Center. 1994. *Punished Twice-Punished Collectively*, Jerusalem, Feb.

Amin, Mustapha. 1984. "The Beautiful Leader" (in Arabic). In *Masa'il shakhsiyya* (Personal matters), 59–68. Cairo: Tihama Publications.

Amin, Qasim. 1899. *Tahrir al-mar'a* (The liberation of women: a document in the history of Egyptian feminism). Cairo: Maktabat al-Taraqqi.

———. 1900. *Al-Mar'a al-jadida* (The new woman). Cairo: Matba'at al-Ma'arif.

———. 1992. *The Liberation of Women: A Document in the History of Egyptian Feminism*. Translated by Samiha Sidhom Peterson. Cairo: American Univ. in Cairo Press.

Amireh, Amal. 1996a. Review of *Men, Women, and God(s): Nawal El Saadawi and Arab Feminist Poetics*, by Fedwa Malti-Douglas. *Middle East Studies Association Bulletin* 30, no. 2: 230–31.

———. 1996b. "Publishing in the West: Problems and Prospects for Arab Women Writers." *Al Jadid: A Record of Arab Culture and the Arts* 2: 10.

Amireh, Amal, and Lisa Suhair Majaj. 2000. *Going Global: The Transnational Reception of Third World Women Writers*. New York: Garland.

al-Aqqad, Abbas Mahmud. 1938. *Sarah*. Cairo, n. p.

———. 1978. *Sara*. Translated by M. M. Badawi. Cairo: General Egyptian Book Organization.

Arebi, Saddeka. 1994. *Women and Words in Saudi Arabia: The Politics of Literary Discourse*. New York: Columbia Univ. Press.

Aruri, Naseer, and John J. Carroll. 1994. "A New Palestinian Charter." *Journal of Palestine Studies* 23, no. 4: 5–17.

Augustin, Ebba, ed. 1993. *Palestinian Women: Identity and Experience*. London: Zed Books.

al-'Azm, Sadiq Jalal. 1968. *al-Naqd al-dhati ba'd al-hazimah*. Beirut: Dar al-Tali'ah.

Baalbakki, Layla. 1958. *Ana ahya* (I live). Beirut: al-Maktab al-Tijari 'l-Tiba'ah wa-al-Tawzi' wa-al-Nashr.

———. 1960. *al-Alihah al-mamsukhah*. Beirut: Dar Majallat Shi'r.

———. 1963. *Safinat hanan ila l-qamar* (Spaceship of tenderness to the moon). Beirut: al-Mu'assasa al-wataniyya l'l-Tiba'a wa al-Nashr.

Badr, Liana. 1979. *Buslah min ajl ʿabbad al-shams* (*Compass for the Sunflower*). Bayrut, Lubnan: Dar Ibn Rushd.

———. 1985. *Shurfah ʿala al-Fakihani* (*Balcony over the Fakihani*). Al-Quds: al-Wahdah.

———. 1989. *A Compass for the Sunflower.* Translated by Catherine Cobham. London: Women's Press.

———. 1991. *ʿAyn al-mirʾah* (*Eye of the Mirror*). Al-Dar al-Bayda, al-Maghrib: Dar Tubqal lil Nashr.

———. 1993a. *A Balcony over the Fakihani.* Translated by Peter Clark and Christopher Tingley. New York: Interlink.

———. 1993b. *Najoum Ariha.* Cairo: Dar al-Hilal.

———. 1994. *The Eye of the Mirror.* Translated by Samira Kawar. Reading, UK: Garnet Publishing.

———. Forthcoming. From *The Stars over Jericho.* Translated by S. V. Atallah. PROTA Press.

Badran, Margot. 1988. "Dual Liberation: Feminism and Nationalism in Egypt, 1870–1925." *Feminist Issues,* spring: 15–34.

Badran, Margot, and miriam cooke, eds. 1990. *Opening the Gates: A Century of Arab Feminist Writing.* Bloomington: Indiana Univ. Press.

Bahri, Deepika. 1995. "Once More with Feeling: What Is Postcolonialism?" *Ariel: A Review of International English Literature* 26, no. 1: 51–82.

Bakhtin, M. M. 1981. *The Dialogic Imagination.* Edited by Michael Holquist and translated by Caryl Emerson and Michael Holquist. Austin: Univ. of Texas Press.

Bakr, Salwa. 1986. *Zeinat fi janazat al-raʾis* (Zeinat at the president's funeral). Cairo: Private printing by the author.

———. 1991. *Al-ʿaraba al-dhahabiyya la-tas ʿad ila al-samaʾ* (*The Golden Chariot*). Cairo: Dar Sina.

———. 1992a. *Such a Beautiful Voice.* Translated by Hoda El-Sadda. Cairo: General Egyptian Book Organization.

———. 1992b. *The Wiles of Men and Other Stories.* Translated by Denys Johnson-Davies. London: Quartet.

———. 1995a. "Baʿidan ʿan firashihi" (Far from his bed). *Al-Hilal,* 88–91.

———. 1995b. *The Golden Chariot.* Translated by Dinah Manisty. Reading, UK: Garnet Publishing.

Barakat, Hoda. 1985. *Zaʾirat* (The visitors). Bayrut: Dar al-Matbʿu at al-Sharqiyah.

————. 1990. *Hajar al-dohk* (*The Stone of Laughter*). London: Riyad al-Rayyes Books.

————. 1993a. *Ahl al-hawa* (People of love). Bayrut: Dar al-Nahar.

————. 1993b. "Thukura Wa Unutha" (Masculine/feminine). *al-Katiba*, Dec 1: 18.

————. 1995. *The Stone of Laughter.* Translated by Sophie Bennett. London: Garland Press.

————. 1998. *Harith al-miyaah* (*The Tiller of Waters*). Bayrut: Dar al-Nahar.

————. 2001. *The Tiller of Waters.* Translated by Marilyn Booth. Cairo: American University in Cairo Press.

Basu, Amrita. 1982. Letter. *New York Times,* May 2, late city final ed., sec. 7, p. 41.

Ben Jelloun, Tahar. 1990. "Towards a World Literature." Interview with Miriam Rosen. *Middle East Report* (Mar.-Apr.): 30–33.

Bensaoud, Ali. 1991. "Ta'riyat al-Harb" (Stripping the war). Review of *Hajar al-dohk,* by Hoda Barakat. *al-Naqid* 39 (Sept.): 70–71.

Bensmaia, Réda. 1996. "La nouba des femmes du Mont Chenoua: Introduction to the Cinematic Fragment." *World Literature Today* 70, no. 4 (autumn): 877–84.

Bhabha, Homi K., ed. 1990. *Nation and Narration.* London: Routledge.

————. 1994. *The Location of Culture.* New York: Routledge.

Blain, Virginia, Patricia Clements, and Isobel Grundy, eds. 1990. *The Feminist Companion to Literature in English: Women Writers from the Middle Ages to the Present.* New Haven: Yale Univ. Press.

Booth, Wayne. 1974. *A Rhetoric of Irony.* Chicago: Univ. of Chicago Press.

Boullata, Issa J. 1990. *Trends and Issues in Contemporary Arab Thought.* Albany: State Univ. of New York Press.

Boullata, Kamal, ed. 1978. *Women of the Fertile Crescent: Modern Poetry by Arab Women.* Washington, D.C.: Three Continents Press.

Bowen, Donna Lee, and Evelyn Early, eds. 1993. *Everyday Life in the Muslim Middle East.* Bloomington: Indiana Univ. Press.

Braidotti, Rosi. 1994. *Nomadic Subjects: Embodiment and Sexual Difference in Contemporary Feminist Theory.* New York: Columbia Univ. Press.

Bruner, Charlotte H., ed. 1993. *The Heinemann Book of African Women's Writing.* London: Heinemann.

Buck, Claire, ed. 1992. *Bloomsbury Guide to Women's Literature.* London: Bloomsbury.

Butler, Judith. 1993. *Bodies That Matter: On the Discursive Limits of "Sex."* New York: Routledge.

Cassidy, Madeline. 1995. " 'Love is a Supreme Violence': The Deconstruction of Gendered Space in Etel Adnan's *Sitt Marie Rose*." In *Violence, Silence and Anger: Women's Writing as Transgression,* edited by Deirdre Lashgari, 282–90. Charlottesville: Univ. Press of Virginia.

Chedid, Andrée. 1952a. *Jonathan*. Paris: Seuil.

———. 1952b; 1976. *Le Sommeil délivré* (*From Sleep Unbound*). Paris: Flammarion.

———. 1960. *Le Sixième jour* (*The Sixth Day*). Paris: R. Julliard.

———. 1963. *Le survivant*. Paris: R. Julliard.

———. 1969. *L'Autre*. Paris: Flammarion.

———. 1972. *La Cité fertile*. Paris: Flammarion.

———. 1974. *Néfertiti et le rêve d'Akhnaton*. Paris: Flammarion.

———. 1981. *Les Marches de sable*. Paris: Flammarion.

———. 1982. *Le Suivant*. Paris: Flammarion.

———. 1983. *From Sleep Unbound*. Translated by Sharon Spencer. Athens, Ohio: Swallow Press.

———. 1985. *La Maison sans racines* (*The Return to Beirut*). Paris: Flammarion.

———. 1987. *The Sixth Day*. Translated by Isobel Strachey. London: Serpent's Tail.

———. 1989a. *L'Énfant multiple* (*The Multiple Child*). Paris: Flammarion.

———. 1989b. *The Return to Beirut*. Translated by Ros Schwartz. London: Serpent's Tail.

———. 1990. *The Prose and Poetry of Andrée Chedid: Selected Poems, Short Stories, and Essays*. Translated and with an introduction by Renée Linkhorn. Birmingham, UK: Summa Publications.

———. 1992. *A la mort, à la vie: nouvelles*. Paris: Flammarion.

———. 1995. *The Multiple Child*. Translated by Judith Radke. San Francisco: Mercury House.

———. 1998. *Lucy: la femme verticale*. Paris: Flammarion.

———. 2000. *Le Message*. Paris: Flammarion.

Chow, Rey. 1991. "Violence in the Other Country: China as Crisis, Spectacle, and Woman." In *Third World Women and the Politics of Feminism,* edited by Chandra Talpade Mohanty, Ann Russo, and Lourdes Torres, 81–100. Bloomington: Indiana Univ. Press.

———. 1993. *Writing Diaspora: Tactics of Intervention in Contemporary Cul-*

tural Studies. Bloomington: Indiana Univ. Press.

Cixous, Hélène. 1981. "The Laugh of the Medusa." In *New French Feminisms,* edited by Elaine Marks and Isabelle de Courtivron, 245–65. New York: Shocken Books. First published in English in *Signs* (summer 1976) as a revised version of "Le rire de la méduse," which appeared in *L'arc* in 1975.

A Committee of Scholars. 1980. "Fi qadaya al-mar'a" (On women's issues). In *Hasad al-fikr al-'Arabi al-hadith* (Harvest of modern Arab thought). Beirut: Mu'assasat Nasir li al-Thaqafa.

cooke, miriam. 1988. *War's Other Voices: Women Writers on the Lebanese Civil War.* Cambridge, UK: Cambridge Univ. Press.

———. 1997. *Women and the War Story*. Berkeley: Univ. of California Press.

Croucher, Michael. 1995. Letter. *Guardian,* Aug. 22, sec. Guardian Features, p. 14.

Cumming, Laura. 1994. "Books." Review of *The Innocence of the Devil,* by Nawal El Saadawi. *Guardian,* Mar. 15, sec. Guardian Features, p. 8.

Darraj, Faysl. 1992. "Riwaya Bab al-saha: Al-mawdu' al-lataqlidi fi al-manzur al-taqlidi." *Dalalat al-'alaqa al riwayiya*. Damascus: Dar al-Kana'an.

Darwaza, Muhammad 'Izzat. 1993. *Mudhakkarat Muhammad 'Izzat Darwaza: sijill hafil bi masirat al-haraka al-'Arabiyya wa al-qadiyya al-Filastiniyya khilal qarnin min al-zaman 1305–1404/1887–1984* (The memoirs of Muhammad 'Izzat Darwaza: a full record of a century 1305–1404/1887–1984 of the development of the Arab [political] movement and the Palestine issue). Beirut: Dar al-Gharb al-Islami.

Davis, Natalie Zemon, and Randolph Starn. 1989. Introduction to *Representations* 26 (spring): 1–6.

de Lauretis, Teresa. 1987. *Technologies of Gender: Essays on Theory, Film, and Fiction*. Bloomington: Indiana Univ. Press.

Djebar, Assia. 1969a. *Poèmes pour l'Algérie heureuse*. Alger: SNED.

———. 1969b. *Rouge l'aube*. Alger: SNED.

———. 1980. *Femmes d'Alger dans leur appartement*. Paris: Des Femmes.

———. 1985. *L'amour, la fantasia*. Paris: Editions Jean-Claude Lattès.

———. 1987. *Ombre sultane* (*A Sister to Scheherazade*). Paris: Editions Jean-Claude Lattès.

———. 1988. *A Sister to Scheherazade*. Translated by Dorothy S. Blair. London: Quartet.

———. 1992. *Women of Algiers in Their Apartment*. Translated by Marjolijn De Jager. Charlottesville: Univ. Press of Virginia.

———. 1993. *Fantasia: An Algerian Cavalcade.* Translated by Dorothy S. Blair. Portsmouth, N.H.: Heinemann.

———. 1995. *Vaste est la prison.* Paris: A. Michel.

———. 1999. *So Vast the Prison.* Translated by Betsy Wing. New York: Seven Stories Press.

Donnell, Alison. 1995. "She Ties Her Tongue: The Problem of Cultural Paralysis in Postcolonial Criticism." *Ariel: A Review of International English Literature* 26, no. 1: 101–16.

Dullea, Georgia. 1980. "Female Circumcision a Topic at UN Parley." *New York Times,* July 18, late city final ed., p. B4.

Eco, Umberto. 1983. *Travels in Hyper Reality.* Orlando, Fla.: Harcourt Brace and Company.

Elia, Nada. 2001. *Trances, Dances, and Vociferations: Agency and Resistance in Africana Women's Narratives.* New York: Garland.

Emberley, Julia V. 1993. *Thresholds of Difference: Feminist Critique, Native Women's Writings, Postcolonial Theory.* Toronto: Univ. of Toronto Press.

Fabian, Johannes. 1983. *Time and the Other: How Anthropology Makes Its Object.* New York: Columbia Univ. Press.

el-Faizy, Monique. 1994. "Between the Devil and the Big Black Book." *Guardian,* Mar. 21, sec. Guardian Features, p. 15.

Faqir, Fadia. 1994. Introduction to *The Eye of the Mirror.* By Liana Badr. Translated by Samira Kawar, v-x. Reading, UK: Garnet Publishing.

———, ed. 1998. *In the House of Silence: Autobiographical Essays by Arab Women Writers.* Translated by Shirley Eber and Fadia Faqir. Reading, UK: Garnet Publishing.

Faraj, Afif. 1985. *al-Hurriyya fee adab al-mar'a* (Freedom in women's literature). Beirut: Arab Research Institute.

Ferguson, Charles A. 1959. "Diglossia." *Word* 15: 325–40.

Fernea, Elizabeth Warnock, ed. 1985. *Women and the Family in the Middle East: New Voices of Change.* Austin: Univ. of Texas Press.

Foster, Thomas. 1995. "Circles of Oppression, Circles of Repression: Etel Adnan's *Sitt Marie Rose.*" *PMLA: Publications of the Modern Language Association of America* 110, no. 1 (Jan.): 59–74.

Franco, Jean. 1988. "Beyond Ethnocentrism: Gender, Power and the Third-World Intelligentsia." In *Marxism and the Interpretation of Culture,* edited by Cary Nelson and Lawrence Grossberg, 503–15. Urbana: Univ. of Illinois Press.

Fullerton, John. 1989. "Egypt's Saadawi Champions Woman's Struggle in a Male World." *Reuters Library Report,* Aug. 6, BC cycle.

Gauch, Sarah. 1991. "A Troublemaker in Egypt Stands up to Her Government." *Chicago Tribune,* Oct. 27, final ed., sec. Womanews, p. 1.

Genette, Gerard. 1980. *Narrative Discourse: An Essay in Method.* Translated by Jane E. Lewin. Ithaca, N.Y.: Cornell Univ. Press.

Germain, Christine. 1985. "Andrée Chedid." *Auteurs Contemporains: Marguerite Yourcenar, Jean Jeverzy, Andrée Chedid.* Brussels: Didier-Hatier.

Al-Ghalayini, Shaikh Mustafa. 1346/1928. *Nazarat fi kitab al-sufur wa al-hijab, al-mansoub ila al-'Anisa Nazira Zeiniddin* (A look at the book, *Lifting the veil, wearing the veil,* ascribed to Miss Nazira Zeineddin). Beirut: Matabi' Quzma.

Ghandour, Sabah. 1993. Foreword to *Gates of the City,* by Elias Khoury, xiv-xv. Minneapolis: Univ. of Minnesota Press.

Ghaussy, Soheila. 1994. "A Stepmother Tongue: 'Feminine Writing' in Assia Djebar's *Fantasia: An Algerian Cavalcade.*" *World Literature Today* 68, no. 3 (summer): 457–62.

Ghazoul, Ferial. 1990. "Balaghat al-ghalaba." In *Contemporary Arab Thought and Women: Papers of the Arab Women Solidarity Association 2nd International Conference,* 107-24. Cairo: Arab Women's Solidarity Association.

al-Ghitani, Jamal. 1971. *al-Zayni Barakat.* Damascus: Wizarat al-Thaqafah.

———. 1988. *Zayni Barakat.* Translated by Farouk Abdel Wahab. New York: Viking.

Ghosh, Bishnupriya, and Brinda Bose, eds. 1996. *Interventions: Feminist Dialogues on Third World Women's Literature and Film.* New York: Garland.

Gilmour, David. 1983. *Lebanon: The Fractured Country.* New York: St. Martin's Press.

Gindi, Hoda. 1995. Letter. *Guardian,* Aug. 22, sec. Guardian Features, p. 14.

Gingell, Susan. 1995. "Nawal El Saadawi." E-mail to the author.

Gluck, Sherna. 1994. *An American Feminist in Palestine.* Philadelphia: Temple Univ. Press.

Gornick, Vivian. 1982. "About the Mutilated Half." *New York Times,* Mar. 14, late city final ed., sec. 7, p. 3.

Green, Mary Jean, et al., eds. 1996. *Postcolonial Subjects: Francophone Women Writers.* Minneapolis: Univ. of Minnesota Press.

Grewal, Inderpal, and Caren Kaplan, eds. 1994. *Scattered Hegemonies.* Minneapolis: Univ. of Minnesota Press.

Guha, Ranajit. 1988. "The Prose of Counter-Insurgency." In *Subaltern Studies II: Writings on South Asian History and Society,* edited by Ranajit Guha and Gayatri Spivak, 1–42. New Delhi: Oxford Univ. Press.

Hafez, Sabry. 1989. "Intentions and Realization in the Narratives of Nawal El-Saadawi." *Third World Quarterly* 11, no. 3: 188–99.

———. 1995. "Women's Narrative in Modern Arabic Literature: A Typology." In *Love and Sexuality in Modern Arabic Literature,* edited by Roger Moore, Hilary Kilpatrick, and Ed de Moor, 154–74. London: Saqi.

al-Hamidi, Ahmad Jasim. 1986. *al-Mar'ah fee kitabatiha: untha bourjwaziyya fee 'alam al-rajul* (Woman in her writing: a bourgeois female in a man's world). Damascus: Dar Ibn Hani.

Harlow, Barabara. 1987. *Resistance Literature.* New York: Methuen.

———. 1992. *Barred: Women, Writing, and Political Detention.* Hanover, N.H.: Wesleyan Univ. Press.

Haykal, Muhammad Husayn. 1914. *Zaynab.* Cairo: Maktabat Nahdat Misr [1963].

———. 1989. *Zainab.* Translated by John Mohammed Grinsted. London: Darf.

Hedges, Chris. 1994. "Palestinians in Jordan See Bleak Future after Accord." *New York Times,* May 30, late final edition, sec.1, p. 5.

Al-Hibri, Azizah, ed. 1982. *Women and Islam.* Oxford: Pergamon Press.

Hiltermann, Joost. 1991. *Behind the Intifada.* Princeton, N.J.: Princeton Univ. Press.

Hitchcock, Peter. 1993. "Firdaus; or, The Politics of Positioning." *Dialogics of the Oppressed,* 25–52. Minneapolis: Univ. of Minnesota Press.

Husayn, Taha. 1934. *Du'a' al-karawan.* Cairo: Matba'at al-Ma'arif [1942].

———. 1980. *The Call of the Curlew.* Translated by A. B. al-Sari. Leiden: E. J. Brill.

Ibrahim, Emily Faris. n.d. *Adibat lubnaniyyat* (Lebanese women writers). Beirut: Dar al-Raihani li al-Tiba'a wa al-Nashr.

Ibrahim, Son'allah. 1992. *Dhat.* Cairo: Dar al-Mustaqbal al-'Arabi.

———. 1997. *Sharaf.* Cairo: Dar al-Hilal.

"The Innocence of the Devil: Book Reviews." 1994. Review of *The Innocence of the Devil,* by Nawal El Saadawi. *Publishers Weekly,* Oct. 24: 54.

Irigaray, Luce. 1985. *Speculum of the Other Woman.* Translated by Gillian Gill. Ithaca, N.Y.: Cornell Univ. Press.

Izoard, Jacques. 1977. *Andrée Chedid.* Paris: Seghers.

Jacoby, Susan. 1994. "Nawal El Saadawi: A Woman Who Broke the Silence." Review of *Memoirs from the Women's Prison* and *The Innocence of the Devil,* by Nawal El Saadawi. *Washington Post,* Nov. 27, final ed., sec. Book World, p. X3.

Jayyusi, Salma Khadra. 1977. *Trends and Movements in Modern Arabic Poetry, II.* Leiden: E. J. Brill.

Johnson, Penny J. 1990. Introduction to "Our Fate, Our House," by Sahar Khalifeh. Translated by Vera Tamari. *Middle East Report* May–August: 29–31.

Jones, Ann Rosalind. 1985. "Writing the Body: Toward an Understanding of L'écriture féminine." In *The New Feminist Criticism: Essays on Women, Literature, and Theory,* edited by Elaine Showalter, 361–77. New York: Pantheon.

Kaplan, Caren. 1994. "The Politics of Location as Transnational Feminist Critical Practice." In *Scattered Hegemonies: Postmodernity and Transnational Feminist Practices,* edited by Inderpal Grewal and Caren Kaplan, 137–52. Minneapolis: Univ. of Minnesota Press.

Kensinger, Loretta. 1995. "Nawal El Saadawi." E-mail to the author. Mar. 6.

Khalifa, Iglal. 1973. *Al-Haraka al-nisa'iyya al-haditha, qissat al-mar'a al-'Arabiyya 'ala ard Misr* (The modern women's movement, the story of the Arab woman in the land of Egypt). Cairo: al-Matba'a al-'Arabiyya al-Haditha.

Khalifeh, Sahar. 1980. *'Abbad al-shams* (Sunflower). al-Quds: Kar al-Katib.

———. 1985. *Wild Thorns.* Translated by Trevor LeGassick and Elizabeth Fernea. London: Al-Saqi Books.

———. 1986. *Mudhakkirat imra'ah ghayr w aqi'iyah* (Memoirs of an unrealistic woman). Bayrut: Dar al-Adab.

———. 1990. *Bab al-saha* (The courtyard's gate). Bayrut: Dar al-Adab.

———. 1997. *al-Mirath* (The inheritance). Bayrut: Dar al-Adab.

Al-Khansa, d. 1885. *Anis al-julasa fi mulakhkhas sharh Diwan al-Khansa.* Beirut: al-Matba'h al-Kathulikiyah.

Kharrat, Edward. 1989. *City of Saffron.* Translated by Francis Liardet. London: Quartet.

al-Khuri, Colette. 1959. *Ayyam ma'ahu.* Beirut: al-Maktab al-Tijari li-al-Tiba'wa-al-Nashr wa-al-Tawzi'.

Kilpatrick, Hilary. 1985. "Interview with Etel Adnan (Lebanon)." In *Unheard Words: Women and Literature in Africa, the Arab World, Asia, the Caribbean and Latin America,* edited by Mineke Schipper, 114–20. London: Allison and Busby.

———. 1992. "The Egyptian Novel from *Zaynab* to 1980." In *Modern Arabic Literature,* edited by M. M. Badawi, 223–69. Cambridge, UK: Cambridge Univ. Press.

Knapp, Bettina. 1984. *Andrée Chedid*. Amsterdam: Rodopi.

Kristeva, Julia. 1988. *Étrangers à nous-mêmes*. Paris: Fayard.

———. 1991. *Strangers to Ourselves*. Translated by Léon Roudiez. New York: Columbia Univ. Press.

La Guardia, Anton. 1992. "Egyptian Pens Terrorised by Islam's Sword." *Sunday Telegraph*, Aug. 2, p. 18.

Lacan, Jacques. 1977. *Écrits: A Selection*. Translated by Alan Sheridan. New York: Norton Books.

Lashin, Mahmud Tahir. 1934. *Hawwa bila Adam*. Cairo: al-Hay'a al-Misriyya al-'Amma li al-Kitab.

———. 1986. *Eve Without Adam*. Translated by Saad el-Gabalawy. In *Three Pioneering Egyptian Novels*, edited by Saad el-Gabalawy, 49–94. Fredericton, N.B., Canada: York Press.

Layoun, Mary. 1994. "The Female Body and Transnational Reproduction: or, Rape by Any Other Name?" In *Scattered Hegemonies: Postmodernity and Transnational Feminist Practices*, edited by Inderpal Grewal and Caren Kaplan, 63–75. Minneapolis: Univ. of Minnesota Press.

Le Gassick, Trevor. 1992. "The Arabic Novel in English Translation." *Mundus Arabicus* 5: 47–60. (Special issue entitled "The Arabic Novel since 1950: Critical Essays, Interviews, and Bibliography," edited by Issa Boulata.)

Le Guin, Ursula K. 1989. Introduction to "Left Hand of Darkness." In *The Language of the Night: Essays on Fantasy and Science Fiction*, 150–54. New York: Harper Collins.

Lemaire, Anika. 1977. *Jacques Lacan*. Translated by David Macey. London: Routledge and Kegan Paul.

Lennon, Peter. 1994. "Speaking Out in a Volatile Climate." *Guardian*, May 28, p. 29.

Levis-Mano, Guy. 1974. *Étude de Andrée Chedid et Pierre Torreilles*. Paris: Seghers.

Lionnet, Françoise. 1995. "Dissymmetry Embodies: Nawal El Saadawi's *Woman and Point Zero* and the Practice of Excision." In *Postcolonial Representations: Women, Literature, and Identity*, 129–53. Ithaca, N.Y.: Cornell Univ. Press.

Liu, Lydia. 1994. "The Female Body and Nationalist Discourse: *The Field of Death* Revisited." In *Scattered Hegemonies: Postmodernity and Transnational Feminist Practices*, edited by Inderpal Grewal and Caren Kaplan, 37–62. Minneapolis: Univ. of Minneapolis Press.

Loflin, Christine A. 1995. "Nawal El Saadawi." E-mail to the author. June 2.

Mahfouz, Naguib. 1960a. *Bayna al-qasrayn* (*Palace Walk*). Cairo: Maktabat Misr.

———. 1960b. *Qasr al-shawq* (*Palace of Desire*). Cairo: Maktabat Misr.

———. 1962. *Al-Sukkariyah*. Cairo: Maktabat Misr.

———. 1990. *Palace Walk*. Translated by William Maynard Hutchins and Olive E. Kenny. New York: Anchor Books/Doubleday.

———. 1991. *Palace of Desire*. Translated by William Maynard Hutchins and Olive E. Kenny. New York: Doubleday.

———. 1993. *Sugar Street*. Translated by William Maynard Hutchins and Angele Botros Samaan. New York: Anchor Books.

Majaj, Lisa, and Amal Amireh. Forthcoming. *Etel Adnan: Critical Reflections*. Jefferson, N.C.: McFarland.

Al-Mala'ika, Nazik. 1949. *Shazaya wa-ramad* (Ashes and shrapnel). Baghdad: Matba't al-Ma'rif.

———. 1962. *Qadaya al-shi'r al-mu'asir* (Issues in contemporary poetry). Beirut: Dar al-Adab.

———. 1974. *Al-Tajzi'iyya fi al-mujtama' al-'Arabi* (Fragmentation in Arab society). Beirut: Dar al-'Ilm li al-malayin.

Malti-Douglas, Fedwa. 1991. *Woman's Body, Woman's Word: Gender and Discourse in Arabo-Islamic Writing*. Princeton, N.J.: Princeton Univ. Press.

———. 1995a. *Men, Women and God(s): Nawal El Saadawi and Arab Feminist Poetics*. Berkeley: Univ. of California Press.

———. 1995b. "Writing Nawal El Saadawi." In *Feminism Beside Itself*, edited by Diane Elam and Robyn Wiegman, 283–96. New York: Routledge.

Mamdouh, Alia. 1996. "Translating the Life of the Arab Woman." *Al-Hayat*, May 20: 12.

Marxist-Feminist Literature Collective. 1996. "Women Writing: Jane Eyre, Shirly, Vilette, Aurora Leigh." In *Marxist Literary Theory*, edited by Terry Eagleton and Drew Milne, 328–50. Oxford, UK: Blackwell.

al-Mazini, Ibrahim Abd al-Qadir. 1931. *Ibrahim al-katib*. Cairo: Matba'at dar al-Taraqqi.

———. 1976. *Ibrahim the Writer*. Translated by Magdi Wahba. Cairo: General Egyptian Book Organization.

Meese, E., and A. Parker, eds. 1989. *The Difference Within: Feminism and Critical Theory*. Amsterdam: J. Benjamin Pub. Co.

Mehrez, Samia. 1994. *Egyptian Writers Between History and Fiction: Essays on Naguib Mahfouz, Sonallah Ibrahim, and Gamal al-Ghitani*. Cairo: American Univ. in Cairo Press.

"Memoirs from the Women's Prison: Book Reviews." Review of *Memoirs from the Women's Prison*, by Nawal El Saadawi. *Publishers Weekly* 19 (Sept.): 63.

Mernissi, Fatima. 1975. *Beyond the Veil: Male-Female Dynamics in Modern Muslim Society*. New York: John Wiley and Sons.

Michel, Martina. 1995. "Positioning the Subject: Locating Postcolonial Studies." *Ariel: A Review of International English Literature* 26, no. 1: 81–99.

Middle East Watch. 1993. *A License to Kill: Israeli Undercover Operations Against Wanted and Masked Palestinians*. New York and Washington, D.C.

———. 1994. *Torture and Ill-Treatment: Israel's Interrogation of Palestinians from the Occupied Territories*. New York and Washington, D.C.

Mikhail, Mona. 1988. *Images of Arab Women: Fact and Fiction*. Washington, D.C.: Three Continents Press.

Mitchell, W.J.T. 1995. "Postcolonial Culture, Postimperial Criticism." In *The Post-Colonial Studies Reader*, edited by Bill Ashcroft, Gareth Griffiths, and Helen Tiffen, 475–79. London: Routledge.

Mitra, Indrani, and Madhu Mitra. 1991. "The Discourse of Liberal Feminism and Third World Women's Texts: Some Issues of Pedagogy." *College Literature* 18, no. 3: 55–63.

Mitra, Madhuchhanda. 1995. "Angry Eyes and Closed Lips: Forces of Revolution in Nawal el Saadawi's *God Dies by the Nile*." In *Violence, Silence, and Anger: Women's Writing and Transgression*, edited by Deirdre Lashgari, 147–57. Charlottesville: Univ. Press of Virginia.

Mohanty, Chandra Talpade. 1991. "Under Western Eyes: Feminist Scholarship and Colonial Discourses." In *Third World Women and the Politics of Feminism*, edited by Chandra Talpade Mohanty, Ann Russo, and Lourdes Torres, 51–80. Bloomington: Indiana Univ. Press.

Mohanty, Chandra Talpade, Ann Russo, and Lourdes Toures, eds. 1991. *Third World Women and the Politics of Feminism*. Bloomington: Indiana Univ. Press.

Morgan, Robin, ed. *Sisterhood Is Global: The International Women's Movement Anthology*. New York: Anchor Press.

Mortimer, Mildred. 1996. "Reappropriating the Gaze in Assia Djebar's Fiction and Film." *World Literature Today* 70, no. 4 (autumn): 859–66.

Mukherjee, Bharati. 1986. "Betrayed by Blind Faith." Review of *God Dies by the Nile*, by Nawal El Saadawi. *New York Times*, July 27, late city ed., section 7, p. 14.

Muslih, Muhammad. 1990. *Toward Coexistence: An Analysis of the Resolutions of the Palestine National Council.* Washington, D.C.: Institute for Palestine Studies.

Najjar, Orayb Aref, with Kitty Warnock. 1992. *Portraits of Palestinian Women.* Salt Lake City: Univ. of Utah Press.

Nancy, Jean-Luc. 1994. "Corpus." In *Thinking Bodies,* edited by Juliet Flower MacCannell and Laura Zakarin, 17–31. Stanford, Calif.: Stanford Univ. Press.

al-Naqqash, Raga'. 1995. "Imra'ah li-kul al-'usur" (A woman for all times). *al-Musawwar* 18 (Aug.): 28, 73.

Nelson, Cynthia. 1996. *Doria Shafik, Egyptian Feminist: A Woman Apart.* Gainesville: Univ. Press of Florida.

Nora, Pierre. 1989. "Between Memory & History: Les Lieux de Mémoire." *Representations* 26 (spring): 7–25.

Al-Nowaihi, Magda M. 1999. "Constructions of Masculinity in Two Egyptian Novels." In *Intimate Selving: Self, Gender, and Identity in Arab Families,* edited by Suad Joseph, 235–63. Syracuse, N.Y.: Syracuse Univ. Press.

———. 2001. "Resisting Silence in Arab Women's Autobiographies." In *International Journal of Middle East Studies* 33, no. 4.

Nuweihed, Nadia. 1998. "Nazira Zeineddin, the Woman More Mysterious." *Al-Duha Review* (Beirut), May.

Ouyang, Wen-Chin. 1996. Review of *Woman at Point Zero* and *The Circling Song,* by Nawal El Saadawi. *International Journal of Middle East Studies* 28, no. 3: 457–60.

———. 1997. "Feminist Discourse Between Art and Ideology: Four Novels by Nawal Al-Saadawi." *Al-'Arabiyya* 30: 95–115.

Parker, Andrew, Mary Russo, Doris Sommer, and Patricia Yaeger, eds. 1992. *Nationalism and Sexualities.* New York: Routledge.

Payne, Kenneth. 1992. *"Woman at Point Zero:* Nawal El Saadawi's Feminist Picaresque." *Southern Humanities Review* 26 (winter): 11–18.

Peteet, Julie M. 1991. *Gender in Crisis: Women and the Palestinian Resistance Movement.* New York: Columbia Univ. Press.

Plato. 1952. *Gorgias.* Translated by W. C. Hembold. Indianapolis, Ind.: Bobbs-Merrill.

———. 1971. *Gorgias.* Loeb Classical Library, vol. 3. London: Heinemann.

al-Qa'id, Muhammad Yusuf. 1969. *al-Hidad.* Cairo: n.p.

Rabbani, Mouin. 2001. "Commentary." *Toronto Globe and Mail,* Jan. 22.

Radhakrishnan, R. 1989. "Feminist Historiography and Post-Structuralism: Intersections and Departures." In *The Difference Within: Feminism and Critical Theory*, edited by E. Meese and A. Parker, 189–205. Amsterdam: J. Benjamin.

Rida, Muhammad Rashid. 1932. *Nida' ila al-jins al-latif, yaum al-mawled al-nabawiyy al-sharif sanat 1351: fi huquq al-nisa' fi al-Islam wa hazzuhunna min al-islah al Muhammadi al-'aam.* (A call to the fair sex on the occasion of the Prophet's birthday, 1351: regarding the rights of women in Islam and their share of the general Muhammadan reform). Cairo: Matba'at al-Manar.

Roberts, Paul William. 1993. "Novels of an Arab Feminist." Review of *Well of Life*, by Nawal El Saadawi. *Toronto Star*, May 15, weekend sec., p. J14.

Roth, Katherine. 1991. "Nawal El Saadawi: An Egyptian Feminist's Fight to Protect Hard-Won Gains." *San Francisco Chronicle*, Sept. 23, sec. Briefing, p. A10.

El Saadawi, Nawal. 1958. *Mudhakkirat tabiba*. Cairo: Dar el-Ma'aref.

———. 1965. *Al-Gha'ib*. Cairo: al-Kitab al-Zahabi.

———. 1968. *Imra'atani fi-mara'a*. Cairo: Dar al-Kitab.

———. 1971. *al-Mar'a wal-jins*. Cairo: el-Sha'b.

———. 1974a. *Mawt al-rajul al-wahid 'ala al-ard*. Beirut: Dar al-Adab.

———. 1974b. *al-Untha hiya al-asl*. Cairo: Maktabat Madbuli.

———. 1976a. *al-Mar'ah wal-sira' al-nafsi*. Beirut: al-Mu'assasa al-'Arabiyah lil-Dirasat wa-al-Nashr.

———. 1976b. *al-Rajul wal jins*. Beirut: al-Mu'assasa al-'Arabiyah lil-Dirasat wal-Nashr.

———. 1977. *al-Wajh al-'ari lil-mar'a al-'arabiyyah*. Beirut: al-Mu'assasa al-'Arabiyah lil-Dirasat wa-al-Nashr.

———. 1979. *Imra'a 'ind nuqtat al-sifr*. Beirut: Dar al-Adab.

———. 1980a. "Arab Women and Western Feminism: An Interview with Nawal El Saadawi." *Race and Class* 22, no. 2: 175–82.

———. 1980b. "Creative Women in Changing Societies: A Personal Reflection." *Race and Class* 22, no. 2: 159–73.

———. 1980c. *The Hidden Face of Eve: Women in the Arab World*. London: Zed Books.

———. 1981. "Feminism in Egypt: A Conversation with Nawal Saadawi." Interviewed by Sarah Graham Brown. *MERIP*. Reports: Middle East Research and Information Project no. 95 (Mar.-Apr.): 24–27.

———. 1982. *The Hidden Face of Eve: Women in the Arab World*. Translated and edited by Sherif Hetata, with a foreword by Irene Gendzier. Boston: Beacon Press.

———. 1983a. *Mudhakkirati fi sijn al-nisa'*. Cairo: Dar al-Mustaqbal al-'Arabi.

———. 1983b. *Woman at Point Zero*. London: Zed Books.

———. 1984. "When a Woman Rebels." Translated by Sherif Hetata. In *Sisterhood Is Global: The International Women's Movement Anthology*, edited by Robin Morgan, 199–206. New York: Anchor Press.

———. 1985a. "Challenging a Taboo: Going to Jail for Politics, Sex and Religion." *Worldpaper*, June: 6.

———. 1985b. *God Dies by the Nile*. Translated by Sherif Hetata. London: Zed Books.

———. 1985c. *Two Women in One*. Translated by Osman Nusairi and Jana Gough. London: Saqi.

———. 1986. *Memoirs from the Women's Prison*. Translated by Marilyn Booth. London: Women's Press.

———. 1987a. *Death of an Ex-Minister*. Translated by Shirley Eber. London: Methuen.

———. 1987b. *She Has No Place in Paradise*. Translated by Shirley Eber. London: Methuen.

———. 1987c. *Suqut al-imam* (*The Fall of the Imam*). Cairo: Dar al-Mustaqbal al-'Arabi.

———. 1988a. *The Fall of the Imam*. Translated by Sherif Hetata. London: Methuen.

———. 1988b. *Memoirs of a Woman Doctor*. Translated by Catherine Cobham. London: Saqi.

———. 1990a. "In Conversation with Nawal El Saadawi." Interview by Marcel Farry. *Spare Rib* 217 (Oct.): 22–26.

———. 1990b. "An Overview of My Life." *Contemporary Authors Autobiography Series*, edited by Mark Zadrozny, 11:61–72. Detroit: Gale Research Co.

———. 1990c. "Reflections of a Feminist." In *Opening the Gates: A Century of Arab Feminist Writing*, edited by Margot Badran and miriam cooke, 395–404. Bloomington: Indiana Univ. Press.

———. 1991a. *My Travels Around the World*. Translated by Shirley Eber. London: Metheun.

———. 1991b. "Nawal El Saadawi." In *Critical Fictions: The Politics of Imaginative Writing*, edited by Philomena Marian, 155–56. Seattle: Bay.

———. 1991c. *Searching*. Translated by Shirley Eber. London: Zed Books.

———. 1991d. "Time to Come Together: In Conversation with Nawal El Saadawi." Interview by Marcel Farry. *Spare Rib,* Mar.: 221.

———. 1992a. *Jannat wa-Iblis.* Beirut: Dar al-Adab.

———. 1992b. "The Progressive Interview: Nawal el Saadawi." Interview by George Lerner. *The Progressive* 56, no. 4: 32–35.

———. 1993a. "Feminism and Arab Humanism: An Interview with Nawal El Saadawi and Sherif Hetata." With Gaurav Desai and David Chioni Moore. *Sapina-Bulletin* 5, no. 1 (Jan.-June 1993): 28–51.

———. 1993b. "Living the Struggle: Nawal el Saadawi Talks about Writing and Resistance with Sherif Hetata and Peter Hitchcock." *Transitions* 61: 170–79.

———. 1994a. "The Bitter Lot of Women: In Conversation with Nawal el Saadawi." Interview by Hanny Lightfoot-Klein. *Freedom Review* 25 (May 1): 22–25.

———. 1994b. *The Innocence of the Devil.* Translated by Sherif Hetata. Berkeley: Univ. of California Press.

———. 1994c. *Memoirs from the Women's Prison.* Translated by Marilyn Booth. Berkeley: Univ. of California Press.

———. 1995a. "But Have Some Art with You": An Interview with Nawal El Saadawi. Interviewed by Jennifer Cohen. *Literature and Medicine* 14 (spring): 53–71.

———. 1995b. "A Cure for Blushing: An Obituary of Amina el-Said." *Guardian,* Aug. 17: 13.

———. 1997. *The Nawal El Saadawi Reader.* London: Zed Books.

———. 1999. *A Daughter of Isis: The Autobiography of Nawal El Saadawi.* London: Zed Books.

Sabbagh, Suha. 1989. "Palestinian Women Writers and the *Intifada.*" *Social Text* 22: 62–78.

Sabri, Ismail. 1938. "Liwa' al-husn" (Banner of beauty). In *Diwan Isma'il Sabri Pasha,* compiled by Hasan Rif'at and edited by Ahmad al-Zein, 107–9. Cairo: Matba'at Lajnat al-Ta'lif wa al-Tarjama wa al-Nashr.

El-Sadda, Hoda. 1996. "Women's Writing in Egypt: Reflections on Salwa Bakr." In *Gendering the Middle East,* edited by Deniz Kandiyoti, 127–44. Syracuse, N.Y.: Syracuse Univ. Press.

Sagar, Aparajita. 1995. "Nawal El Saadawi." E-mail to the author. Mar. 5.

al-Said, Amina. 1950. *al-Jamihah* (The defiant). Reprint, 1987. Cairo: Dar al-Ma'arif.

Said, Edward. 1983. "Introduction: Secular Criticism." In *The World, the Text and the Critic*, 1–30. Cambridge, Mass.: Harvard Univ. Press.

———. 1989. Foreword to *Little Mountain*, by Elias Khoury, ix-xxi. Minneapolis: Univ. of Minnesota Press.

———. 1990a. "Embargoed Literature." *Nation* 251, no. 8 (Sept. 17): 280–85.

———. 1990b. "Reflections on Exile." In *Out There: Marginalization and Contemporary Cultures*, edited by Russell Ferguson, Martha Gever, Trinh T. Minh-ha, and Cornel West, 357–66. New York: New Museum of Contemporary Cultures.

———. 1992. "Intellectuals and the War: An Interview," by Barbara Harlow. *Middle East Report*, July/Aug.: 15–20.

Said, Khalida. 1970. "al-Mar'a al-'arabiyyah: ka'in bi ghayrihi la bi-dhatihi" (The Arab woman: being through the other, not through the self). *Mawaqif* 12: 90–100.

Saliba, Therese. 1995. "On the Bodies of Third World Women: Cultural Impurity, Prostitution, and Other Nervous Conditions." *College Literature* 22, no. 1: 131–46.

Salman, Magda. 1981. Review of *The Hidden Face of Eve*, by Nawal El Saadawi. *Khamsin* 8: 121–24.

Salti, Ramzi. 1994. "Paradise, Heaven, and Other Oppressive Spaces: A Critical Examination of the Life and Works of Nawal El-Saadawi." *Journal of Arabic Literature* 25, no. 2: 152–74.

Sayigh, Rosemary. 1988. "Palestinians in Lebanon: Status, Ambiguity, Insecurity, and Flux." *Race & Class* 30, no. 1: 13–32.

———. 1993. "Palestinian Women and Politics in Lebanon." In *Arab Women: Old Boundaries, New Frontiers*, edited by Judith Tucker, 175–92. Bloomington: Indiana Univ. Press.

———. 1994. *Too Many Enemies: The Palestinian Experience in Lebanon*. London: Zed Books.

Sayigh, Tawfiq, ed. 1962. *Al-Adab al-'Arabi al-mu'asir* (Contemporary Arabic literature). Paris: n.p.

Scarry, Elaine. 1985. *The Body in Pain: The Making and Unmaking of the World*. New York: Oxford Univ. Press.

Semah, David. 1974. *Four Egyptian Literary Critics*. Leiden: Brill.

Shaaban, Bouthaina. 1988. *Both Right and Left Handed: Arab Women Talk about Their Lives*. London: The Women's Press.

Shafik, Doria. 1947. "The New Woman." *La Femme Nouvelle,* Dec.

―――. 1949. "A Bond Between Civilizations." *La Femme Nouvelle,* Dec.

―――. 1953. "Egypt's Renaissance." *La Femme Nouvelle,* 27–28.

―――. 1979a. *Avec Dante aux Enfers* (With Dante in hell). Paris: Pierre Fanlac.

―――. 1979b. *Larmes d'Isis* (Tears of Isis). Paris: Pierre Fanlac.

Sharabi, Hisham. 1975. *Muqqadimah li-dirasat al-mujtama' al-'arabi* (An introduction to the study of Arab society). Jerusalem: Salah al-Din.

―――. 1988. *Neopatriarchy: A Theory of Distorted Change in Arab Society.* New York: Oxford Univ. Press.

―――. 1990. "The Scholarly Point of View: Politics, Perspective, Paradigm." In *Theory, Politics and the Arab World: Critical Responses,* edited by Hisham Sharabi, 1–51. New York: Routledge.

al-Sharqawi, Abd al-Rahman. 1953. *al-Ard.* Cairo: Naadii al-Qissah.

―――. 1962. *Egyptian Earth.* Translated by Desmond Stewart. London: Heinemann.

al-Shaykh, Hanan. 1970. *Intihar rajul mayyit* (Suicide of a dead man). Bayrut: Dar al-Nahar.

―――. 1975. *Faras al-Shaytan* (Praying mantis). Bayrut: Dar al-Nahar il-al-Nashr.

―――. 1982. *Wardat al-sarha'* (Desert rose). Bayrut: al-Mu'assasah al-Jami'iyah.

―――. 1987. *The Story of Zahra.* Translated by Peter Ford with the cooperation of the author. London: Pan Books Ltd. (Pavanne edition). First published in English translation in 1986 by Quartet Books (London).

―――. 1988. *Misk al-Ghazal* (*Women of Sand and Myrrh*). Bayrut: Dar al-Adab.

―――. 1989. *Hikayat Zahra.* Beirut: Dar al-Adab. First published in Arabic in 1980.

―――. 1992a. *Barid Bayrut* (*Beirut Blues*). al-Qahirah: Dar al-Hilal.

―――. 1992b. *Women of Sand and Myrrh.* Translated by Catherine Cobham. New York: Doubleday.

―――. 1994. *Aknus al-shams 'an al sutuh* (*I Sweep the Sun off Rooftops*). Bayrut: Dar al-Adab.

―――. 1995. *Beirut Blues.* Translated by Catherine Cobham. London: Chatto and Windus.

―――. 1998. *I Sweep the Sun off Rooftops.* Translated by Catherine Cobham. New York: Doubleday.

———. 2001a. *Innaha Landan ya ʿazizi*. Bayrut: Dar al-Adab.

———. 2001b. *Only in London*. Translated by Catherine Cobham. London: Bloomsbury.

Shehadeh, Raja. 1982. *The Third Way: A Journal of Life in the West Bank*. London: Quartet.

———. 1994. *The Declaration of Principles and the Legal System in the West Bank*. Jerusalem: PASSIA.

Shohat, Ella. 1992. "Notes on the Post-Colonial." *Social Text* 10, nos. 2, 3: 99–113.

Siddiq, Muhammad. 1986. "The Fiction of Sahar Khalifah: Between Defiance and Deliverance." *Arab Studies Quarterly* 8, no. 2: 143–60.

Silverman, Kaja. 1989. "White Skin, Brown Masks: The Double Mimesis, or with Lawrence in Arabia." *differences* 1, no. 3 (fall): 3–54.

Slade, Margot, and Tom Ferrell. 1980. "Ideas and Trends." *New York Times*, July 20, late city final ed., sec. 4, p. 7.

Smith, Sidonie, and Julia Watson, eds. 1992. *Decolonizing the Subject: The Politics of Gender in Women's Autobiography*. Minneapolis: Univ. of Minnesota Press.

Sontag, Susan. 1994. *Los Angeles Times*, Aug. 17, p. 7.

Soueif, Ahdaf. 1996. "Translating the Life of the Arab Woman." *Al-Hayat*, May 20, p. 12.

Spivak, Gayatri Chakravorty. 1988. "Can the Subaltern Speak?" In *Marxism and the Interpretation of Culture*, edited by Cary Nelson and Lawrence Grossberg, 271–313. Urbana: Univ. of Illinois Press.

Strum, Philippa. 1992. *The Women Are Marching: The Second Sex and the Palestinian Revolution*. Chicago: Lawrence Hill Books.

Talhami, Ghada Hashem. 1966. *The Mobilization of Muslim Women in Egypt*. Gainesville: Univ. Press of Florida.

Tammam, Abu. 1979. *Diwan al-hamasah*. Lahur: al-Maktabah al-Salafiyah.

Tarabishi, George. 1978. "Untha Nawal El Saʿdawi wa usturat al-tafarrud" (The female of Nawal El Saadawi and the myth of individuation)." In *Al-Adab min al-dakhil* (Literature from the inside), edited by George Tarabishi, 10–50. Beirut: Dar al-Taleeʿa.

———. 1982. *ʿUqdat Odeeb fee al-riwaya al-ʿarabiyah* (The Oedipus complex in the Arabic novel). Beirut: Dar al-Taleeʿa.

———. 1983. *al-Rujulah wa aydyoulojyat al-rujulah fee al-riwaya al-ʿarabiyah* (Manhood and the ideology of manhood in the Arabic novel). Beirut: Dar al-Taleeʿa.

———. 1988. *Woman Against Her Sex.* Translated by Basil Hatim and Elisabeth Orsini. London: Saqi.

Thornhill, Theresa. 1992. *Making Women Talk: The Interrogation of Palestinian Women Detainees.* London: Lawyers for Palestinian Human Rights.

Tierney-Tello, Mary Beth. 1996. *Allegories of Transgression and Transformation: Experimental Fiction by Women Writing under Dictatorship.* Albany: State Univ. of New York Press.

Verdery, Katherine. 1994. "Beyond the Nation in Eastern Europe." *Social Text* 38: 1–19.

Wallach, John, and Janet Wallach. 1992. *The New Palestinians: The Emerging Generation of Leaders.* Rocklin, Calif.: Prima Publishing.

Werner, Louis. 1991. "Arab Feminist Pens Powerful Prose." *Christian Science Monitor* 25 (June): 3.

Winokur, Julie. 1994. "Uncensored: Egypt's Most Outspoken Feminist Sets Up Her Soapbox at the UW." *Seattle Times,* Apr. 24, final ed., sec. Pacific, p. 12.

Woodhull, Winifred. 1993. *Transfigurations of the Maghreb: Feminism, Decolonization, and Literatures.* Minneapolis: Univ. of Minnesota Press.

Woolf, Virginia. 1929. *A Room of One's Own.* New York: Harcourt, Brace and Co.

Young, Elise G. 1992. *Keepers of the History: Women and the Israeli-Palestinian Conflict.* New York: Teachers College Press.

Zayour, Ali. 1977. *al-Tahlil al-nafsi lil-dhat al-'arabiyyah: Anmat al-sulukiyyah al-usturiyyah* (The analysis of the Arab self). Beirut: Dar al-Tali'ah.

al-Zayyat, Latifa. 1960. *al-Bab al-maftuh* (The open door). Cairo: Maktabat al-Anglo al-Misriyyah.

———. 1992a. *Hamlat taftish: awraq shakhsiyya.* Cairo: Dar al-Hilal.

———. 1992b. "Qira'a fi riwayat Salwa Bakr al-'araba al-dhahabiyya la-tas'ad ila al-sama'." *Fusul* 11, no. 1: 273–77.

———. 1994. "On Political Commitment and Feminist Writing." In *The View from Within: Writers and Critics on Contemporary Arabic Literature. A Selection from "Alif: Journal of Comparative Poetics,"* edited by Ferial J. Ghazoul and Barbara Harlow, 240–60. Cairo: American Univ. in Cairo Press.

———. 1996. *The Search: Personal Papers.* Translated by Sophie Bennett. London: Quartet.

Zeidan, Joseph T. 1995. *Arab Women Novelists: The Formative Years and Beyond.* Albany: State Univ. of New York Press.

Zeineddin, Nazira. 1928. *Al-Sufur wa al-hijab* (Lifting the veil, wearing the veil). Beirut: Matabi' Quzma.

————. 1929. *Al-Fatat wa al-shuyukh* (The young woman and the savants). Privately published by her father, Sa'id Zeinedden.

Zimra, Clarisse. 1992. Afterword to *Women of Algiers in their Apartment,* by Assia Djebar, translated by Marjolijn DeJager, 159–211. Charlottesville: Univ. Press of Virginia.

Ziyada, Mai. 1975. *Al-Saha'if.* Beirut: Muassasat Nawfil.

————. 1982. *Al-Mu'allafat al-kamila* (Complete works). Edited by Salma al-Haffar al-Kuzbari. Beirut: Muassasat Nawfil.

Index